Suffragettes, Suffragists and Antis –

the fight of the vote in the Surrey Hills

To Kathy
Best wishes
from Kathy.

Kathy Atherton

First published in 2017 by The Cockerel Press
Copyright © 2017 Kathy Atherton

ISBN 978-1-909871-11-3

The Cockerel Press is an imprint of Dorking Museum and Heritage Centre, The Old Foundry, 62 West Street Dorking, RH4 1BS
www.dorkingmuseum.org.uk Enquiries to: admin@dorkingmuseum.org.uk

Printed and bound by Short Run Press Limited, Exeter

Acknowledgments and thanks:

This book has been ten years in the research. It could not have been completed without the help of the following: the team at Dorking Museum; Margaret Kyriacou at Shere Museum; Lucy Neal for material on Mary Neal; Emma and William Corke for material on the Farrer family; Sandra Wedgwood for material on the Gordon-Clark and Lawrence families; Beverley Cook at the Museum of London; the London School of Economics Library and Women's Library; Adam Green at the library of Trinity College, Cambridge; the Bodleian Library, Oxford; Frank Pemberton of Dorking Labour Party for material on Pethick-Lawrence House; Di Stiff at Surrey History Centre; Terry Wooden of Westcott Local History Group; John Callcut of Newdigate Local History Group; Mary Day; Lorraine Spindler of Leatherhead Museum; the Pethick family for allowing access to letters to Emmeline; Ray Wilson for information on policing; Jenny Overton and Joan Mant for their research on the village of Peaslake; Irene Cockcroft for information on the campaign in Cornwall, John Molyneux for information on the waste paper supply depot; and JJ Heath Caldwell for information on the Heath family. My thanks to all who have provided images and granted permission to reproduce them. And to Susannah Horne and Peter Camp of the Cockerel Press for proofreading, wisdom and moral support.
Once again I must thank my family and friends - Richard, Tom and Ulysses Fedrick, Don and Betty Attwood, Erica Chambers and Yvonne Brown - for encouragement and tolerance.

Contents

Introduction

From as early as the 1860s women (and men) of the Surrey Hills played an active part in the campaign for the vote for women. Perhaps surprisingly, a significant number from the quiet villages around Leith Hill chose to involve themselves with the militant 'suffragette' campaign rather than the more respectable 'constitutional' movement. Mrs Pankhurst's Women's Social and Political Union had its beginnings in the radical politics of Manchester, but the support of middle-class women was vital to its success - and by the early twentieth century Surrey was home to educated, comfortably-off women who had time, energy and money to offer.

Many of these women were inspired by the example of Emmeline Pethick-Lawrence, whose home in Holmwood was dubbed 'the unofficial home' of the 'suffragettes'. As the WSPU's treasurer, it was Emmeline's business acumen, contacts, and fortitude that provided the organization's firm foundation. Nicknamed 'Godfather' by the women, Emmeline's husband, Fred, was the only man to take a leadership role in an organization he was not entitled to join. All of the WSPU's leadership, including the Pankhursts, spent time in the Holmwood, socializing, recuperating, and developing strategy, while hundreds of supporters converged on the village for a six week-long campaign in 1912.

The nearby village of Peaslake was just as significant. Home to the movement's first hunger striker, and to the wealthy and influential Brackenbury family, many a stone that was aimed at London windows came from its secluded lanes. And when the Pethick-Lawrences moved to Peaslake after the First World War, they gathered about them an extraordinary community of thinkers, activists and campaigners.

In part this is the story of an extraordinary couple, and of their lives, not on the national stage but in the Surrey villages of Holmwood and Peaslake. It is the story of the militant 'suffragettes' of the Surrey Hills. But it is also the story of the non-militant 'constitutional' campaigners who spurned the violent action that Emmeline Pethick-Lawrence advocated and distanced themselves from it, and of her neighbours who were not convinced of the rightness of the cause and who campaigned against it. It is the story of local communities participating in the national debate.

The inhabitants of the towns and villages of the Surrey Hills played their part, not just in the campaign for the vote, but in the wider struggle for justice, freedom, and human equality. Denied the conventional male routes to power of the ballot box and public office, women organised themselves to improve the lives of their neighbours by other means. They sought to bring medical and 'social' care to communities where there was little safety net for those without money. They established and supported schools. They pushed for legal reform and for the entry of women into the professions and the highest political office, with a view to improving the lot of women and children. They responded to international crises by founding charities that are still working across the world today. They established the lasting legacy of the Leith Hill Musical Festival that has brought music to people of all classes for over a century; and their efforts were crucial to the English folk song revival that reclaimed the music of the ordinary working person from obscurity.

The campaign for the vote for women did not take place in a vacuum, and this book attempts to put local participation into the context of the many initiatives engaged in by women seeking to transform their communities and their world. Their legacy has been much more than the vote.

I hope that this book provides a new perspective, not just on our understanding of the campaign for the vote and the divisions within it, but also on the ambitions and achievements of the women of the Surrey Hills in the early years of the twentieth century.

In 1908 Emmeline Pethick-Lawrence was well enough known to be modelled in wax at Madame Tussauds. In a eulogy to her husband, Frederick, Clement Attlee acknowledged how unusual it was for one man to have played a leading part in two great movements of emancipation. And the memorial plaque placed outside Dorking Labour Party headquarters in 1962 confidently announced that the work of Fred and Emmeline for the emancipation of women and for world peace would be remembered for 'countless generations'. Without them we might never have heard of Mrs Pankhurst or her 'suffragettes', for it is quite possible that had they not met Fred and Emmeline the Pankhursts would be no more than a footnote in history, the WSPU just one of many competing voices in the campaign for the vote. Yet today the Pankhursts are revered, whilst the Pethick-Lawrences are largely forgotten. (LSE Library)

5

A suffrage Christmas card. Suffrage campaigners were ingenious in finding ways to keep the campaign for the vote in the public eye at all times, as in this card by C. Hedley Charlton. The Museum of London has in its collections a copy of this card, doctored to read 'from the Surrey Hills', rather than the Alps. (LSE library)

A short note on spelling:

The house owned by Fred and Emmeline Pethick-Lawrence in Holmwood was known as the Dutch House before they bought it, and reverted to that name, by which it is still known, when they sold it. During the twenty years of their ownership it was known as The Mascotte. Whenever it appears in print, in biographies, autobiographies, on postcards or in local histories, it is generally spelled 'Mascot'. However in all correspondence the Pethick-Lawrences referred to it as the 'Mascotte', which is French for 'lucky charm'. Emmeline was a fluent French speaker and presumably wished her house to bring luck to those who lived within it.

1866 and all that

When Emmeline Pankhurst founded the Women's Social and Political Union (WSPU) in 1903 campaigners had been working to win the vote for women for forty years. Women from the villages of the Surrey Hills had been involved from the start: when John Stuart Mill introduced the first women's suffrage petition to Parliament in 1866 two of its signatories, Harriet Grote and Augusta Spottiswoode, were living in the village of Shere, between Dorking and Guildford.

Both had dedicated their lives to the improvement of their communities. They knew one another well and worked together to establish an experimental farm in Shere. The older of the two, Harriet Grote nee Lewin (1792-1878), was a writer and radical. Her family moved in influential circles: her father had had a relationship with Princess Tallyrand before their respective marriages and her godparents were the Alderseys of Stoke Park in Guildford.

In childhood Harriet rejected feminine amusements, recalling in later life that: *'I could never content myself with the insipid recreations common to girls at that time, but sought amusements which required bodily agility, nerve and innovation'*. Tree-climbing, skating, and making fires pleased her better. In 1820, when unable to obtain permission to marry, 28-year-old Harriet eloped with the historian of ancient Greece and radical thinker, George Grote (1794-1871). The couple kept their marriage secret for a month.

Tall and square of face, Harriet had penetrating eyes and dressed in an eccentric manner. She also had a passion for 'discordant colours'. Highly intelligent, she was nick-named the Empress by her family, suggesting an imperious manner. Her nephew, Thomas Herbert Lewin, (who later lived at Parkhurst in nearby Abinger), recalled that she treated everyone as a subject. *'She never seemed aware in the slightest degree of the startling effect she produced on her conventional listeners'*, he wrote. *'Hers was a mind to lead and rule, decided, clear, judicial, courageous and generous beyond the average of either men or women and possessing a quality of rare wit and humour.'* She was, said fellow radical and leader of the Anti Corn-Law

Harriet Grote of Shere. (The Lewin Letters, Cornell University)

League, Richard Cobden (1804-1865), *'a remarkable woman'*, though, (he could not help adding), *'desperately blue in the stocking'*. Setting up home in London in the 1820s Harriet Grote became involved in politics when her husband became a Member of Parliament. Prior to 1832 entitlement to vote depended on ownership of land in rural counties, and on payment of sufficient rents in urban boroughs. Constituency sizes varied hugely as boundaries had not been revised to reflect changes in population distribution so that ancestral landowners controlled who was returned to Parliament from semi-deserted villages, whilst the new industrial centres of the Midlands and North had relatively few seats and thousands of voters. The Great Reform Act of 1832 addressed both eligibility to vote, and size of constituency, so that the new industrial 'millocracy' was adequately represented. It took the electorate to some the 20% of the male population who could meet the threshold for eligibility. But the use of the term 'male persons', in the definition of those eligible to vote, explicitly excluded women. The vast majority of the population, therefore, and all women, remained without any voice in the government of their country.

Such reform was not sufficient for the Grotes and their followers. The 'Philosophic Radicals', as they called themselves, advocated further democratic reform, as well as minimal government interference in economic matters and a utilitarian approach to ethics. Based at the couple's London home in Ecclestone Street, the 'Grote conclave' argued for further extension to the franchise and for secret ballots to prevent voters coming under pressure from their landlords or employers. In return for crucial parliamentary support, their MPs pushed Lord Melbourne's Whig government for concessions. Unable to vote, let alone stand for Parliament, Harriet was deeply involved in deliberations and the radicals were soon referred to as *'Mrs Grote's party'*. Sydney Smith referred to her as *'queen of the radicals'*. Another observer described her as *'more of a man, but not a better man than her husband.'*, whilst Cobden referred to the couple as *'Mrs and Mr Grote'*, on the grounds that she was the greater politician of the two. Had she been a man, he wrote, she would have been a party leader. Prefiguring later radical leaders, she had a reputation for boldness and advocated bringing down the government if necessary

Harriet Grote always assumed equality with men and that was reflected in her manner. One observer wrote of going to see *'the two Mr Grotes'*, another that she was like *'a regular politician in breeches.'* Some comments could be snide: *'Who is the gentleman in the white muslin gown?'* asked one observer. And even amongst those who came to know her, acceptance was usually accompanied by amused reference to her eccentricities: *'I like the Grotes,'* said Sydney Smith. *'He is so ladylike and she is a perfect gentleman.'* Certainly she lamented being born a woman and when an organised movement to secure the vote for women began to emerge in mid-century she embraced it.

It is unsurprising, therefore, that she was a signatory to the women's suffrage petition when reform of the political system was under discussion again in 1866. When the bill that would become the Reform Act of 1867 was in draft form, various groups sought to influence Parliament as to its contents. The accepted argument was that there should be no taxation without representation - and many women paid taxes in their own right. The petition therefore proposed voting rights for single and widowed women who were property-owners and taxpayers. (Though the favouring of women who had 'failed' in their role in life in not having secured – or having lost - a husband, over married women whose financial affairs were in the hands of their husbands, was controversial.)

The petition marked the start of the women's suffrage campaign. Signed by Harriet Grote and by Augusta Spottiswoode, it was presented to Parliament by MPs John Stuart Mill and Henry Fawcett (1833-84). When voting rights for women did not appear in the 1867 Reform Bill, Mill proposed an amendment. It was following the defeat of this amendment, and with no prospect of further reform, that women's suffrage committees were set up all over the country.

Harriet Grote was instrumental in setting up the London National Society for Women's Suffrage. A great patron of the arts - Mendelssohn, Chopin and Liszt were all guests at her London home – she had been responsible for bringing the Swedish singer Jenny Lind, to England. With Lind she had founded the Society of Women Artists and it was at the Society's headquarters at the Architectural Association that the first meeting of the London National Society was held in 1867. With the young Millicent Fawcett (1847-1929), she spoke at its first public meeting in 1869. She had never, wrote her biographer, Lady Eastlake, *'been engaged in any work in which her feelings were more completely seconded by her reason'* than this. She claimed that she had always felt that the arguments against women's

John Stuart Mill (1806-1873) presented the first petition in support of the vote for women to Parliament. Mill's philosopher father rented a house for his family in Dorking in 1822 and the family spent six months of every year in the town. The Mills were amongst the first 'ramblers' to take long walks for pleasure on Box Hill. In 1830 the family moved to a house behind The Running Horses at Mickleham and Mill campaigned against a proposal to site a railway through the Mickleham valley. He was a visitor to Harriet Grote in Shere, but visited the area less frequently once he had become involved with Harriet Taylor and the campaign for the vote. (Library of Congress)

suffrage were so feeble and limited and ineffectual that it was a wonder they were ever put. It was a cause of regret to her that the campaign had not got under way thirty years earlier when she might have led it. (Eventually that role fell to Millicent Fawcett who served with her on the committee of the London National Society and who later led the umbrella National Union of Women's Suffrage Societies (NUWSS) which brought together all the local societies in 1897.)

Harriet Grote acquired The Ridgeway – named after her childhood home in Hampshire - in Shere's Hook Lane in 1865, just as she became involved with the campaign for the vote. John Stuart Mill stayed with her there in 1872. With Gomshall station within easy reach, George Grote was able to attend to his parliamentary business from Shere. The couple led increasingly separate lives, however. He had his duties with the newly-founded University of London and as a trustee of the British Museum; Harriet went to London less frequently. She stayed in Shere for months at a time, writing and walking on Albury Heath with her dog, Pixie. *'The Ridgeway is now a perfect paradise,'* she wrote to a friend, *'trees tall and umbraceous, two alcoves to chat under the acacias, croquet lawn where I gave a party to the neighbours on Thursday with tea.'*

One of the neighbours was Thomas Henry Farrer (1819-1899) - later Lord Farrer of Abinger - who lived at Abinger Hall. In 1876 Harriet Grote hosted Farrer, and the Brays of Shere Manor, to dinner with Prime Minister Gladstone at her London home. She described Farrer as *'a very enlightened neighbour'* and his family became strong suffrage supporters. In Surrey she worked to the public good. She established a mission house in nearby Peaslake and acquired a piece of land in Ewhurst Lane from Sir Reginald Bray on which to establish an inn for the isolated village. She proposed to call it The Little Fir Tree. Sadly, it remained uncompleted at her death at the age of 86 in 1878.

Harriet Grote is buried in Shere. She was fondly remembered in the villages for her generosity towards staff and villagers. And so eminently was she regarded generally that her biography was written and published within two years of her death, followed shortly by her letters. In the 1870s Harriet Grote had collaborated with her co-signatory to the 1866 petition, Augusta Spottiswoode, on a local venture. With Spottiswoode's sister, Rosa, the two women bought a piece of land near The Ridgeway where they established a small 'farm' with orchards. It was run with Grote's niece, Jessie Lewin. Thirty years younger than Grote, Augusta Spottiswoode (1824-1912) was the daughter of the Queen's printer, Andrew Spottiswoode (1787-1866). (The firm was later known as Eyre and Spottiswoode). It was an intellectual family: Augusta's brother was the mathematician, physicist and president of the Royal Society, William Spottiswoode (1825-1883). The Longman printing family, (who also had local residences), were cousins, as were the Brays of Shere. In Augusta's youth the family had lived at Broome Hall on the hillside between Ockley and Coldharbour, but by late mid-century she and Rosa were living at Drydown, close to Grote in Shere. Augusta was an early member of Grote's London National

Society for Women's Suffrage and the family firm printed the Society's first headed notepaper and early reports.

Augusta Spottiswoode actively sought public office; she served as a poor law guardian, and in 1894 she was elected to Guildford Rural District Council as a councillor, one of the first women in the country to hold such a position. (Women were eligible to stand for election in new rural and urban districts from 1894, but not for borough or county councils.)

Augusta and Rosa rented out a string of cottages in the neighbouring village of Peaslake, where they expressed a patrician concern for the morality of the villagers by imposing strict conditions on their tenants' behaviour. Augusta was a supporter of the temperance movement; she funded school treats and ran a Red Riding Hood charity which gave out cloaks to girls too poor to afford them. She also

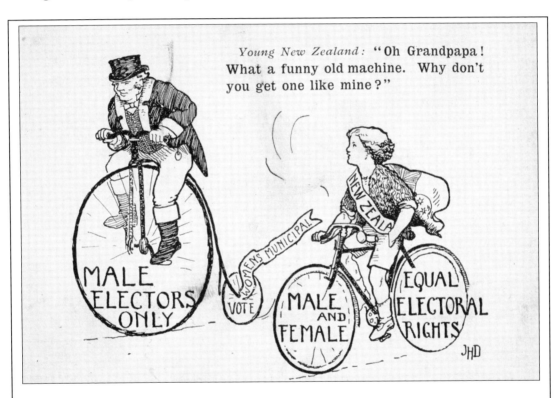

The bicycle became something of a symbol of liberation for women. A young Emmeline Pethick-Lawrence and her sisters shocked polite society in Weston-super-Mare when she went out cycling. In Holmwood Margaret Pennington recalled that it had given women freedom, though in Dorking early women cyclists had to battle the attitude of hotel owners who refused entry to women wearing 'rational' cycling dress rather than voluminous skirts. This postcard by the Artists' Suffrage League shows the modern forward-thinking New Zealand, powered by electoral equality, overtaking the elderly Britain with its unequal electoral system that allowed women to vote only in municipal elections. (LSE library)

provided land for a village schoolroom, and in 1888 she proposed a new mission hall for the village, donating £300 to the fund. When George Cubitt (1828-1917) of Denbies (near Dorking) - son of the master-builder, Thomas – and Sir Reginald Bray also made large donations it proved possible to build a church. Augusta and Rosa laid the foundation stone. The village hall in Peaslake, established after the First World War, was named the Eyre and Spottiswoode War Memorial Club and Institute in joint commemoration of the sisters. The legacy of these benevolent and strong-minded suffrage supporters is therefore embedded in the infrastructure of Peaslake, a village that came to play a major part in campaigns for the vote.

The Spottiswoodes were succeeded at Broome Hall (after a short period of ownership by the Labouchere banking family) by the Penningtons. They were related by marriage to those at the very heart of the developing women's suffrage movement. Radical Liberal MP for Stockport, Frederick Pennington (1819-1914) was a wealthy east-India merchant and had been a member of the council of the Anti Corn-Law League. One of his sisters was married to Thomas Thomasson (1808-76), a founder of the League and an early supporter of women's suffrage. Like Grote and Spottiswoode, Pennington's Thomasson nieces had been signatories to the 1866 petition. A niece by another sister, Ursula Bright (nee Mellor) (1835-1915), was married to the radical Liberal MP Jacob Bright (1821-99) who took over parliamentary stewardship of suffrage bills after John Stuart Mill's death in 1873. Close friends with Richard and Emmeline Pankhurst, Ursula was instrumental in the founding of Manchester's women's suffrage movement that drew strength from the radical tradition of that city. Her sister-in-law, Priscilla Bright McLaren (1815-1906), was president of the Edinburgh National Society for Women's Suffrage and - drawing on the anti-corn-law rallies with which her family's name is synonymous - she promoted the Grand Demonstrations held in Manchester in the run up to the Reform Act of 1884.

With his family instrumental in the promulgation of the campaign for the women's vote in the north, Frederick Pennington and his wife, Margaret Landall

---

Alice Bell Le Geyt

The village of Peaslake was home to Jersey-born novelist and journalist, Alice Bell Le Geyt (c.1840-1934), who occupied The Chalet at the beginning of the twentieth century. As a girl of 14 she had won a gold medal for bravery whilst on holiday at Lyme Regis when she rowed out in heavy surf to save two young boys from drowning. She was a temperance campaigner who not only wrote articles on the social evils of drink, but attempted to establish coffee houses as alternatives to the public house. She also wrote a three-volume novel, 'Which Will Triumph?' (1867). She was an early treasurer of the Bath National Society for Women's Suffrage when it was established there in the 1870s and sat with the Penningtons on the committee of the Central Committee of the National Society for Women's Suffrage. In the 1880s she was a speaker at suffrage meetings in Bristol.

Pennington nee Sharp (1828-1929) were ideally placed to promote the translation of the cause south. A member of both the Manchester National Society for Women's Suffrage and Harriet Grote's London National Society, Margaret became a founder member of the new Central Committee of the National Society for Women's Suffrage in 1872. (Her sister-in-law, Priscilla Bright McLaren, was also on the committee.) It was hoped that the support of a national committee, based in London, would enable the numerous local societies to exert greater pressure on government. The Central Committee was initially run from the Penningtons' London home at 17 Hyde Park Terrace; Margaret Pennington served as honorary secretary. She was still supporting the cause 35 years later. In 1908 she advised the NUWSS on election policy and in June 1910 – in her eighties - she was spreading the word for the first meeting of a proposed women's suffrage society in Cranleigh.

At Broome Hall the Penningtons hosted weekend parties with guests from the worlds of the arts, politics and letters and they built a private road to the house from Holmwood station to enable their political guests to visit in comfort. The presence of Priscilla Bright McLaren, her MP husband, and the Thomassons provided direct access to the Manchester radical heartland of the suffrage movement. Margaret Pennington also subscribed to other causes that sought to improve the lot of women: she was a member of the Society for the Promotion of Employment of Women, was on the executives of the Married Women's Property Committee and the Ladies' National Association, and gave money to Sophia Jex-Blake's university

In the mid-1870s the Member of Parliament for Mid-Surrey was the Conservative Sir James John Trevor Lawrence (1831-1913). He lived at Burford Lodge, at the foot of Box Hill, where he created a celebrated garden. Orchids were his particular interest; he had collected specimens in the Himalayas whilst working in the Indian Medical Service as a young man and had one of the world's leading orchid collections. In 1913 he became president of the Royal Horticultural Society.

Sir Trevor, as he was known, was a strong supporter of women's suffrage. He spoke in favour of granting the vote to women at Primrose League meetings in the 1880s and 1890s. When his constituency was abolished in 1885 he became the member for Reigate, which then included the Dorking area. (The Gardeners' Chronicle) endowment scheme for women.

'You and I worked as hard as any of them,' she wrote to fellow campaigner Elizabeth Malleson (1828-1916) in 1905, *'and in times of much greater difficulty. How we poor pioneers were reviled and ridiculed.'* For in the late nineteenth century it appalled many that a married woman should show herself on stage in public, let alone speak; at least one press commentator declined to mention names in print for fear of adding to their 'shame'. *'Our successors don't know at what cost to some of us their comparative emancipation has been attained,'* she commented. For though they had not attained the vote, the lives of relatively affluent women had changed in noticeable practical ways over the forty years of Margaret Pennington's campaigning. In particular the bicycle, she thought, had been a great emancipation: *'It is nothing short of a social revolution for women,'* she wrote of this seemingly innocuous innovation.

For thirty years the campaign for the vote had been conducted by argument and persuasion, via public meeting, pamphlet and petition. The first petition from the villages of the Surrey Hills – which in the late 1860s and 1870s were seeing an influx of wealthy Londoners as the coming of the railways opened up the area to the professional classes - came from Capel, Ockley and the surrounding area and was presented in May 1870, probably at the behest of the Penningtons. The vote was certainly a topic of conversation, even in the smallest villages.

The issue was debated throughout the 1870s. Jacob Bright presented several women's suffrage bills in Parliament, all of which were defeated at the behest of the party whips despite large numbers of MPs pledging personal support. But the vote for women was not yet an issue which generated widespread interest: for millions of middle and working-class women, gender was hardly an issue; the property requirements of the Reform Act of 1867 had left two thirds of the male population unqualified to vote. So if women were to be enfranchised on the same terms as men, few – and none who were married – would meet the property requirement.

That situation was set to change with the prospect of another reform bill in the 1880s. Suffrage meetings were held in bigger centres of population. In 1883 Margaret Chorley Crosfield (1859-1952) hosted visiting speakers to a meeting at The Dingle in Reigate, after which her father, Joseph, chaired a public meeting at the town's Public Halls. But when it came, the Reform Act of 1884 enfranchised whole sections of the male population, extending the vote to the majority of men, but not to women. Gender was no longer one of many grounds for disqualification from eligibility to vote; it was the principal ground. Female suffrage became a cause, not just of wealthy women, but of the educated middle-classes. It became an issue of individual and group fitness, for if the main argument against granting the vote to working-class men was of their perceived fecklessness and ignorance, then women of whatever social class or education found themselves classed with the pathetic and the despised. A suffrage poster drew attention to the fact that no matter how accomplished a woman was, politically her voice counted for less than the lowest of the low: under the heading *'What a women may be and yet not have a vote'* were depicted female mayors, nurses, mothers, doctors, teachers and factory hands. These upstanding women were contrasted with depictions of men who were unfit for service, drunkards, convicts, lunatics, and proprietors of white slaves under the heading *'What a man may have been and yet not lose the vote'.*

The sense of injustice engendered by the 1884 Act was compounded by the fact that by the late nineteenth century a professional middle-class had arisen whose womenfolk had begun to play a greater role in public life. Such women were, as a result of the educational reforms of the 1870s, increasingly educated. The newly established 'professions', with their examinations at which women might prove their ability on equal terms with male applicants, were obvious battlegrounds for those seeking the advancement of women. Women like Elizabeth Garrett Anderson (1836-1917) and Sophia Jex-Blake (1840-1912) had taken on the medical establishment; others had the law in their sights. By 1900 increasing numbers of women – including the many female writers, illustrators and artists of the Surrey Hills - were taxpayers; others, like Augusta Spottiswoode, sat in a legally responsible capacity on the boards of hospitals and charities, or served as guardians of the poor.

Many found that their responsibilities lead them to question women's exclusion from political influence. One such was Wilhelmina Lydia Brodie-Hall (1845-1939). A great-granddaughter of John Walter, founder of 'The Times' newspaper, in 1908 she made a bid to take control of the paper with her Walter cousins. She spent most of her life in Eastbourne, where she was a founder member of the town's Natural History Society. By the early twentieth century she was living at The Haven in Peaslake. She had come to politics after 25 years on the board of Eastbourne's poor law guardians (often as the only women). Her particular concerns were for the welfare of children, the elderly, and paupers with mental health problems. As secretary of the Association for the Advancement of Boarding Out, she advocated the fostering of children dependent on the poor rates (and thus consigned to the workhouse with their parents). She urged poor law guardians to place workhouse children with families or in settings where they might have a more natural

---

Ethel Akers-Douglas

Wilhelmina Brodie Hall's companion in later years in Peaslake was Ethel Margaret Akers-Douglas (1879-1951), the daughter of Aretas Akers-Douglas, 1st Viscount Chilston, (a former home secretary). In 1908 she qualified as a doctor. Her studies probably precluded her from having campaigned actively for women's suffrage. It was unusual even for militant WSPU supporting medical students to risk getting into trouble for the cause until after they had qualified for fear of being accused of not conducting themselves in a manner appropriate to their desired professional status. Even after qualification they had to consider the dignity of the profession. Mrs Pankhurst told female medical students that qualifying to practice was sufficient support for the cause.

upbringing in the community, an education, and the chance to learn a trade. She was a prolific speaker in favour of female doctors; she advised the Royal College of Nursing to press for women to be allowed to sit on hospital boards, and addressed a Commons select committee on infant mortality. She was also involved with the Girls' Friendly Society and spoke about ending prostitution in order to raise women to 'a higher nobler' life. A Conservative, she was a member of the Eastbourne Women's Suffrage Society and took the chair when Millicent Fawcett spoke there in 1909. And she was a vice-president of Harriet Grote's Liberal-leaning London National Society for Women's Suffrage.

Some women, like Margaret Pennington, were directly active in party politics, fund-raising and campaigning for the established political parties in the hope that if they proved themselves responsible and intelligent citizens their efforts would be rewarded and their fitness to vote recognised. Though denying them the vote, the 1884 Act's enfranchisement of large numbers of new male voters served to increase women's involvement in politics as the campaigning that must be undertaken to reach such voters required a party structure. Women were therefore drawn into organising and fundraising, into hand-shaking and tea-making, into speaking and distributing. By the end of the century much of the legwork of the major parties was being done by women who had no vote themselves.

Anomalies in entitlements to vote at the end of nineteenth century are highlighted in this suffrage poster. Men of all social classes and capabilities, from the manual labourer to the influential grandee, make their way to the polling station to cast their vote whilst accomplished female graduates, lawyers, teachers, nurses, artists, musicians, and mothers, are turned away. Depicting the huge advances made by women and the contribution they were making to society by the end of the century, it reflects the frustrations of campaigners. Women had based their claim to the vote on proving themselves to be responsible, hardworking, taxpaying citizens; it infuriated campaigners that only gender was considered relevant. (LSE Library)

With no immediate prospect of government sponsored legislation to extend the franchise to the lower orders (on which the vote for women might piggy-back its way through Parliament) it had become clear that women would have to fight for a

16

specific women's vote. But decades of reasoned persuasion by groups such as those sponsored by Grote and Pennington had resulted in nothing by way of legislation. Though women's suffrage was a non-party issue and many MPs, including the member for Mid-Surrey, Sir Trevor Lawrence, professed to be in favour, neither Conservatives nor Liberals wished to risk doing something that might give electoral advantage to the other. (The fledgling Labour party was unwilling to support limited female enfranchisement – which would benefit the wealthy – rather than universal suffrage that would give all working men the vote. It was too small in any event to wield influence.) Women were reliant therefore on a favourably-minded MP winning the ballot for a private member's bill and choosing to introduce a female suffrage bill which would in all likelihood be voted down or talked out at the behest of party whips. Repeated such disappointments left many campaigners frustrated.

By 1900 the leading campaigning organisation was the National Union of Women's Suffrage Societies (NUWSS). With thousands of members, it had affiliated branches all over the country. Its members tended to be respectable members of society, of professional and, in many cases eminent, families, for whom 'militant' action would have been inconceivable. They had written, petitioned and lectured for nearly forty years; they would wait as long as it took. There were others, however, who were not willing to wait. And they would seek not to convince - but to coerce.

Margaret Chorley Crosfield

Margaret Chorley Crosfield (1859-1952) was born at Wray Park, the daughter of a tea merchant. Her Quaker school was one of the first to send girls to university and she went to Newnham, Cambridge. But as a woman she could not be awarded a degree, nor be affiliated to an academic institution. Nonetheless her fieldwork and research, much of it undertaken with Ethel Skeat, was published in academic journals. She made a significant contribution to our understanding of the Silurian and Ordovician stratigraphy of north-east Wales and discovered a new species of trilobite. An early member of The Geologists' Association, she was elected to the British Association for the Advancement of Science in 1894 and was one of the first female fellows of the Geological Society.

She hosted a suffrage meeting at The Dingle in Reigate in 1883. By the early twentieth century she had moved to Undercroft in Raglan Road and was an active member of The Reigate and Redhill Women's Suffrage Society. Some of her field notes are written on the back of suffrage notepaper.

In 1918 Lord Farrer urged the Reigate WSS to oppose the 'flapper finance bill', suggesting that as a wife's expenses were a drain on a man he ought to be allowed a tax allowance in respect of keeping a wife. Crosfield retorted that in a wife a man had a slave or an unpaid housekeeper; therefore to claim the expense of keeping her as a burden for which he ought to be given an allowance was like a slave owner complaining at the unfair expense of keeping slaves!

Women's suffrage and Holmwood vicarage

Women's suffrage was being discussed in the Surrey village of Holmwood as early as 1873, only six years after John Stuart Mill's first petition. *'My father does not see why women should not have votes'*, wrote Agnes Wickham (1841-?), youngest daughter of St Mary Magdalene's vicar, Edmund Dawe Wickham, to her anti-suffragist associate in community works, Bertha Broadwood of Lyne House in Capel. The Wickham family of six girls and two boys was wealthy and well-connected with intellectual interests. They employed a German governess, the sisters married influential writers and scholars, and the Reverend took an interest in 'women's issues'. (One of their friends, Lucy Waters, travelled alone to New Zealand in 1862.) *'He seems to have a better opinion of our sex than we venture to have,'* Agnes went on, seemingly inclined to take her father's view: *'Are '£12 men' superior to women of the same rank? Well! Probably ye and all will have to submit to whatever comes.'* For Agnes Wickham the idea of women voting was not so outlandish that it might not be expected to happen imminently. In fact 45 years would pass before the vote became a reality for women.

There were suffrage campaigners in Agnes Wickham's family. Her cousin Emmeline Agnes Fawcett (daughter of the Reverend's sister Mary Agnes) married into the wealthy Huguenot Cazalet family and settled with her husband William Clement Cazalet and their nine daughters (and one son) at Grenehurst in Capel. Women's suffrage was without doubt a topic of discussion in the household as their aunt, (and Emmeline's sister-in-law, married to her husband's brother, Edward), was a member of the National Society for Women's suffrage and their cousin, William Marshall Cazalet (son of Edward), went on to marry suffrage campaigner, Maud Lucia Heron-Maxwell (1868-1952) who was a confidante of Mrs Pankhurst. She owned land with Eva McLaren of Minnickfold, with whom she went out campaigning. Maud and William's daughter, Thelma Cazalet (later Keir) (1899-1989) became a Conservative MP in 1931, serving in Parliament alongside her brother, Victor. She went on to work with Emmeline Pethick-Lawrence as chair of the Equal Pay Campaign.

The Wickham family at Holmwood vicarage. (Dorking Museum)

Minnickfold and the Bright-McLarens

In 1898 Eva Maria McLaren (nee Muller) (1853-1921) and her brother-in-law, Liberal MP Sir Charles Benjamin Bright McLaren (1850-1934), leased Minnickfold, between Holmwood and Coldharbour. It was close to the home of Frederick and Margaret Pennington, to whom Sir Charles was closely related. His wife was suffrage campaigner Laura Bright nee Pochin (1854-1933), whose father was a radical Liberal MP. Sir Charles had given up his legal career in order to help with his wife's business affairs when Laura was left with her family businesses (rather than her disreputable brother).

Eva Maria was married to Sir Charles' brother, Walter Stowe Bright McLaren MP. The daughter of a German businessman, she and her and sister, Henrietta Muller (c1851-1906) were both committed suffrage campaigners. Eva worked with Octavia Hill in housing management, trained as a nurse, campaigned with Josephine Butler to repeal the Contagious Diseases Acts, and was one of the earliest women poor law guardians (in Lambeth in 1884). From its foundation in 1886 she was treasurer and national organizer of the Women's Liberal Federation, working from within the party to promote the vote for women through local women's Liberal associations. She also sat on the executive of the national suffrage societies. Eva and Walter devoted their lives to women's issues. She insisted on being known as 'Mrs Eva McLaren', rather than 'Mrs Walter McLaren', a move unusual even amongst suffrage campaigners, arguing that it was more important that people knew who she was than who she was married to. Walter supported women's emancipation throughout his career and wrote 'The Political Emancipation of Women'. Eva wrote on women's civil rights, on the election of women to parish and district councils, and an early history of the women's suffrage movement. She was also a public speaker.

The McLarens were committed to women's suffrage, but, like many Liberals, they were often conflicted as to the means by which it might be achieved, and the terms on which it would be acceptable.

Minnickfold, left, the home of the Bright-McLarens, and Broome Hall, right, the home of the Spottiswoodes and the Penningtons. (Dorking Museum)

Diana of the Crossways –
George Meredith of Box Hill and property rights for women

The lack of the vote was just one of the injustices suffered by women that were under scrutiny by radical thinkers in the mid to late nineteenth century. An issue with more practical ramifications was that of property. Until 1882, when a woman married she ceased to have a separate legal identity to that of her husband, meaning that she could no longer hold property in her own right. Even if a woman was independently wealthy, or earned money during her marriage, that money belonged to her husband. So a married woman was vulnerable even in the best of marriages. Wealthy families protected their daughters by way of legally enforceable marriage settlements that provided incomes for them; but for most women financial security was a matter of a husband's whim - as Caroline Norton (1808-1877) discovered in 1835.

Caroline Sheridan was the grand-daughter of the playwright Richard Brinsley Sheridan (1761-1816) of Polesden Lacey. In 1827 she married George Norton. He was abusive and the marriage disintegrated in 1835. Caroline was barred from the family home and denied access to her children. (Norton's accusations of adultery with the Prime Minister, Lord Melbourne, made her notorious but failed to convince.) As a married woman with no status in law there was no possibility of her taking action against Norton for money or for access to her children. She therefore set to campaigning for the rights of separated and divorced women: the resulting Custody of Infants Act 1839 gave custody of children under seven to the mother and access rights thereafter. (Norton, however, removed their sons to Scotland where the law did not apply.)

She took to campaigning again in 1851, when, on the death of her mother, her husband stood to inherit her mother's interest in the family estate. This brought a round of legal battles over his responsibility for her debts and her entitlement to her own earnings. The result of her efforts was the Matrimonial

Causes Act 1857 which gave separated women access to a financial settlement.

Caroline Norton never saw herself as a campaigner for women's rights, nor did she consider women equal to men; she was simply, she argued, seeking to right a wrong. She did not campaign for married women's property rights – only those of separated women – but the issue was taken to its logical conclusion by other campaigners. In 1882 the Married Women's Property Act gave married women a legal identity separate from that of their husbands. This allowed them to own property and made them responsible for their own debts.

A writer herself, Norton was a friend of the novelist, George Meredith (1828-1909) who lived at Flint Cottage on Box Hill. He based his best-known novel, 'Diana of the Crossways' (1885), on the events of her life, setting it at Crossways Farm in Abinger. Meredith advocated women's emancipation and in his old age became known for his support of female suffrage. Amongst his local circle were pioneering female foreign correspondent Flora Shaw of Little Parkhurst in Abinger and Harriet Grote's nephew, Colonel Thomas Herbert Lewin of Parkhurst. He was also responsible for introducing the formidable Brackenbury women to Peaslake. Lines from his works were regularly quoted by suffrage supporters: a column in the 'Dorking Advertiser' in 1912, by non-militant Isabel Hecht of Westcott, references his 'Ballad of Fair Ladies in Revolt'. She claimed that his every novel preached emancipation and the rights of women.

His attitude to the militancy of the Pankhursts seems to have been ambivalent. In correspondence he declared that militant demonstrations were a flawed tactic and that women should instead concentrate on proving their intellect. He advised the Leith Hill Women's Suffrage Society to follow Mrs Fawcett for *'the combative suffragists play the enemy's game.'* But he wrote to 'The Times' in support of Emmeline Pethick-Lawrence when she was imprisoned in 1906, and his claim to Millicent Fawcett that he could not *'quite excuse those suffragists who have given a weapon to their adversaries by their [militant] behaviour'*, was hardly an unambiguous condemnation.

Crowds came to his funeral at Dorking cemetery when he was denied burial at Westminster Abbey. Attendees included Colonel Lewin, Sylvia Drew of the Leith Hill Women's Suffrage Society, and Isabel Hecht. *'In reverence and gratitude to one who to women was ever critic, counsellor and friend'* read the Leith Hill society's crown of lilies, with a quote from his 'Ballad of Fair Ladies in Revolt': *'Then are there fresher mornings mounting east than ever yet have dawned.'* *'To our noble champion with undying gratitude'* read that of the Godalming Women's Suffrage Society, whilst Millicent Fawcett's tribute read simply: *'In grateful memory'*. Tributes were paid by both the Leith Hill Women's Suffrage Society and the Redhill and Reigate Women's Suffrage Society at subsequent meetings. *Caroline Norton by Emma Fergusson. (National Portrait Gallery of Scotland. Image courtesy of Stephen Dickson); George Meredith by Samuel Hollyer (Library of Congress)*

A new century and a new campaign: the Pankhursts

In 1903 Emmeline Pankhurst decided that women should stop putting their faith and their fates into the hands of male MPs who put party politics before commitment to an issue that to them was just one of many. The major parties had repeatedly failed women, she argued, and should be deprived of their female support. Rather than joining a mainstream party and raising funds for it in the hope of winning influence and gratitude, women should join an organisation with one aim – to win the vote for women.

Emmeline Pankhurst was a regular visitor to Holmwood, and lived for a time in Peaslake. Her daughter, Christabel, lived with the Pethick-Lawrences for five years in London and Holmwood. The handsome femininity of mother and daughter won over nervous potential supporters. (Postcard from the collection of the family of Alice Hawkins, www.alicesuffragette.co.uk)

The widow of Dr Richard Pankhurst (1835-1898), a reforming Manchester lawyer and founding member of the Independent Labour Party, Emmeline Pankhurst nee Goulden (1858-1928) was registrar for births, marriages and deaths in Manchester. She formed the Women's Social and Political Union (WSPU) with a group of women from Manchester's Independent Labour Party. Her eldest daughter Christabel Harriette Pankhurst (1880-1958) was studying law in the city – though with no hope of practising since the profession was closed to women. Her second daughter, (Estelle) Sylvia Pankhurst (1882-1960), was at art school in London. A third daughter, Adela Constantia Mary Pankhurst (1885-1961), and her young son, Harry, also became involved.

The WSPU began life as a small and somewhat disorganised fringe group. It initially differed from its long-established rivals not so much in tactics as in the nature of its support as Mrs Pankhurst sought to educate and convert Manchester's working women to the cause. This was not a straightforward matter since many working class men did not have the vote. Despite criticism from the Labour movement, however, that she was putting the interests of wealthy and propertied women above those of the disenfranchised working man, she remained committed to what would become the organisation's catch-phrase: 'Votes for Women' - on the same terms as men. Women's commitment would no longer be divided by class to the advantage of men. Universal adult suffrage must follow the women's vote.

In 1905, after two years of opinion-forming amongst local radical groups, the WSPU witnessed yet another private member's suffrage bill talked out in Parliament at the second reading stage. It never reached a vote due to the filibustering of Northampton MP Henry

Christabel Pankhurst. (Postcard from the collection of the family of Alice Hawkins, www.alicesuffragette.co.uk)

Labouchere (1831-1912) who deliberately talked at inordinate length on the previous bill, (concerning lights being fitted to carts after the hours of darkness), which ensured that the suffrage bill would run out of time and therefore never make it to the statute books. Mrs Pankhurst called the meeting held in protest outside the Houses of Parliament the WSPU's first 'militant' action.

In response to such contempt the Pankhursts initiated a campaign aimed at forcing the issue of the vote into the papers to provoke public debate. Supporters began to appear with banners at political meetings and to question candidates at hustings. Their first headline-grabbing action came in October 1905 when Christabel, accompanied by mill girl Annie Kenney (1879-1953), interrupted a meeting held by Sir Edward Grey (1862-1933) at the Free Trade Hall in Manchester to ask *'Will the Liberal government give women the vote?'* When they deliberately got themselves arrested, the two women made the national papers. Their youth and passion caught the public imagination in a way that 40 years of respectful campaigning had failed to do.

In the run up to the general election of January 1906 women of the WSPU, together with London-based sympathisers, demanded to be allowed to question candidates at the hustings. They may have attracted jeers and abuse but they raised the profile of the issue.

With the Liberal landslide of 1906 the prospect of achieving the vote appeared promising. The Liberal Party, with its radical element, had traditionally been less opposed to the idea than the Conservatives. Prime Minister Sir Henry Campbell-Bannerman (1862-1933) was known to be sympathetic, as were several of his cabinet, and the (mainly) sympathetic Labour Party had achieved 29 MPs. It was full of hope, therefore, that the WSPU set off to lobby the new parliament.

The organisation needed a London base. Mrs Pankhurst's job was funding the organisation, so she was precluded from leaving Manchester, and Christabel had not completed her law degree. It therefore fell to Annie Kenney and Sylvia Pankhurst to establish the organisation in the capital. The story goes that Annie had never been south, knew no-one in London but Sylvia, and set off to establish the WSPU's London office with just two pounds in her pocket. In fact Annie had campaigned in London during the election campaign and the WSPU had powerful friends in the capital. One of them was Keir Hardie, leader of the Independent Labour Party, its first MP, life-long Pankhurst family friend, and long-time suffrage supporter. He recommended the services of one Emmeline Pethick-Lawrence. It was her involvement, and those of other middle-class women like her, that would make the villages of Surrey rather than the radical industrial heartlands of the north, the home of the WSPU.

Liberal anti-suffragist MP Henry Labouchere (1831-1912) talked out the private member's bill that would have given some women the vote in 1905. A rakish character who owned a theatre, his living arrangements summed up the moral leeway allowed to wealthy men of the period: he lived with a married actress with whom he had fathered a child but whom he could not marry until the death of her husband.

Labouchere's banker father, John, had occupied Broome Hall near Coldharbour - sometime home of the suffrage-supporting Penningtons and of Augusta Spottiswoode. John Labouchere is credited with having brought the railway south from Dorking to Horsham through Holmwood. After his father's death Henry Labouchere's widowed mother, Mary Louisa (nee Du Pre), established the great estate of Oakdene (later known as Capel Leyse) near South Holmwood.
(Library of Congress)

Sylvia Pankhurst and Keir Hardie

The leader of the Independent Labour Party and MP for Merthyr Tydfil, James Keir Hardie was a life-long women's suffrage supporter. Women were *'more and more taking part in the world's work',* he argued, therefore *'it surely follows that they ought also to enjoy the chief rights of citizenship otherwise they will suffer from sex legislation quite as much as men have suffered from class legislation'.*

Hardie recommended Emmeline Pethick-Lawrence to the Pankhursts when they were trying to establish the WSPU in London. A long-time family friend, he knew Emmeline Pethick-Lawrence through her mission work. He became close to Frederick Pethick-Lawrence when Fred was editor and owner of 'The Echo', and he and his family spent weekends with the couple in Holmwood. Emmeline gave Hardie's daughter, Maggie, detailed instructions on what to do if arrested: wear no jewellery or furs; say nothing; insist on your own clothes; do not use prison combs, brushes or hairpins for fear of nits, and insist on air and exercise.

Sylvia Pankhurst was a life-long friend of the Pethick-Lawrences and a frequent visitor to their homes. A talented artist, she was denied access to the opening of Pankhurst Hall in Salford, (despite having been commissioned to execute the murals there in memory of her father), because she was a woman. In 1903 she won a scholarship to the Royal College of Art and her artistic influence can be seen on WSPU banners and merchandising. Her designs complemented the heightened religiose rhetoric of Emmeline Pethick-Lawrence. Sylvia always saw the campaign for the vote as part of the larger struggle for social change and was torn between loyalty to the WSPU, her involvement with the labour movement, and her artistic career.

Sylvia and Hardie conducted a long-running affair. In 1915 Emmeline was speaking against conscription with Sylvia in Trafalgar Square when Sylvia spotted a newspaper billboard announcing Hardie's death and collapsed. *(Library of Congress)*

Annie Kenney

Annie Kenney began her working life as a mill-girl in Manchester at the age of 10. By her mid-20s she had been a union organizer for many years. Taking her into their entourage, the Pethick-Lawrences dressed her, educated her, and took her on their travels in Europe. A regular visitor to Holmwood she practically lived at The Mascot in 1906. Several of her sisters were involved in the campaign and one of them, Jessie, worked as secretary to the Pethick-Lawrences for a time.

The relationship between Emmeline Pethick-Lawrence and Annie was intense, to the extent that some had concerns about it. Fellow campaigner Theresa Billington-Grieg wrote that it was *'so emotional and so openly paraded that it frightened me as I saw it as unbalanced and primitive and possibly dangerous to the movement.'* When the Pethick-Lawrences split with the Pankhursts, however, Annie stayed with the Pankhursts.

Fred continued to visit Annie into old age, calling in at her home in Letchworth whenever he visited his sister who lived nearby.
(Postcard from the collection of the family of Alice Hawkins, www.alicesuffragette.co.uk)

A bit of singing and dancing:
Emmeline Pethick, Mary Neal and the Esperance Club

Emmeline Pethick (1867-1954) was the eldest surviving child of a large middle-class, non-conformist family from Bristol. Her father, to whom she was close, was forward-thinking; she and her sisters were amongst the first girls to ride bicycles in Weston-super-Mare, scandalizing some. Emmeline was elegant, striking, and had great charm. Years later, her friend Mary Neal recalled her beautiful eyes and dignified, attractive voice, which was described by one of her secretaries as being

Emmeline Pethick-Lawrence in a postcard put out by the Women's Social and Political Union. (Copyright People's History Museum NMLH 2001.15.15)

like golden syrup. She was 'finished' for marriage in France and Germany where, with her gift for languages, she picked up fluent French and German. But Emmeline had inherited her father's passion for social justice, and in 1890, at the age of 23, she left Bristol for London to work with the West London Methodist Mission. The poverty and social deprivation that she encountered in the London slums lead her to socialism. It also lead her to another pioneering worker for the poor, her life-long friend, Clara Sophia 'Mary' Neal (1860-1944).

Neal had also left a comfortable home (in Birmingham) to work as 'Sister Mary' with the Mission, where she ran a girl's club. Emmeline Pethick was assigned to assist. She was, recommended her mentor (and another life-long friend), the Rev Mark Guy Pearse (1842-1930), *'an idealist and very sensitive and wouldn't believe anyone was unhelpable'*. She would get a shock, he warned Neal, but she would hold on to her belief. The two young women became immediate friends. But shortly after Emmeline's arrival, Neal was taken ill with suspected TB. Emmeline took over the running of the club. After Neal's recovery she and Emmeline ran the club together and Emmeline discovered her talent for public speaking: *'Should women preach?'* asked one report of the club's activities: *'If they can preach like Sister Emmie they ought to do nothing else.'* Many years later Gladys Groom Smith recalled an anti-war meeting at the Home and Empire on Kingsway where Emmeline was so compelling a speaker that three men in the audience were reduced to tears.

Club work was not for the faint-hearted lady; on one occasion a riot almost resulted in destruction of the club, and Pethick and Neal came across all manner of social distress from drunkenness to incest. Conventional advocates of temperance, they were initially anxious to improve the character of the urban poor. But they came to have misgivings about the work of the Mission. They felt that that the Mission household, with its maids and servants, was too middle-class and comfortable, isolating the volunteers from those with whom they worked. A waning of their conventional Christian faith was accompanied by ambition for social change as they came to understand more of the lives of the girls and their families. The realisation that despite long days in the clothing trade the girls were unable to make enough money to live on, whilst the profits of their labours supported the middle-class daughters of business owners like themselves to live in comfort, lead to a questioning of the whole economic system.

In 1895 Neal and Pethick resigned from the Mission and set about a social experiment of their own. They took a small flat in a block designated for working men, number 20 Somerset Terrace, behind St Pancras church. Unusually for young women of their class, they cooked and cleaned for themselves, and entertained radical thinkers, politicians and campaigners. Edward Carpenter, Havelock Ellis, Ramsay MacDonald, George Lansbury and Keir Hardie all visited them. They also established their own girls' club. Opening for two hours nightly, the aim of the Esperance Girls' Club in Cumberland Market was to improve the lives of those who toiled in the sweatshops of the West End clothing trade. For a short time the girls might escape the drudgery of work and home. Evenings were given over to games, sewing and cooking, lectures and talks, and to music and dance, activities by which Neal and Pethick believed they might develop socially, intellectually and spiritually.

The pair were criticized by socialists for wasting their time in seeking to extend to a handful of youngsters the benefits that the economic regime had bestowed on their own class, rather than throwing their energies into an attempt to change the system to the benefit of the working class generally. The foundation of Maison Esperance in 1897 went some way to addressing such issues. The dressmaking business was established in Great Portland Street on a new model. It paid its female employees what Neal and Pethick calculated to be the minimum required to maintain a decent standard of living (and therefore more than the wage that the girls might otherwise have commanded). It kept limited working hours and guaranteed annual leave. In 1899 a philanthropic young man named Frederick Lawrence bought some shares in Maison Esperance. Emmeline later explained to him that her commitment to socialism was in her bones, that it was her touch-stone and her standard of values. She claimed that her commitment stemmed from her *clearest, strongest and most inveterate sense of the dignity and worth of the human body and soul above everything else*' which, she said, had forced her '*into a life long campaign – against every sort of bondage, against all sorts of established authorities: and it... has kept me (not by choice but by inward necessity) always against the stream... This is the great context of the coming century: the life and death struggle of human life against material mastery.'*

It was part of the Esperance philosophy that the aspirations of the young women of the club should be raised by the sharing of experiences. Emmeline therefore described her excursions by train to walk in the Leith Hill countryside. Most of the girls had never left the city, so she and Mary Neal decided to take them on holiday to experience the countryside for themselves.

Following the success of the first Esperance holiday to Bisley, the club holidayed for three years at Broadmoor, described by Mary Neal as *'a tiny hamlet in Surrey at the foot of Leith Hill'*. The girls saved all year to contribute their ten shillings towards the cost of staying in set of holiday cottages rented out by the wife of Brooke Bond tea magnate, Arthur Brooke of Leylands, in Abinger. So unusual was the concept of time off work for working people that Neal and Pethick had to obtain written confirmation from every employer that the girls would not be dismissed for their week's absence (for which they were, of course, not paid). Later in life Mary Neal recalled with fondness their visits to Leith Hill, singing as they walked, and the old lady who kept the key to the tower there.

The cottages in Broadmoor which were let to the Esperance Club had a communal reading room and are thought to have been designed by Arnold Dunbar Smith, who later designed The Sundial for Fred and Emmeline. (Dorking Museum)

Lily Montagu was the daughter of Anglo-Jewish philanthropist and Liberal MP for Whitechapel, Samuel Montagu (later Lord Swaythling) (1832-1911). She was introduced to club work by her school-friend, Margaret Gladstone, who married another of Emmeline's associates, future Prime Minister, James Ramsay MacDonald. Lily was later instrumental in the founding of the Liberal Jewish synagogue in London. She was a supporter of women's suffrage; in 1911 the West Central Girls' Club passed a resolution declaring itself in favour of the cause, and she was vice-president of the Jewish League for Women's Suffrage. But Emmeline's influence was not sufficient to convert her to militancy.

The house in East Street is now known as Ormsby House.
(The Jewish Museum, London)

Neal and Pethick were in the vanguard of a movement that would eventually see the development of holiday camps for working people and the establishment of the youth hostel movement. Their next move was to buy a house near the sea at Littlehampton. They joined forces in this venture with Lily Montagu (1873-1963). Lily and her sister, Marion, had established a similar club to the Esperance, the West Central Club, for Jewish girls. Together they converted the house into a hostel for working people. Lily Montagu's father donated money, as did new Emmeline's husband when she married in 1901. The money was used to add a storey to the building so that it could sleep sixty people.

The hostel was named The Green Lady after the myth of Demeter and her daughter, Persephone. It was intended to signify the rejuvenation of modern urban woman through contact with the pure air and freedom of the countryside. When not in use by the Esperance or the West Central, The Green Lady was rented by clubs of all denominations for working people and children, not at a profit but at a price calculated to cover the costs. The catering at the Green Lady, recalled Lily Montagu, could be curious and unsatisfying, the windows inadequate, the mattresses soft and the crockery chipped, but *'no house in the world could ever have entertained happier groups of girls and women.'*

Mary Neal said that Emmeline Pethick-Lawrence would not have considered herself a mystic, but, asserted Neal: *'if living in close touch with the unseen forces and in touch with the beautifying vivifying forces of earth and sky and sea and a power to transmute these life giving spiritual forces into the sternest practical work is not being a mystic then [the term] would have no meaning for me.'*

Neal and Pethick's belief in the restorative powers of the countryside was allied to nostalgia for the perceived purity of the pre-industrial past. In 1908 Emmeline was the dedicatee of a playlet, 'Dear Mother Earth', by Alfred Sayers (later the WSPU's auditor). Performed by the Esperance girls under Emmeline's direction, it is the mystical tale of a town girl going to the country where she is awakened and her heart set singing. It neatly sums Pethick and Neal's view of town folk as disinherited from the earth that is their birthright. These strands of thought fed into many of the Esperance's activities, but none more so than the dancing for which the Esperance girls would become famous.

Emmeline started a singing class at the club which was later taken over by Herbert MacIlwaine. In 1905 Mary Neal approached Cecil Sharp (1862-1933), a music teacher who had collected and published a volume of folk songs, to ask whether she might have some of these traditional songs for the Esperance girls to sing. When this proved a success she approached him for dances, and was passed on to William Kimber (1872-1961) of the Headington Quarrymen Morris dance group in Oxford. Traditional Morris dancing had more or less died out and in many areas it was unknown.

The influence of mystical progressive thinker Edward Carpenter (1844-1929) can be seen in many of Emmeline's initiatives. A visitor to the home that she shared with Mary Neal, Carpenter had left the Church in the 1870s to teach in deprived areas and to establish a rural community. His advocacy of self-sufficiency and the simple life was taken up by FE Green and the smallholders' organisation in Newdigate and his radical social ideas inspired the Kibbo Kift youth movement which Emmeline and many of her left-leaning, pacifist, anti-imperialist friends joined after the First World War. In 1921 he moved to Guildford; mutual friends Evelyn Sharp, EM Forster and Henry Nevinson all visited him there. In 1944 Emmeline marked the centenary of Carpenter's birth with a celebration in Peaslake at which Forster gave a speech.
A verse from Carpenter's 'Children of Freedom' is inscribed below the portrait of the Pethick-Lawrences which hangs in Peaslake Village Hall. (Photograph by Fred Holland Day)

Kimber, however, was able to provide the Esperance Club with dancers to teach the girls. The tuition was received with such enthusiasm that the Esperance Morris Guild was formed to give public performances.

There was growing nostalgia at the beginning of the twentieth century for aspects of times past that had been lost to industrialization and the movement of working people to the cities. This manifested itself in such developments as the Arts and Crafts movement and in the return to a rustic style of architecture. Much of the impulse was romantic; towns and cities were smoggy, filthy, crime-ridden and overcrowded; the past, and the countryside, offered an alternative, pre-lapserian vision. So whilst city men built miniature pleasure farms within railway distance of London, Sharp and his collaborators collected and recorded songs and dances that had been handed down from generation to generation. (Lucy Broadwood of Lyne House in Capel and Ralph Vaughan Williams of Leith Hill Place were undertaking a similar exercise in the villages and fields and would collaborate with Sharp in the founding of the English Folk Dance and Song Society). The Esperance girls and their obsolete dances found themselves the object of much attention. They were invited to perform at the country houses of their benefactors, (raising money for her projects was one of Emmeline Pethick's talents), and in schools. Soon they were travelling the country giving demonstrations. And eventually, after school teachers had received lessons, country dancing was incorporated into school curricula.

Cecil Sharp published the first book of Morris dances; it was followed by 'The Esperance Morris Book'. Morris troupes were formed all over the country and Sharp went out into the countryside to record more dances from remaining practitioners, which he then published in a second book, greatly increasing the repertoire that is available to dancers today. Though Neal and Sharp fell out over the question of authenticity, each played a part in the revival that ensured the survival of Morris dancing. The Esperance girls played a key role in establishing Morris as the dance form that symbolises rural England to this day, rather than one encountered only in academic journals.

Emmeline Pethick, meanwhile, had been advancing the club's aims by other means, resulting in the dancers being often seen in the Surrey village of Holmwood. Soon her activities outside the club would see the dancers, together with Mary Neal, and Cecil Sharp's sisters, drawn into the campaign for the vote.

Mary Neal – a life-long friendship

Emmeline recruited Mary Neal onto the London committee of the WSPU in 1906 and onto the national committee (which seldom met) the following year. Neal spoke for the WSPU, but she was never an active militant. She was too preoccupied with the Esperance dancers. Nonetheless she gave Emmeline practical help and took care of her Surrey home and staff during Emmeline's imprisonments.

As she became embroiled in the suffrage campaign, Emmeline had less involvement with the Esperance Club, though she continued to holiday with the girls and to take an interest in individuals. It was Mary Neal who was responsible for the growing reputation of the Esperance dancers. In 1910 she and Florence 'Florrie' Warren undertook a teaching tour of America. Warren married in the United States and named one of her daughters after Neal, another after Emmeline. Another protégé was Esther Knowles, who spent her life working for Fred and Emmeline; she was introduced to the couple through an older sister and brother-in-law who were Esperance dancers.

Mary Neal originally worked closely with the dance-collector, Cecil Sharp, but a rift opened between them over the authenticity of the dance as practised by the Esperance girls. Sharp felt that Neal valued enthusiasm over accuracy. His misgivings increased as she began to emphasize the role of dance in social reform. Neal saw dance as a means to promote social inclusivity, by giving confidence and a sense of belonging to the socially excluded girls of the urban poor. Sharp grew alienated at the use of dance as a tool for social empowerment with little regard to the accuracy of the original dances. He dissociated himself from her and from the Esperance. The disagreement was bitter and public: the composer and folk song collector, Ralph Vaughan Williams (1872-1958), (who grew up at Leith Hill Place and later lived in Dorking), attended a fancy-dress party dressed as Neal with a placard hung about him reading *'Power not accuracy'*. The Esperance's singing director, Herbert MacIlwaine, resigned rather than be associated with Neal and her friends because of their political opinions. (Though quite likely Neal's proximity to Emmeline Pethick-Lawrence and the increasingly notorious suffragettes was as much a concern as Neal's opinions on dance.) Others, like the teacher and promoter, Nellie Chaplin and her Whall cousins, stayed loyal to Neal.

In 1908 Lady Constance Lytton met Emmeline through the Esperance dancers. The organisation that had brought underprivileged girls into the limelight now brought to the WSPU the political commitment of a woman who was able to publicize the inequality of treatment experienced by upper-class women like herself whilst in prison, and that endured by working-class girls.

Mary Neal left the WSPU with the Pethick-Lawrences in 1912, and joined them in the United Suffragists. During the First World War she worked in the pensions office, whilst raising funds for the United Suffragists' Southwark working women's club with the Esperance dancers. After the explosion at the Silvertown munitions factory in 1917, (which blew in the windows of her home), an exhausted Neal suffered a mental breakdown and a prolonged period of illness. In 1925 a group of admirers collected 100 guineas to enable her to recuperate, or, as they put it: to give her *the gifts of happiness and pleasure to which you have yourself so generously dispensed to many'*. Those contributing included Emmeline's family – her sister and brother-in-law, Nancy and Mortimer Budgett and her brother Harold – their secretary, Esther Knowles, their architect, Arnold Dunbar Smith, suffrage colleagues Betty Balfour and her brother, Neville Lytton, and folk revival contacts including Nellie Chaplin, Lucy Broadwood and Florrie Warren. Neal moved to Amberley in Sussex, (which she had visited from The Green Lady), and offered a home to two boys aged six and seven. She went on to adopt Anthony MacIlwaine, the orphaned son of Herbert MacIlwaine. (On one occasion Emmeline turned up to tea to find the boys delivering coal in their best clothes.)

Neal introduced Emmeline Pethick-Lawrence to the youth leader, Rolf Gardiner (1902-1971), who also saw dance as a life-giving force with the potential to be harnessed for the public good. Both women became supporters of his Kibbo Kift movement. Between the wars Neal moved to Littlehampton where she sat as a magistrate, specializing in juvenile courts. She named her home 'Green Bushes' after a popular folk song. In 1937 she was awarded the CBE for her services to English song and dance. Emmeline Pethick-Lawrence and Rolf Gardiner spoke at the celebratory lunch at Claridges. As she aged, however, a more spiritual and mystical Mary Neal came to feel that in upsetting the masculine rhythm of the original folk dances she had interfered with a cosmic ritual and been responsible for stirring up spiritual disharmony.

When Littlehampton was bombed during the Second World War – an event which brought back the trauma of Silvertown - she joined the Pethick-Lawrences in the growing ex-suffragette community of Peaslake. She rented a room in a cottage in Rad Lane, close to their home at Fourways, and ate her meals and spent her days with Emmeline. During these years Fred was away much of the time on parliamentary business in London. Though her primary friendship was with Emmeline, Neal got on well with him: when the couple married in 1901 she had claimed that she had not lost a sister but gained a brother. *'Frederick Lawrence and I have always been good pals'*, she wrote, though he found her insistence on having the last word in an argument a trial in later years. Mrs Plaw, the Pethick-Lawrences' cook in Peaslake, witnessed her will.

When Mary Neal died in 1944 Emmeline wrote her obituary, read the eulogy at her cremation in Woking, and tried to get her memoirs, 'A Tale that is Told', published. It is only in recent years that Neal's contribution to the survival of English folk song and dance, and her attempts to combat the de-humanising effects of urban poverty, have been recognised. (*English Folk Song and Dance Society*)

Margaret Vaughan Williams, Evangeline Farrer and the Leith Hill Musical Competitions

The Leith Hill Musical Competition for village choirs was founded by Margaret 'Meggie' Vaughan Williams and Evangeline 'Eva', Lady Farrer of Abinger Hall. The first competition was held at Dorking Public Halls in May 1905. Eight choirs from villages within a ten mile radius competed. Meggie's brother, the composer Ralph Vaughan Williams, chose the music with Lucy Broadwood.

Thereafter the competition was held annually. The competitions generated huge excitement. In 1908 Eva wrote that *'Dorking was worked up to an unknown pitch of excitement. Such a concert has never been in Dorking before. Hundreds were turned away from the door – but they stood outside and heard a good deal and joined loudly in the applause!'*

The involvement of Vaughan Williams attracted some of the most distinguished musicians of the day to participate. The composer, Gustav Holst, came in 1909 as an adjudicator and Hubert Parry presented the awards in 1911. Vaughan Williams was devoted to the festival. He took village choir practices and inspired members to achieve difficult works. *'The composer must not shut himself up and think about art,'* he wrote. *'He must live with his fellows and make his art an expression of the whole community.'* With the Leith Hill Musical Competitions Meggie Vaughan Williams and Eva Farrer fostered musical participation of the highest quality for the whole community, rich and poor.

Like Eva Farrer, Joan Drew, who designed posters for the LHMC, and her sister Sylvia, who conducted festival choirs, were committed suffrage supporters. But there is no evidence of Meggie Vaughan Williams having any involvement in the cause, and competition vice-president Mrs Carey Druce of Rokefield in Westcott was an active anti-suffrage campaigner.

Left: Margaret Vaughan Williams. Right: Mrs Carey Druce and the Westcott choir at Rokefield in 1905. (Dorking Museum)

Anne Cobden-Sanderson, Veronica Whall, and the Chaplins

Veronica Whall (1887-1970) was born and spent much of her childhood at Ada Cottage at Blackbrook near Holmwood. Her father was the renowned Arts and Crafts stained glass artist, Christopher Whall. Her mother, Florence (nee Chaplin), was a portrait painter and her aunt, Alice Chaplin, a sculptor who had modelled animals for Queen Victoria. When the family moved to London in 1896 they became part of a Hammersmith colony of Arts and Crafts artists centred on Ravenscourt Park with the book-binder James Cobden Sanderson. Sanderson's wife, (Julia Sarah) Anne Cobden Sanderson (1853-1926), was the daughter of Richard Cobden of the Anti-Corn Law League. She was a suffrage campaigner and a pacifist. She and Emmeline Pethick-Lawrence were arrested together in October 1906. Despite Anne Cobden-Sanderson leaving the militant WSPU to become a founder member of the Women's Freedom League, she and Emmeline remained friends.

Veronica Whall may not have been active in the suffrage movement, but her family had close links to it through the Sandersons and through Mary Neal. Three of Veronica's many Chaplin cousins, Kate, Mabel and Nellie, were musicians who performed as the Chaplin Trio and (with others) the Chaplin Quartet. Nellie, (who played piano and harpsichord), was a well-known folk dance teacher at the Hampstead conservatoire, a publisher of traditional folk dances and promoter of folk dance events. Embroiled in the battle between Mary Neal and Cecil Sharp, Nellie Chaplin and her Whall cousins, who were also involved in the folk revival, fell on Mary Neal's side of the divide. Cecil Sharp on one occasion described a festival in Blackpool as *'the worst type of Chaplin come Esperance dancing'*.

Left: Anne Cobden Sanderson depicted in the New York papers speaking at a suffragette event in 1907. (Library of Congress)
Centre; Veronica Whall as a young girl in 1900. (The William Morris Galley)
Right: Mabel, Kate and Nellie Chaplin performing in Berlin.
(Universitätsbibliothek Johann Christian Senckenberg, Frankfurt am Main S36/F08369)

Arts and Crafts, song and dance, in London's playground

Neal and Pethick were not alone in their belief in the purifying and restorative powers of country pursuits. Many who were dismayed at city life in the late 19th century viewed the villages of the Surrey hills as places of retreat.

The countryside represented more than just a relief from the crowding of the city; it symbolized an alternative vision for society. Followers of John Ruskin and William Morris rejected the mechanisation and industrialisation of mass production, which they felt had deprived humanity of its dignity. They idealised the workshops of the pre-industrial past. Their followers left the city to set up craft workshops which often owed more to nostalgia than to the reality of artisan production of previous centuries. Close to London and with good transport links, the villages of the Surrey hills saw a stream of incomers seeking to establish a more wholesome way of production. The best known craft workshop was Godfrey Blount's Peasant Arts Society in Haslemere. Another who worked locally was Charles Robert Ashbee (1863-1942) of the Guild of Handicrafts who designed and fitted out the extension to Helen Gordon Liddle's cottage in Peaslake; like Emmeline Pethick-Lawrence, he had roots in the settlement movement. The likes of Blount and Ashbee saw a return to hand production as political, believing that the restoration of the simple life through arts and crafts would reform society. Pottery, wood-crafts and hand-loom weaving all saw a revival in interest and there were many small operations, (like Holmwood's fraternity of weavers at Mill Bottom), across Surrey.

The revival in interest in folk song and dance was part of this general desire to re-connect with what had been lost to industrialisation and urbanisation. Locally, Lucy Etheldred Broadwood (1858-1929) of Lyne House in Capel began collecting folk songs, working with Cecil Sharp and Mary Neal. Her 'English Country Songs' (1893) included several items collected from a Holmwood carter. Later her endeavours caught the attention of family friend Ralph Vaughan Williams who was also in the vanguard of efforts to preserve folk traditions. He recorded local gamekeepers and labourers, motivated by the chance of *'picking up some rare old ballad or an exquisitely beautiful melody'*, which might be, he said, *'worthy, within its smaller compass, of a place beside the finest compositions of the greatest composers'*. Themes from traditional songs from all over the country (including Surrey) found their way into his own compositions.

Lucy Broadwood was a member of the Broadwood piano manufacturing family. Her sister, Bertha, was a prominent member of Dorking's anti-suffrage societies, but Lucy appears to have had no involvement with promoting or opposing the vote for women. *(By permission of Surrey History Centre 2185/LEB/9/111)*

Small girls from the Esperance Club, run by Emmeline Pethick and Mary Neal, dancing on Holmwood Common. (Museum of London)

'Godfather':
Frederick Lawrence

Emmeline Pethick met Frederick Lawrence when she took the Esperance girls to dance at the Mansfield House settlement project in Canning Town. When it was discovered that no tea had been provided for the girls, the project's voluntary treasurer dashed out for bread and cake. Afterwards he came to tea with the settlement's founder, Percy Alden (1865-1944), and soon he came calling on 'Sister Emmie'.

Frederick William Lawrence (1871-1961) was a young man of considerable wealth. Originating in Cornwall, his carpenter grandfather had become a master-builder and made a fortune in the development of Cannon Street. Frederick's father died when he was three and his widowed mother was remote, probably an invalid, and never out of her mourning black. Sent to school early, Fred, as he was known, was not a happy child.

Frederick Lawrence at about the time of his marriage. Chivalrous in an old-fashioned way, his relationship with Emmeline was somewhat fatherly even though he was her junior by four years. Rigid in his personal habits, he was extremely flexible in his world-view, always willing to embrace change and to look to the future.

After Eton he took a double first in Maths and Natural Sciences at Trinity College, Cambridge, where he was president of the Union. Initially he planned an academic career.

He became involved in philanthropic work on meeting Percy Alden whilst he was a student. Inspired by the economist Alfred Marshall (1842-1924), he set out to see how the rest of the world lived. In 1892 he travelled to Russia; in 1897 he went to India, Australia, the United States and the Far East. During this time his faith in social justice was called into question and his Christian belief transmuted into a more personal synthesis of eastern and western belief. (Like Emmeline, he never adopted any formal faith; both were agnostics of a rather romantic frame of mind.)

On his return to England Fred studied for the bar and began to give free legal advice to those in need whilst volunteering as treasurer of the Mansfield House project. The death of his older brother - there were also three sisters, Ellen, Annie and Caroline - saw Fred inheriting his father's fortune in 1900. He considered an attempt to emulate the philanthropist Charles Booth (1840-1916) in his great unfinished study of the streets of London. In the longer term he was expected to follow his uncles - his father's brothers, to whom he was close - into the House of Commons.

Fred was efficient, meticulously organised and precise to the point of compulsiveness. (This hampered him as a public speaker; it was said that he was all facts and no sparkle.) He was a man of routine: he took his meals at regular times and holidayed year after year in the same places and with the same people. For a man so controlled, he was openly emotional, however, revealing himself not just in his letters and poems to Emmeline, but also to associates. He was good company, generous, keen on tennis, billiards and golf. He had many friends though he was apt to treat his friendships with the same meticulousness that he applied to his professional life: alphabetizing his Christmas card list, rigorously observing anniversaries and birthdays, and sending condolence and congratulation messages with an almost obsessive punctiliousness. That obsessiveness found expression even in his plain culinary tastes: he was childishly fussy, never taking tea or coffee, and with such a dread of onions and strongly flavoured ingredients that he demanded the exclusion of a raft of foods when visiting. However, for all the rigidity of his character, Fred would prove to be remarkably open-minded.

He seems to have fallen for Emmeline Pethick almost immediately; later he claimed that it was love at first sight. It is not clear that the feeling was mutual. Mary Neal reportedly told Emmeline on the way home from their first meeting that he was the man that she would marry. In June 1900 Fred Lawrence proposed marriage to Emmeline Pethick. But she refused his proposal. She felt that life with him would not allow her the independence to carry on her campaigning and social work and explained to Fred that the meaning of life for both of them lay above the personal and that she had put aside all thoughts of personal choice in her decision. The key issue was his selection as prospective Liberal Unionist MP for North Lambeth; she, as a committed socialist, did not feel that she could support him in his career. She saw the future as a battle between capitalism and freedom, and told him that in allying himself with a political party that stood for capitalism, he had placed himself in opposition to her beliefs, and that if he married her, he would find himself pulled in opposite directions. A particular sticking point was the contentious second Boer War, which Emmeline described as no more than *organised murder for robbery.'* It was not an issue on which she felt able to turn a blind eye: *'Place, position and any sort of pursuit of power are dust and ashes to me compared with the integrity of one man's soul,'* she wrote.

Fred Lawrence travelled to South Africa to see the situation for himself. Convinced of the Boer cause, he renounced his parliamentary candidacy on his return and invested in a socialist London paper, 'The Echo'. His experiences with Mansfield House had brought him to question the domination of working people by the upper classes, his visit to Africa caused him to question the morality of the domination of one race by another; now his relationship with Emmeline Pethick saw him questioning the domination of one sex by the other. *'It was an extraordinary sequence of events, that I, who am not of a revolutionary temperament, was drawn into a revolutionary movement,'* he later wrote of his journey from Liberal Unionist to feminist socialist.

Emmeline began to write for 'The Echo', bringing a practical common sense to its committee. She also, Fred later recalled, brought *'two eyes whose glance penetrated to my inmost being'.* He proposed again on 12th May 1901, on a day out in Regent's Park. For the rest of their lives the couple celebrated her acceptance on the 26th with a special, almost ritual, meal and solemn declarations of their devotion. And every year on 12th and 26th May, and on their wedding anniversary in October, Fred would write a letter to Emmeline, summarizing the achievements of their marriage and what it meant to him. He kept a red rose that she gave him on their engagement and treasured it until it crumbled. On May 27th he took Emmeline to Paddington to tell her family in Weston of their engagement.

In June of the same year Emmeline brought a party of Esperance Club girls and children to stay in cottages in the village of Broadmoor. The party roamed Leith Hill, made 'billie teas', and bathed in the pond at Friday Street. On the 8th and 9th Fred joined them. He cycled to and from the station, and walked with them to Mag's

The isolated hamlet of Friday Street, with its pond, where Emmeline and the Esperance children bathed on their club holiday in 1901. Fred joined them for a few days from London. (Dorking Museum)

41

Well near Coldharbour. He got on very well with the children with whom he, as Emmeline, had a great affinity. Perhaps it was because there was something childlike about him that remained even into later life; in his simple love of winning at tennis and at billiards, in his joy at Christmas, and in his visceral reactions to food, as there was in her stubborn fondness for tales of fairies and life-long reliance on surrogate parents, particularly the father figure which Fred now provided.

Fred and Emmeline were married at Canning Town Hall on 2nd October 1901. She was thirty-four, he thirty. Members of Parliament mixed with slum-dwelling club girls at an unconventional ceremony organized by Mary Neal. The wedding was held during the midday dinner hour to enable working guests to attend. Fishermen came from Littlehampton and the bathing girl from the beach there. One guest stole a teaspoon only to return it to Mary Neal a week later. Fred's MP uncles made it a condition of attendance that they should not have to mix with Lloyd George, who, like Fred, had opposed the Boer War.

Fred later recalled that he had married his wife because she smoked, could get off a moving bus, and went out walking without gloves. Respectful of her desire to keep her own identity, he added her name to his. He soon acquired the nickname 'Pethick' which stayed with him into later life. His own affectionate name for Emmeline was 'Partsie'.

Fred seems to have been determined to find in his marriage all the affection that his childhood had lacked. Every year on his wedding anniversary he meticulously summed his feelings and the achievements of the union in letters and verse. He wrote and sent cards whenever he and Emmeline were apart – on separate holidays with friends, with the Esperance Club or on Maison Esperance or Echo business - and sometimes accompanied them with poems. When he was leaving for London before she awoke, he left her notes to wake to, signing himself 'Laddie'.

Both were determined that their marriage should embrace the values of equality. They took an apartment in a serviced block at Clement's Inn, near the

The plaque which marks the site of the Pethick-Lawrences' flat in Clement's Inn, off the Strand in London. The symbol was worn as a badge by WSPU members who had suffered imprisonment. It depicts the gates to Holloway women's prison, with an arrow in the WSPU colours of purple, white and green.

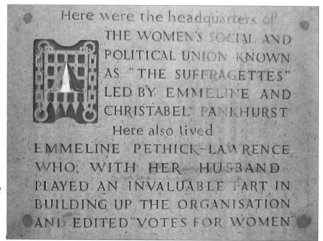

Here were the headquarters of THE WOMEN'S SOCIAL AND POLITICAL UNION KNOWN AS "THE SUFFRAGETTES" LED BY EMMELINE AND CHRISTABEL PANKHURST
Here also lived
EMMELINE PETHICK-LAWRENCE WHO, WITH HER HUSBAND PLAYED AN INVALUABLE PART IN BUILDING UP THE ORGANISATION AND EDITED "VOTES FOR WOMEN"

offices of 'The Echo' and next to the Royal Courts of Justice on the Strand. On their first wedding anniversary, Fred demonstrated his belief in Emmeline's independence by giving her the keys to a separate flat for her own use. Even he was not to have a key.

Their main home was to be in the country. In the July before their marriage, they considered properties in Weybridge, Leatherhead, Box Hill and Dorking before coming across the house that they rented and subsequently bought. On the Dorking to Horsham road in Holmwood The Dutch House had been designed by Sir Edwin Lutyens (1869-1944) for local developer Stephen Wildman Cattley of the nearby mansion at Oakdene. Pevsner describes it as *'somewhat outré'* as it is Y-shaped, with rooms radiating in three directions from a central hallway. Originally it stood in eight acres. Emmeline was immediately taken with it, recalling that: *'before entering the garden gate, I cried, "This is our house!"'* It stood opposite Holmwood Common backing on to the slopes of Redlands woods and Leith Hill, a mile or so from Holmwood station and a five-mile horse-taxi ride from the station in Dorking. The garden path, wide enough for a carriage, was bordered by yew hedges and led to a circular pillared porch. *'If I have ten springs here'*, she wrote, *'I shall be happy with my lot.'*

Fred said simply: *'it caught our fancy and we closed the offer at once.'*

The Mascot, Holmwood.

The Dutch House at Holmwood was known as The Mascot during Fred and Emmeline's ownership. The country home of the WSPU had views of Redlands woods and Leith Hill. It has subsequently been altered with the addition of dormer windows and roof extensions. (Sue Goodwin)

In the months before her wedding Emmeline took detours from The Green Lady to visit The Dutch House to sort out the furnishings. Whilst on their honeymoon at the Abinger Hatch Hotel she and Fred walked over to the house in Holmwood. Once in occupation they renamed the house 'The Mascotte'. They took on the caretaker, (28 year-old William Rapley, a groom/gardener who had been living at the house with his wife, Beatrice, one year-old daughter, Alice, and his dog), as a gardener; he stayed with them fifty years. When they bought a car, (one of the first in the village), he became their chauffeur. To house the car the couple bought a 'motor garage' with petrol store and inspection pit a short walk away in Norfolk Road; it eventually housed several cars. They also bought two cottages known as White Cottages in Buckingham Road. Mr Rapley occupied one, paying his employers 5/- 6d a week in rent; the other was tenanted. Close enough to London to offer hospitality to her many friends, The Mascot saw some of the happiest days of Emmeline's life and she claimed to have blessed Lutyens' genius all the years that they lived there. With their friends and guests they lunched on home-grown vegetables under the trees, played croquet on the lawns, and rode to the nearby pond to play with Podge the dog.

The tree platforms in the garden at The Mascot where suffragettes practiced their speeches and slept out on warm nights. (Illustration by Elliot Seabrooke from The Surrey Hills by FE Green, published by Chatto & Windus. Reprinted by permission of The Random House Group Ltd)

The couple referred to the house as their 'cottage'. The furnishings were by Liberty (as they were in Emmeline's flat at Clements Inn). Mary Gawthorpe recalled that: *'All was in keeping. Surrey was not London and the Liberty fabrics, like the leadless glaze from which we ate, spoke of innocent, if costly simplicity. Sweetness and quietness and poet's coolth are what I felt most at my first visit to The Mascot when Mrs Pethick-Lawrence took me to a casemented room for the night and, placing candle and drink nearby, left me to myself. Letting that unutterable peace and quiet of the silent house within matching and enveloping quietness of the garden without sink in, I picked up a book and read...'*

The list of visitors to The Mascot is a roll-call of the suffragette and socialist movements: Annie Kenney practically lived there in 1906; Olive Schreiner stayed; Emmeline, Sylvia and Christabel Pankhurst, Lady Constance Lytton, and Labour leaders Keir Hardie, George Lansbury and future prime minister Ramsay MacDonald were all visitors. All took away fond memories, of the stillness of the night and of singing folk songs. Annie Kenney wrote that she had *'never enjoyed home life as I did when I visited the country house in summer; it was a privilege and a deep pleasure.'*

In the garden of The Mascot the couple built two tree platforms, one for sleeping out in fine weather, the other with seats. They put in a rose garden and a fish pond, and commissioned a stone model of their Airedale dog. Fred had Lutyens add a billiard room with a hearth, spectator space and a bath and dressing room (now a separate dwelling, Oak Tree House). Emmeline learned to drive whilst Fred - known in the village as 'Great Pethick' - involved himself in local issues, taking up matters such as proposed enclosures of the Common on behalf of those affected. They shared their riches, hosting cricket teas and fetes, taking part in charitable tennis tournaments, and donating a billiard table to the village club and books to its library.

They also set aside a large room at the top of the house as a weekend retreat for the Esperance girls. When the room did not prove big enough they bought some land and a few cottages to the north of The Mascot on which to build a place of respite for impoverished mothers and their children. Fred claimed to have got the idea from the cottages let by Mrs Brooke at Broadmoor, where he and Emmeline had stayed with the Esperance girls in 1901[1]. They retained the existing three brick and slate Wayside Cottages, letting them to tenants, and engaged a friend from their London philanthropic milieu to design a modern cottage on the remaining land. Arnold Dunbar Smith had designed the Passmore Edwards (now Mary Ward) Centre in Tavistock Square with his partner Claude Brewer[2].

---

[1] The Brooke Bond tea merchant, Arthur Brooke (1845-1918) lived at Leylands near Abinger. The row of cottages at Broadmoor, which are thought to also have been designed by Arnold Dunbar Smith, have a communal reading room. Goddards at Abinger Common, two cottages with a shared bowling alley which was built in 1898 by Frederick Mirrielees to provide holiday accommodation for 'ladies of small means' and designed by Lutyens, may also have provided inspiration.

[2] Trading as Smith and Brewer, the pair worked for Brooke at Leylands in 1909.

Left: May Start was the Pethick-Lawrence's housekeeper during their years in Holmwood. She is photographed outside The Sundial, overlooking Holmwood Common. May stayed with the Pethick-Lawrences for many years and taught games to the Esperance children. During the suffrage campaigns she took care of recuperating suffragettes at The Mascot, amongst them Lady Constance Lytton. (The Esperance Morris book vol. 1)
Right: Emmeline poses with some of her Esperance children in one of Holmwood's first cars outside The Mascot. (Museum of London)

The Sundial stands a few hundred metres to the north of The Mascot, its mural and cheerful inscription visible from Holmwood Common: *'Let others tell of storms and showers, I tell of sunny morning hours.'* Close to the road, its stairs and cloakrooms face the highway, leaving the back living rooms which face the woods and hills. Long latticed windows let in light and Dutch blue tiles adorned the walls. The front garden was flagged with a formal design of beds and dwarf pyramid trees. There was a wooden seat on each side of the doorway and two at the gate. Inside it had two dormitories and an inscription in the hallway which read: *'In Praise of Mother Earth and of her daughter The Green Lady'.*

The Sundial opened on 4th June 1904. At the opening ceremony local children were invited to knock at the door, where they were greeted by a fairy who led them inside, then out into the garden. Fred, the local vicar, and Dr Robertson[3] made

---

[3] The father of the novelist, critic and radio presenter E. (Eileen) Arnot Robertson (1903-1961)

speeches and Emmeline spoke of the joy of sharing what made her happy. When The Mascot played host to garden fetes the village children would be entertained by holidaying girls from the Esperance Club who taught their dances to the locals. Emmeline never tired of looking back at her creation from a rise on the Common opposite, but nobody, she said, *'appreciated its beauty more than the schoolchildren and their tutors that came with them. Nothing but happiness… slept under that roof.'*

In November 1904 Emmeline travelled with her sister May and her cousin, Hetty Lawes, to Egypt. Hetty acted as their guide as she had worked with Flinders Petrie on archaeological excavations near Cairo. The party travelled from London to Dover, then by train to Marseilles whence they sailed through the Mediterranean to Port Said, took the train to Cairo and then a boat to Aswan. In Luxor they were joined by Fred and his sister, Carrie, who had been staying at The Sundial. The party arrived back in England at the end of January 1905; they planned to travel to South Africa later in the year.

In the meantime, they returned to their political and philanthropic activities. 'The Echo' was not a success. When it ceased publication Fred took on the 'Labour Record and Review'. Emmeline regularly contributed articles – in her uplifting spiritual style – to its 'Page About Women'. Rather than circumscribing her activities, marriage brought her new opportunities for Fred supported her in her determination to share the good fortune of their wealth. At Clement's Inn and in Holmwood friends, like-minded colleagues, and Esperance girls became an extended 'family'. Husband and wife shared a sense of purpose and of destiny: *'You and I*

The newly-built Sundial in Holmwood. (Dorking Museum)

were born to fight, dear; ourselves and all the world and all the powers of darkness...' wrote Fred with characteristic solemnity to his wife in 1902. *'Courage, lady, sing a poem, beloved, that you and I are found worthy to stand up together and fight. Fight for light as the darkness, for truth as the lie, for life against death.'* The cause for which these semi-spiritual exhortations would find real purpose had not as yet manifested itself to them, however. For the moment it was the relief of poverty that was the focus of their attention.

Dancing was part of the Esperance strategy for the improvement of the Esperance girls, and it undoubtedly cheered the lives of many of its participants. But Emmeline had concluded that offering temporary relief from hardship was not enough. Lives must be changed, not simply made bearable and socially acceptable. Studying the working conditions of the girls, as well as their home lives, she advocated a move away from pure charity and towards political action as an aim for such organisations as the Esperance. The Club, therefore, developed a political as well as a philanthropic mission, and the girls were introduced to the idea of political action, and in particular to the concept of trades unions with whom they might work to improve their conditions.

In such an atmosphere it inevitably occurred to Emmeline and to Mary Neal, (as it had to Mrs Pankhurst and many others working in public or charitable roles within their communities), that if the poverty and suffering of women and children were really to be relieved then women must have a voice in the government of their nation. It was a realisation that was to have a profound effect on Emmeline's life, and on those of many of the dancers and their benefactors.

The Pethick-Lawrences were away visiting Olive Schreiner in South Africa in October 1905 when Christabel Pankhurst and Annie Kenney took on Sir Edward Grey at the Manchester Free Trade Hall. Mary Neal read an account of the incident in the papers and proposed to write a piece on the women's activities for Fred's 'Labour Record and Review'. When Emmeline returned to England Mary Neal consulted her for an opinion. Emmeline immediately expressed a desire to meet Mrs Pankhurst. Through mutual friend, Keir Hardie, a meeting was arranged and in early 1906 Emmeline Pankhurst arrived to see Emmeline Pethick-Lawrence.

The Dunbar Smiths and Mary Ward

The Sundial's architect, Arnold Dunbar Smith (1866-1933), was very much of Fred and Emmeline's London campaigning milieu. He met his business partner, Cecil Claude Brewer (1871-1918), whilst both were working at the University Settlement in Bloomsbury. In 1895 the pair designed the Passmore Edwards Settlement in Tavistock Square. As a result they acquired a clientele of intellectual social reformers. Another of their commissions was Heath Cottage in Oxshott, the home of pro-suffrage philosopher Bernard Bosanquet. They also worked for the Brookes of Leylands near Wotton.

Fred and Emmeline knew Dunbar-Smith before they commissioned him; in January 1901 he had been a guest at the flat that Emmeline shared with Mary Neal. The Passmore Edwards Settlement was also familiar to them as Mary Neal had set up a play scheme there and it was the venue for Esperance parties. Dunbar Smith and his adoptive step-daughter, Margaret Dean-Smith (1899-1997), (born Lillian Gracie Copeman), were there in early 1906 to watch the Esperance girls dance. Margaret became involved with Mary Neal's folk dance revival and in later life she was librarian to the English Folk Dance and Song Society at Cecil Sharp House and editor of its journal. She was responsible for the establishment of the Society's Vaughan Williams Memorial Library and wrote an influential article on Lucy Broadwood. Margaret Dean Smith died in Guildford in 1997, probably the last surviving member of the Pethick-Lawrence 'circle'.

Ironically the novelist and philanthropist responsible for establishing the Passmore Edwards Settlement and after whom it is now named, Mary Ward nee Arnold (1851-1920), was an anti-suffragist. Known as Mrs Humphrey Ward, her stance was opposed by most involved with the Settlement. In July 1910 she wrote to 'The Times' claiming that women did not want the vote; Lord Farrer of Abinger replied on behalf of the women of Surrey, that they very much did.

Left: Margaret Dean Smith (The English Folk Song and Dance Society. Right: Mrs Humphrey Ward (Library of Congress)

Labour leaders - Ramsay MacDonald and George Lansbury

The future Labour Prime Minister, James Ramsay MacDonald (1866-1937) and his wife visited Fred and Emmeline at The Mascot. The couples had much in common: MacDonald wrote for 'The Echo'; Margaret MacDonald nee Gladstone (1870-1911) had studied political economy under Millicent Fawcett, was a school-friend of Emmeline's associate, Lily Montagu, and, like Emmeline, had come to socialism through voluntary work in London boys' clubs. The MacDonalds' home, often visited by Emmeline with Mary Neal, was close to the Pethick-Lawrences' Clement's Inn apartment, in Lincoln's Inn Fields. Margaret was on the executive of the National Union of Women's Suffrage Societies, but the vote was never the focus of her attention, nor was she converted to militancy.

Another visitor to The Mascot was George Lansbury (1869-1940), MP for Bow and Bromley. A committed supporter of the WSPU, Lansbury founded 'The Daily Herald', a left-wing, feminist (and subsequently pacifist) newspaper in 1912. He resigned his parliamentary seat over women's suffrage and in 1913 was imprisoned after giving a speech which was deemed to have condoned the suffragette arson campaign. Emmeline pressed him to recuperate from his hunger strike in Holmwood. Lansbury and his wife Bessie arrived for the weekend on 31st May and were regularly re-invited.

Lansbury was returned to Parliament with Fred in the 1920s. He held a cabinet position in MacDonald's second government, but, like Fred, he opposed MacDonald's National Government. He led the Labour Party from 1931. Responding to an invitation to recuperate from illness at Fourways in 1934, the Labour leader told Emmeline that his late wife had never forgotten their happy time in Holmwood and neither had he. Lansbury resigned the Labour leadership in 1935, unable to reconcile his pacifism with impending conflict with Germany. He became president of the Peace Pledge Union. The pacifist's dilemma in the face of Nazism was one which Emmeline also faced.

Left: James Ramsay McDonald; right: George Lansbury. (Library of Congress)

'This pathetic little committee': leadership of the WSPU

Emmeline Pethick-Lawrence in 1908.

Emmeline was not initially keen to get involved with Mrs Pankhurst's Women's Social and Political Union. Struggling to establish themselves in London, Annie Kenney and Sylvia Pankhurst had no experience of managing money, which was in any event scarce. The London branch may have talked of rousing the city but to Emmeline Pethick-Lawrence its committee seemed helpless. *'To tell the truth,'* she says in her autobiography: *'I had no fancy to be drawn into a small group of brave and reckless and quite helpless people who were prepared to dash themselves against the oldest tradition of human civilization as well as one of the strongest governments of modern times.'*

Emmeline declined appeals from a dejected Mrs Pankhurst, citing her multiple other responsibilities. But she was persuaded to reconsider on meeting Annie Kenney, and agreed to attend a meeting at Sylvia Pankhurst's studio. She took Mary Neal along to the first meeting of the London committee of the WSPU. There, on Keir Hardie's recommendation, (his secretary had been performing the role), she accepted the role of treasurer of the London office. Mary Neal took the minutes. *'What is to become of my friends and what to become of my country home I do not know,'* she told Neal, *'for this is going to take all my time and interest, but it is worthwhile'.*

'It was a great day when Mrs Pethick-Lawrence joined,' recalled Christabel Pankhurst. *'The pace was greatly accelerated onto a much wider field because*

Emmeline and you came to the little struggling WSPU and gave so much to it. None of us should forget that,' Sylvia Pankhurst told Fred in a letter many years later.

'From this time,' wrote Fred in his autobiography, *'the suffragettes surged up into my life. They invaded my flat and almost took possession of it and everything in it. They engrossed the attention of my wife who had become their honorary treasurer. They brought with them an inexhaustible fund of logic and laughter, courage and charm, reason and raillery.'*

If Mrs Pankhurst was the charismatic figurehead of the movement and Christabel its guerrilla tactician, the Pethick-Lawrences provided the WSPU's practical business foundation. Without them it is doubtful that the organisation would have expanded at anything like the rate that it did on its move to London, or made the impact that it did. The Pankhursts, Emmeline later wrote: *'possessed extraordinary qualities, [but] they did not understand organisation and they had absolutely no idea of finance. Theirs was the guerrilla method of political warfare. It became my business to give their genius a solid foundation.'* Emmeline brought business sense and experience to the WSPU. With the Esperance Club, and at Maison Esperance in particular, she had been an employer. One of her conditions for accepting the post of treasurer was that Alfred Sayers, with whom she had worked at the Esperance Club, should be appointed to the position of auditor.

Emmeline recognised that if the WSPU was to unite women behind it, it needed a firm national base. That base was established in the Clement's Inn apartment that she shared with her husband. Close to the Law Courts and Fleet Street, it was a serviced building which provided meals, leaving the occupants free to work. The WSPU's first London office was Emmeline's secretary's room. Only when the Union's finances were on a firmer footing and able to rent offices of its own within the building, did Fred and Emmeline get their flat back to themselves. Emmeline's own garden flat became something of a secret refuge for those needing a place of retreat; Lady Constance Lytton called it the 'upstairs rest room'. It later served as a hiding place from the police.

The Pethick-Lawrences also brought wealth to the organisation. Fred paid off the WSPU's debts (with Keir Hardie). But he initially played little part in the WSPU's activities. His sympathies were more naturally with the deprived and impoverished than with middle-class women. However, his concern for human rights soon saw him promoting the cause. (*'Deep as is the love between us he never took up the women's cause for my sake but as a result of our common outlook,'* wrote Emmeline.) He published character sketches of the WSPU's leading figures in his 'Labour Record and Review' and published its events programmes. Emmeline's women's page was soon entirely devoted to the cause. But the day had gone, said Fred, when the 'ladies' expected 'gentlemen' to *'be kind enough to tell them how to get the vote'*.

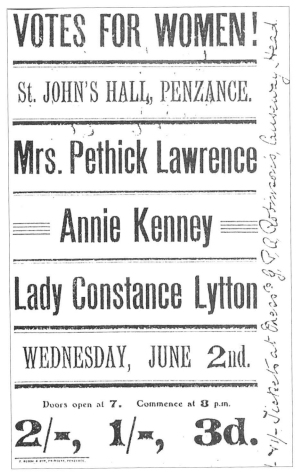

VOTES FOR WOMEN !

St. JOHN'S HALL, PENZANCE.

Mrs. Pethick Lawrence

Annie Kenney

Lady Constance Lytton

WEDNESDAY, JUNE 2nd.

Doors open at **7.** Commence at **8** p.m.

2/-, 1/-, 3d.

Poster for a WSPU meeting in Penzance featuring Emmeline Pethick-Lawrence who particularly liked to campaign in Cornwall, where she emphasized her family's Cornish roots, and those of her husband[1]. She had spent her summer holidays in St Ives in the 1890s and liked to visit her friend Edith Ellis, (the writer and businesswoman wife of Havelock Ellis), who farmed on the moor above Carbis Bay. Her sister Dorothy worked as a WSPU organizer in Cornwall and invited Emmeline to address a large meeting in Penzance in June 1909. She returned to speak in Launceston and Truro in October. She was in Cornwall again in 1911, accompanied by Vida Goldstein, and in Falmouth in 1912 with Mabel Tuke.

On the launch of 'Votes for Women' magazine in October 1907, Fred brought his business and journalistic experience into play. He and Emmeline established the publication together, and acted as joint editors in a unique partnership. Fred's input ensured that the magazine appealed to male as well as female readers. Emmeline specialized in the inspirational editorial, drawing on her experiences in settlement work to draw attention to the devastating result of inequality on women's lives. Until April 1908 'Votes for Women' appeared monthly, after that weekly on a Friday, with a cover price of one penny. Circulation drives and competitions relieved the seriousness of the campaign material. Sales to middle-class women brought in advertisers from the London department stores which subsidized editorial space and by 1910 30,000 copies a week were being produced, going up to 40,000 at the height of the magazine's popularity.

Among those who wrote for the magazine was the young poet John Masefield (1878-1967). Distribution teams all over the country ensured its availability, enabling remote members to feel part of the national organisation. (Volunteer sellers, unable to stand on the pavement for fear of arrest for obstruction, endured verbal harassment and physical abuse as they stood in the gutter.) Fred went on to establish the WSPU's literature department, the Women's Press, which opened on Charing Cross Road in 1910. It soon had a turnover of £10,000 a year from the sale of books, leaflets, pamphlets, badges, postcards and pictures. Sensitive to the fact that this was the women's campaign, Fred played down his contribution. But his partnership with Emmeline and Christabel put him at the heart of the movement.

With Mrs Pankhurst and Christabel unable to leave Manchester, the WSPU's London office was run by Emmeline Pethick-Lawrence and Sylvia Pankhurst, who was simultaneously trying to establish an artistic career. As the organisation's treasurer Emmeline had a roomful of secretaries, and was responsible for the establishment of a chain of regional offices, for the recruitment and employment of the WSPU's paid organisers, and for the organisation of expenses, training, board and lodging for scores of women, as well as for the day-to-day operation of the London office. She kept a tight rein on the expenses of local branches but, in keeping with her principles, was keen to ensure that her workers took time off. She became something of a mother figure to younger women; on one occasion she took Annie Kenney and Mary Gawthorpe with her to the Continent to recuperate.

Emmeline was far more than a director of finance. She brought gaiety and spectacle to the WSPU with her interest in pageantry, music and dance. She devised the WSPU's grand processions with their imagery of benevolent goddesses and noble heroines. She understood the appeal of symbolism and colour and introduced a celebratory style which set the WSPU apart from longer established suffrage societies. And she introduced the organisation's distinctive colour scheme of purple (which she said symbolized the dignity of every suffragette), white (for purity), and green (symbolizing hope and spring). These colours became a tool in raising awareness of the movement; their use allowed even marginal supporters to demonstrate their allegiance or sympathy. Her writing style in 'Votes for Women' was like her speaking style: uplifting, heroic and apt to veer towards the mystical. It was not to everyone's taste – Virginia Woolf found her florid – but her oratory was highly effective. Each person in the audience, reported contemporaries, was convinced that Emmeline was speaking to them individually and she had the ability to move listeners to tears.

Emmeline's cousin, Ellen 'Nellie' Crocker (1872-1962), was the daughter of a doctor. She became a paid WSPU organizer. Arrested numerous times, she went on hunger strike in prison with Dr Louisa Garrett Anderson and composer Ethel Smyth. ('Votes for Women' by permission of the British Library)

Mabel 'Pansy' Tuke (1871-1962) was in mourning for her second husband who had died of a fever in South Africa when she attended a lunch party given by Emmeline Pethick-Lawrence and was recruited to the WSPU. A frequent visitor to The Mascot, she volunteered with the Esperance dancers as well as acting as the WSPU's secretary. She took over Emmeline's role in Holmwood whilst she was recuperating from imprisonment and nursed Mary Gawthorpe there after a spell in prison.

The daughter of the clerk of works at Woolwich Arsenal, her feminine elegance was emphasised by the WSPU to allay fears of potential supporters that the militants were dreadful, mannish women. Mary Gawthorpe wrote that 'there was truly something velvety about Pansy. She was a great asset to Mrs Pethick-Lawrence. I have noticed her counterpart in other movements. Those treasures happier in the comparative background help the leader on a dozen fronts at once. So was and continued Pansy, whether at Holmwood, at Clement's Inn or Aldwych.'

Huge amounts of campaign revenue was needed to put out 'Votes for Women', to stage and publicize rallies in parks and mass meetings at the Albert Hall, to enable paid organisers to spread the message throughout the country and to fund by-election campaigns. Emmeline was a tireless fundraiser and her contact book was invaluable. She turned her attention from working women to wealthier sympathisers who were able to support the WSPU financially. She was inventive in her appeals for money: she instituted 'self-denial' weeks and jewellery collections and kept running tallies of 'promises' at prominent meetings. She was, it was claimed, the most persuasive beggar in London. By 1909 the WSPU's income was in excess of £40,000 a year (compared to the Labour Party's income of just £9,000).

Emmeline's mystical style and talk of sacrifice, suffering and moral purpose inspired family, friend and casual acquaintance alike. Her sisters, Marie Louise Pethick (1876-1916/7), who had qualified as a doctor, and Dorothy Pethick (1881-1870), became committed campaigners. Both went to prison for the cause. Her cousin, Ellen 'Nellie' Crocker, became an organiser in the West Country. Newly-widowed Mabel Kate Tuke nee Lear (1871-1962) met the Pethick-Lawrences on the boat back from South Africa in 1905. Interested in the Esperance dancers, she was invited to lunch where she was converted to the cause and went directly out to chalk the streets with campaign slogans. Esther Knowles (?1897-1961) was selected by Emmeline as a four-year-old to dance with Mary Neal: ten years later she rejected life in the civil service to work at the WSPU's offices as Fred's secretary. Another of their secretaries, H. Shepherd, who had worked on 'The Echo' and was often sent to Holmwood to make travel arrangements with Mr Rapley, became a hunger-striker.

'Every part of the movement's policy is thought out and controlled by Headquarters as much as is humanly possible,' wrote Emmeline to supporters in 'Votes for Women'. But even when the WSPU's finances allowed Mrs Pankhurst to give up her job in Manchester, she spent little time in London, being on the road at speaking engagement after engagement, whilst the notional committee seldom met. Though posters of the leadership celebrated the trinity of the two Emmelines and Christabel, in reality 'Headquarters' comprised three people who worked – and lived – together at Clement's Inn and Holmwood: Emmeline and Fred, described by Isabel Seymour as being *'really like overshadowing guardian angels'*, and Christabel.

Christabel Pankhurst lived with the Pethick-Lawrences for 5 years, at Clement's Inn and in Holmwood. Here Emmeline and Christabel can be seen out campaigning, surrounded by crowds, with a police presence. (LSE Library)

Great hopes were disappointed after the Liberal landslide of January 1906 when no mention was made of a women's suffrage bill in the following King's Speech. The WSPU marched in protest to the House of Commons where groups of twenty women were allowed into the lobby. Prime Minister Campbell-Bannerman urged patience. But women had had forty years of patience. Annie Kenney and her companions deliberately got themselves arrested on a deputation to Chancellor of the Exchequer, (and bitter opponent of the vote for women), Herbert Asquith (1852-1928). Such acts brought publicity and kept the issue on the political agenda.

In the summer of 1906 Christabel Pankhurst finished her law degree. Her arrival in London saw a stepping up of militant tactics and for the next five years she lodged with the Pethick-Lawrences at Clement's Inn and in Holmwood. Christabel's impulsiveness and Fred's love of order did not sit easily with one another; at The Mascot she would come down first to read the morning papers, which she would leave in such chaos that they had to be reassembled before Fred came down. But in general the arrangement worked: seldom out of one another's company, it was Christabel and the Pethick-Lawrences who formulated WSPU policy for the next six years.

Emmeline Pethick-Lawrence receiving flowers from Flora Drummond and Jennie Baines whilst out campaigning. Fred is on the left of the photo. (LSE Library)

A daring tactician, Christabel gave up trying to convert individual MPs. Arguing that MPs acted in loyalty not to causes but to their own parties, and that they could not be relied upon to put the women's cause first, she advocated attacking the party system itself. She believed that if the governing Liberal party lost MPs as a result of the issue, the cabinet would be forced (rather than persuaded) to bring in legislation in its own defence. So in the summer of 1906 the WSPU began campaigning against Liberal candidates at by-elections, whatever their personal views on women's suffrage, in an attempt to unseat them.

In October 1906 yet another state opening of Parliament went by without mention of a bill to enfranchise women. A delegation was sent to Parliament in protest. The doors were barred. Emmeline Pethick-Lawrence, Mary Gawthorpe and Anne Cobden-Sanderson were amongst those arrested on a charge of disorderly conduct for attempting to speak in the lobby. Prevented from making her case inside, Emmeline had tried to make a speech outside. Speechmaking was not an offence so she could not be convicted of any crime but was instead bound over to keep the peace. Fred stood bail for many of the women, guaranteeing their appearance in court the next day. In the morning he and Thomas Cobden-Sanderson accompanied them to court.

Whilst growing up in Bristol Emmeline had seen that members of the Salvation Army, who were often attacked by bystanders, would rather go to prison than give an undertaking not to speak in public. Her father had campaigned against the injustice of their being imprisoned for refusing to give such an undertaking when they had not deliberately instigated the original breach of the peace. But rather than protest at the injustice now, Emmeline recognized the publicity value of imprisonment. She refused to give the undertaking because it would have amounted to an undertaking not to campaign. She was sent to Holloway women's prison for two months.

As editor of the 'Labour Record and Review' Fred collected messages from the women before they were transported to prison, which he incorporated into pro-suffrage editorials. He criticized the party for professing to be ashamed of militant tactics. If the women had gone to prison in protest at poverty or unemployment the party would have praised them, he said; but the party did not want equality for women, and members cared more for their own respectability than for justice. The women were, he wrote, doing the only thing they could. There was no constitutional means for women to achieve the vote, so they were outside the constitution and had to use unconstitutional methods.

In protest at Emmeline's sentence Fred pledged £10 to the WSPU for every day that his wife remained in prison. He urged others to do likewise. *'It is not a matter of how much you feel',* he wrote, *'but how much are you going to do? I am going to give ten pounds to the WSPU for every day of my wife's sentence, and I should like to know who will follow my example.'* Here, derided the press, was a man so hen-pecked he would willingly pay to keep his harridan of a wife inside: *'Ten pounds a day/He said he'd pay/to keep this face/in Holloway.'*

From Box Hill the novelist George Meredith contributed a letter of support to 'The Times'. *'It is the very excellence of their cause,'* he wrote of the women, *'that inflames them. Nor can they doubt it when they know they are supported in their claims by so thoughtful a man as the chief of the Conservative Party, have the countenance of the chief of the Liberal Party, and a voice on their behalf from the Secretary of State for India, one who weighs what he utters, however warm his feeling. The mistake of the women has been to suppose that John Bull would move sensibly for a single kick.'*

For Emmeline it was the first of seven spells of incarceration. Whilst inside she received a moving letter from her Aunt Lizzie in Bristol: *'Just a line to say I love you, I love you, I love you. I loved you when you were a little girl and you went out for walks on the Downs, singing little songs by the way. I loved you in your girlhood when with all your glowing enthusiasm you gave yourself up to mission work and helped many weak and helpless ones on their way and I love you now, more I think than ever, for you are suffering for others (mistakenly, of course, I think), but none the less truly.'* Her father, with his commitment to justice, was no less supportive. Offered sympathy at the disgrace of his daughter's imprisonment he declared he did not need it; *'I am the proudest father in the England!'* And her husband wrote saying that nothing had moved him more than her action which had stirred him to the depths of his being.

Despite such encouragement Emmeline found prison a profoundly shocking experience. Overcome with claustrophobia in the closed prison van, she suffered something of a breakdown. Fred and her father were sent for. Fred determined to pay bail to secure her immediate release, but he found himself on the receiving end of Mrs Pankhurst's scorn, with a snipe about over-sensitive husbands. *'Do not make it harder for me than it must be,'* he begged. With Mrs Pankhurst's consent, Emmeline was forced into a humiliating climb-down and an undertaking to keep the peace. The *'shock to her extra sensitive nature'* was too much, recalled Mary Neal. Fred brought his wife to Neal on her release. She claimed that Emmeline was so changed that she would never have known her as she was, haggard and dazed, with soiled hands and dishevelled hair. A few days later Mary Neal went down to Holmwood, followed by Mabel Tuke, to take care of matters there whilst Emmeline recuperated in Venice, mortified with shame and embarrassment at her capitulation. There she was joined by her parents, then by Sylvia Pankhurst, also newly released from prison. Sylvia drew and painted scenes of Italian life, and a friendship developed between the two newly-released women which would endure throughout their lives.

Fred now threw his resources behind the movement. He took his wife's place as treasurer while she convalesced, running an orderly and efficient regime with meticulous attention to detail. Emmeline's father represented his daughter at a suffrage fund-raising banquet at The Savoy. Emmeline returned from her convalescence in Italy just before Christmas. Mary Gawthorpe confessed to finding her changed: *'I was startled by the change. Those deep still waters were deep as ever in Emmeline Pethick-Lawrence, but now something was reflected from their mysterious depths. As plainly as words could have spoken, so now those agate eyes streamed forth anguished communication. We had been baptized with fire. But it was only the beginning'.*

Support grew rapidly. Imprisonments brought publicity, converts and money. The organisation established new branches across the country. Office space at Clement's Inn was expanded. By the end of 1908 Emmeline Pethick-Lawrence was managing some forty staff at Clement's Inn, thirty paid organizers and a dozen regional offices. By 1911 the WSPU had 23 rooms at Clement's Inn and 110 employees working there and at the bookshop and publishing press in Charing Cross Road. Membership rose, particularly amongst middle-class women who were inspired by the example of women like themselves facing imprisonment. Many seasoned campaigners switched affiliation to the new organisation, though the long-established, law-abiding suffrage societies also saw their memberships rise as a result of the publicity generated. Some cautiously welcomed the new tactics. Others dissociated themselves from the militants.

The term 'suffragette' was devised as a taunt by the 'Daily Mail'[4].

Fred Pethick-Lawrence was known within the WSPU as 'Godfather'. He was the only man to play an active part in the inner workings of the militant movement. Though his role was unofficial and his influence was seldom publicly acknowledged, the appeal of a strong marriage at the heart of the movement was exploited by the WSPU. Like Emmeline and Christabel Pankhurst's femininity and deliberately conservative dress, it allayed fears of a 'war' between the sexes or of a social revolution that might have deterred more conservative potential supporters (not to mention their husbands and parents.)

The Women's Press shop on Charing Cross Road sold the 'Pethick' tobacco pouch for men.
(Library of Congress)

---

[4] 'The Daily Express' nicknamed them the 'voterettes'.

It suggested a reckless youthful impulsiveness in comparison with their more measured 'suffragists'. The term was taken up with scornful enthusiasm by the women of the WSPU, offering as it did an identity around which to rally. The constitutional (non-militant) movement was, wrote Emmeline Pethick-Lawrence: *'like a beetle on its back that cannot turn itself over and get at its legs to pursue its path.'*

Delegations to Parliament and deputations to Prime Ministers became the WSPU's stock in trade. The women would walk, arms linked, and the police would attempt to turn them back so that they could not speak or deliver their petitions. Arrests for obstruction as women refused to be diverted would often be in the hundreds. On other occasions the women would use stealth, 'rushing' unexpectedly on the Houses of Parliament or chaining themselves to the railings so that they could deliver a speech in the time that it took for the police to remove them.

Fred played no part in the deputations or raids but waited by the telephone at Clement's Inn to be summoned to give defence advice or to stand bail. Over the years he personally stood bail for some 1,000 women, on busy days going from police station to police station, those in custody cheering his arrival. Known to the women as 'Godfather', he was, wrote the composer, Ethel Smyth, *'ever ready to take root at police stations, day or night, his money bag at his feet'.'*

To accusations that such tactics were 'silly', Emmeline responded in 'Votes for Women': *'How silly of women to chain themselves to the railings of Downing Street. Doing something silly is the women's alternative for doing something cruel. The effect is the same. We use no violence because we can win freedom for women without; because we have discovered an alternative.'*

In 1908 the two Emmelines, Christabel and Annie Kenney were represented in wax at Madame Tussauds alongside Stanley and Livingstone, Lord Byron and Robert Burns. A tableau featuring a 'cabinet' meeting of the four militant suffrage campaigners opened in December of that year. The visitor guide informed visitors that Emmeline Pethick-Lawrence was treasurer of the Women's Social and Political Union, and that she had been arrested in the autumn of 1908 for protesting against the arrest of Annie Kenney and sentenced to two month's imprisonment. She was credited with having raised a campaign fund of £20,000.

It was a time of optimism, camaraderie and hope. With their notoriety, money, organization, star speakers and growing support, the women of the militant movement had reason to believe that they would soon achieve what forty years of quiet campaigning had not.

Artists in Peaslake

One of Emmeline Pethick-Lawrence's Surrey associates was the artist Adah Stuart Franks (1872-1916) who lived at Gassons Cottage in Peaslake. The daughter of a Croydon coal merchant, Adah had previously shared lodgings in Croydon with fellow artist Daisy 'Dick' Wood (1878-?1962) who accompanied her to Peaslake.

Adah's tea-dealer older brother, Norman Franks, boarded at the Passmore Edwards Settlement in Tavistock Place with which Mary Neal and the Pethick-Lawrences had long-standing connections. By 1910 he knew the couple well enough for Emmeline to suggest that Fred take his advice on settlement issues. Adah, meanwhile, grew close to the Pethick-Lawrences' housekeeper, May Start. She was also friends with fellow Peaslake artist - and suffragette - Helen Gordon Liddle.

In 1904 Franks and Wood were joined in Peaslake by Belle Elkin 'da Loria' Norman nee Mitchell (1872-1935) who had been living near the Pethick-Lawrences in Holmwood. Born in the United States, she had abandoned her career as a pianist on her marriage to the wealthy chemist John Thomas Norman in 1897. When she left her husband, she brought their three young children to Peaslake and for the next eight years she lived at Gassons with Franks and Wood.

When the Normans formalised their legal separation in court John Norman countered claims of drunkenness and violence with accusations that Adah Franks had 'interfered' in his marriage to Belle – a hint at lesbianism. With her opinions that women should earn a living and live independently of men, she had, he claimed, come between man and wife. The court decided in Belle's favour, awarding her custody of the children. With responsibility for young children it was impossible for Belle to to return to the itinerant life of a musician. Instead she re-named herself da Loria, (after a Spanish ancestor), and took up art to support herself and her children.

The three women set up studios for themselves in the grounds of Gassons and da Loria Norman undertook her first commissions there. She left Peaslake in 1912 to set up studios in London and in 1914 she returned to the United States, where she made a life for herself as an artist. Her work included book illuminations, murals on plaster and canvas, miniatures, magazine illustrations and paintings in oil and watercolour. She married again later in life but never lived with her husband.

Adah Stuart-Franks died in 1916 at the age of 43. Daisy Wood remained in Peaslake and many years later contributed to the Pethick-Lawrences' memorial in the village.

The lifelong secretary - Esther Knowles

Esther Knowles came to Holmwood as a small child, carried on Fred's shoulders at an Esperance event. Born near Tottenham Court Road, she was the daughter of a trades unionist print-worker. Her older sister married one of the young men brought in to dance with the Esperance girls at demonstrations. (Vic Ghirardi became one of Mary Neal's dance teachers and Neal was god-mother to their daughter, Nita). So Esther was part of the extended Pethick-Lawrence 'family'.

Dressed in white with a green sash, the 13-year-old Esperance girl walked with the children's contingent to a rally at the Albert Hall in 1910 and sold 'Votes for Women' outside. Her father hit her mother for allowing her to take part. Esther's intelligence was recognised by the Pethick-Lawrences and when her father would not allow her to stay on at school, they took the teenager to work in the WSPU offices. She worked for them until the arrival of Gladys Groom to work for Emmeline in 1924; then she worked for Fred until her retirement in 1959. In his later letters Fred referred to Esther as an 'ever loving friend'. Esther told him that her working life with him had been happy, free and frank, full and complete, and that she had been fortunate as a young girl when destiny had decreed that the path of her life should run alongside his.

Working long hours for so demanding a character as Fred was not without its trials. He was meticulous to the point of obsession; often he and Emmeline exchanged written memos for the sake of evidence for his filing system. On one occasion Esther told him that he thought he was Jesus Christ; but rather than sack her, he shook her hand and congratulated her for her courage.

Esther was far more than a secretary. She organised the couple's lives in London, in Holmwood and, later, in Peaslake; she paid the staff in London and sent the wages down to Peaslake every Friday. She took her holidays with Emmeline's sister, Dorothy, who initiated her into the Steiner philosophy. (She and Gladys would have liked to have holidayed together but they were seldom allowed to take leave at the same time). When she was bombed out of her flat during the Blitz, she was re-supplied with furniture by Fred and Emmeline, Mary Neal and Emmeline's sister, May.

It would be hard to overestimate the extent of Esther's lifelong devotion to her employers. She described Emmeline as her 'loadstar', though she did not necessarily follow her lead on matters political. A huge row broke out when she joined the Liberals in the 1950s but her working relationship with Fred was unaffected. She was also protective of Fred and Emmeline's reputations, during their lives and after. She initially refused to have anything to do with the Suffragette Fellowship when it was established, considering it another vehicle for the promulgation of the Pankhurst reputation at the expense of Fred and Emmeline's. She was persuaded to join when Grace Roe became embroiled in something of a battle with Mrs Pankhurst's nieces, and she became its secretary. She and Roe were responsible for organising Fred and Emmeline's memorial fund and the commemorative ceremonies held in Dorking and Peaslake in 1962. With Gladys she also salvaged many of the couple's papers on the sale of Fourways and the Lincoln's Inn flat after Fred's death. Hopeful of a biography that would do the couple justice, she entrusted the material to her niece, Nita Needham, for safekeeping until such time as history was ready to give Fred and Emmeline the recognition that she felt was their due.

Esther Knowles died in a car crash in 1974.

Mary Anne Ewart

Women had ambitions not just to vote, but also to stand for political office. They had been able to stand as district councillors since 1894 but were barred from standing for the more powerful county or borough councils. The fight for the right to stand was fought at local and national level.

In 1905, at the age of 85, Mary Anne Ewart (1820-1911) of Coneyhurst in Ewhurst, lobbied her neighbour, Lord Farrer of Abinger, to support a bill allowing women to stand as county and borough councillors. Women had, she claimed, shown their fitness for office in their work as poor law guardians, factory and sanitary inspectors. She also lobbied him for his support for women's suffrage

The daughter of politician William Ewart, she was an advocate of women's education and was involved in the establishment of Newnham College, Cambridge. The money that she left in trust to provide scholarships at Newnham, and at Somerville (Oxford) and Bedford (University of London), is still benefiting female students today. *(Newnham College, Cambridge)*

'The unofficial home of the WSPU': The Mascot

Every weekend the WSPU shut up the offices at Clement's Inn and the Pethick-Lawrences travelled with Christabel down to Holmwood. *'It was only at the weekend in my country house that the three of us had enough leisure to thrash out together any complicated problem',* recalled Fred. Annie Kenney's memories were similar: *'Processions, Albert Hall meetings, raids on Parliament, tactics in prison, the varied forms of advertisement... all were decided, debated, discussed, analysed and counter discussed... round the fire at Holmwood or in the woods around Leith Hill. If the beautiful woods there could have spoken, Scotland Yard would have forestalled many a militant action.'*

Mrs Pankhurst, Annie Kenney and Emmeline Pethick-Lawrence dressed for motoring. The car is probably one of the couple's private cars driven by Holmwood chauffeur William Rapley who was famed for his discretion about WSPU matters. (LSE Library)

The 'Daily News' termed The Mascot: *'the unofficial HQ of the WSPU.'* *'One or two of the motor cars especially kept by Mr and Mrs Lawrence at the service of The Cause generally brings down from town at the week-end some of the most prominent of the Suffragettes,'* it told its readers. *'What Rapley, the chauffeur, does not know about the WSPU is not worth knowing, but if you attempt to draw him out, he has the habit of closing the discussion with the crushing phrase of, "I don't think."* The paper described working-class girls, ladies of fashion and labour leaders playing and plotting in the garden and bowling matches between suffragettes and sympathetic MPs. At the end of the garden it reported, stood a *'high tree, up which has been built a platform where budding speakers can try their lungs amid romantic surroundings.'* A drawing of these tree platforms appeared in a guide to the Surrey Hills published in 1915. The author of that guide was local campaigner FE Green.

The Mascot was a place of plotting but it was also a place of refuge. In her autobiography Emmeline wrote that: *'It was in the peace of our country home that, late, those who had to undergo the strain of the militant suffragette would find recuperation, it was here that beauty and joy kept the cup of life filled to the brim.'*

Frederick Ernest Green (1867-1922) ran an experimental farm at Cudworth in the nearby village of Newdigate. He had made a name for himself as a writer on social and labour issues relating to agriculture. At Cudworth he built a modern cottage from which he extolled the virtues of country life and dispensed advice on bee-keeping, soft fruits and poultry-keeping to would-be homesteaders from the city.

The bee-hives at Baringsfield, FE Green's small-holding at Cudworth near Newdigate. The man tending to the hives is thought to be Green. When Green died in 1922, George Lansbury spoke at his funeral. (John Callcut)

(He envisaged a professional income to fund the rural lifestyle.) Their children, he wrote in 'The Awakening of England', would *live intimately with the winds, the clouds and Mother Earth'*. Such aspirations would have struck a chord with Emmeline.

Green was involved in the establishment of the Workers' Union in Newdigate and was a contributor to Fred's 'Labour Record and Review'. He wrote on rural issues: about the exercise of power in rural affairs; about rural crafts, the lack of rural housing, about land colonisation, youth labour and low wages. He contributed similar articles to 'Votes for Women'. In 1909 Fred donated one of the cars that was used on the suffragette campaign to Green to enable him to bring soft fruit, vegetables and honey to market in Dorking. The motorized delivery of fruit to market was sufficiently unusual to merit a mention in the local paper.

A couple of miles from Holmwood, the village of Newdigate in the early twentieth century was something of a magnet for socialist utopian experimenters of a similar mind to the Pethick-Lawrences with regard to the cleansing and rejuvenating properties of the Surrey countryside. The socialist Smallholdings Association had bought several hundred acres there to provide small-scale farming opportunities to working men in an area where little was grown and where fruit and vegetables were accordingly expensive. (Green had acquired several of the plots.) Around 1910 Charles Lancaster Almond and John Aitcheson, (later secretary of Dorking's branch of the Communist Party), bought a piece of land nearby and set up a summer camp with the similar ideals to The Sundial and The Green Lady. The camp was much larger, and under canvas, with a shop, a common-room and dining room. Its facilities

The Newdigate camp (Mary Day)

were advertised in the London Labour press and used by Labour youth organisations. It is more than likely that Aitcheson and Almond were associates of the Pethick-Lawrences and Green.

Fred's widowed sister, Caroline 'Carrie' Apsland Jones (d. 1937), also moved to Newdigate. She lived at Hatchetts Farm with Marion Martha Mary Leighfield (d. 1942). Close to Fred, Carrie was a supporter of his causes: she stayed at The Sundial and invested in 'The Echo' when it was failing. Though there is no evidence that she was an active suffragette, she and her sister Annie gave money to the WSPU and Marion Leighfield was arrested for the cause in 1908. The two women went on to bring up five 'orphans' at Hatchetts after the war.

On 13th June 1908 the non-militant National Union of Women's Suffrage Societies (NUWSS) processed through London. A week later, on 21st June, the WSPU staged the spectacular Hyde Park 'Great Demonstration'. A vast affair organised by Emmeline Pethick-Lawrence, the 'Great Demonstration' was one of the WSPU's glorious moments. Thousands of suffragettes were marshalled in peaceful procession through London in WSPU colours. Fred persuaded the authorities to remove railings in the park to allow the passage of the expected crowds, one detail in a myriad that allowed for a hugely successful event. The watching crowd heard twenty speakers, each on a different podium – amongst them Emmeline herself, Nellie Crocker, Georgina and Marie Brackenbury, Annie and Nellie Kenney, Emmeline, Adela and Christabel Pankhurst, and Marie Naylor. Thirty special trains ran into London on the day, bringing women in from seventy towns including Redhill and Reigate, which towns shared a branch of the WSPU. Figures for the number attending vary between 250,000 and half a million. The leadership viewed it as a triumphal moment, demonstrating widespread public support. It seemed to them that the argument had been won. Others were less convinced: many, they argued, may simply have been looking on in bemusement.

New Prime Minister Asquith - implacably opposed to women's suffrage - was unimpressed, despite having asked for evidence of support for the vote from the women of the country. When sixty Liberal MPs asked him to allow a private members' bill to be introduced giving women a limited franchise, he refused. *'The possibilities of constitutional agitation culminated on 21st June,'* concluded Emmeline Pethick-Lawrence. *'It would be impossible to have a greater demonstration than that which was held... nothing but militant action is now left.'*

Ticket in WSPU colours for the Hyde Park procession. (Library of Congress)

ALL LONDON IN HYDE PARK.

The largest crowd ever gathered together in London assembled in Hyde Park yesterday to see the suffragists and, above all, to hear t Great Shout. As far as eye could reach the park was a sea of faces, as the above picture shows. One of the leaders is seen in t small photograph shouting " One, two, three !" which preceded the cry, " Votes for Women !"

The Daily Express headline for the Hyde Park rally on 21st June 1908 declares: 'All London in Hyde Park' and the accompanying photograph is captioned: 'The largest crowd ever gathered together in London assembled in Hyde Park yesterday to see the suffragists and, above all to hear the Great Shout. As far as the eye could reach the park was a sea of faces, as the above picture shows. One of the leaders is seen in the small photograph shouting "One, two, three!" which preceded the cry, 'Votes for Women!"
Twenty speakers were assigned a platform each, amongst them Peaslake's Georgina and Marie Brackenbury, Holmwood's Emmeline Pethick-Lawrence, Emmeline's cousin, Nellie Crocker, and regular visitors Annie Kenney, Marie Naylor and the Pankhursts. (Library of Congress)

The WSPU kept up the pressure, arranging deputations (which Asquith refused to meet) and large meetings. Twenty thousand gathered on Clapham Common in July 1908, 150,000 in Manchester, and 100,000 in Leeds. But such demonstrations of public support failed to influence government policy. In frustration tactics turned disruptive. In October 1908 Emmeline and Christabel Pankhurst urged the public to 'rush' Parliament; both were immediately arrested and charged with provoking a breach of the peace. (The 'rush' was instead lead by Marion Wallace Dunlop, later of Peaslake.) Mrs Pankhurst was sentenced to three months, Christabel to ten weeks.

Christabel was due for release on December 22nd, her mother on January 9th. Emmeline Pethick-Lawrence planned a reception and parade for their releases. Probably to thwart these plans, both Pankhursts were released early, in the late afternoon of Saturday 19th December. Knowing that Clement's Inn would be shut up for the weekend and with nowhere to go, the Pankhursts took the train from Waterloo down to Holmwood. The following day they were besieged at The Mascot by London press men.

Christabel took long walks on Leith Hill, soon recovering her spirits. Her mother, however, found it harder to adjust to unexpected freedom. In the days before Christmas they were joined in Holmwood by Flora Drummond nee Gibson (1878-1949). With Emmeline, she set to work re-arranging the planned release celebrations for the following Tuesday (December 22nd). After a couple of days' recuperation Emmeline and Christabel Pankhurst returned to London to a parade lead by standard-bearer Charlotte Marsh (who later organised the Holmwood campaign). Mother and daughter then returned to Holmwood where they spent Christmas and New Year at The Mascot.

GENERAL DRUMMOND.

Flora Drummond was a member of the Manchester WSPU, the Independent Labour Party and the Fabian Society. She had wanted to be a postmistress until a height restriction was introduced that discriminated against women. Arriving in London in 1906, she acquired the nickname 'The General' for her habit of leading her troops dressed in military jacket and peaked cap. Drummond was a fearless campaigner, on one occasion she was released from prison when it was discovered that she was pregnant. She came down to Holmwood in 1908 when Emmeline and Christabel Pankhurst were staying at The Mascot and worked with Emmeline Pethick-Lawrence on plans for the Pankhursts' release parade. Though she stayed with the Pankhursts on the split from the Pethick-Lawrences, she later worked with Emmeline and Viscountess Rhondda with the Six Point Group. (Postcard from the collection of Ann Lewis and Mike Sponder)

Women walking in Redlands wood in the early years of the 20th century. The Mascot directly overlooked the wood and WSPU visitors often went walking there. (Dorking Museum)

Emmeline Pethick-Lawrence braved Holloway again the following February after a breach of the peace on a deputation to the House of Commons. An observer recorded that she, *'who is generally all smiles, nearly broke down'* at the prospect. *'She had to lean forward and cover her eyes with her handkerchief.'* This time she served two months without incident, sending Fred instructions for decorating at The Mascot and letting The Sundial from her cell. He, meanwhile, donated books to the prison library. To the WSPU she sent instructions on the planned Albert Hall demonstration on April 26th. She urged members to sell tickets and to raise the fifty thousand pounds that she had set as a fundraising target for the year. Her tone in the one letter per month that she was permitted to write, on just one sheet of paper, was uplifting, celebrating her *'wonderful movement'*. *'Nothing seems too much to hope, too great to believe and expect'*, she told her followers, with spring bringing life and joy back into the world. *'We will give body and soul and all that we have to minister to this new life,'* she wrote, of the shoots of the suffrage campaign. *'We will accomplish the purpose to which we have been called... in the strong bond of fellowship which unites us all in the movement'*. But Mrs Pankhurst worried about her treasurer's health; Emmeline was not thought to be strong but it would have set an awkward precedent to have had her released on grounds of ill health. Instead Mrs Pankhurst appealed to readers of 'Votes for Women' for contributions to buy a car in WSPU colours for the use of *'our devoted treasurer'*. She urged members to be present on Emmeline's release: *'She must feel that not only is she a leader of a great women's movement, she is the friend and comrade of every woman in the Union and we are there and all of us are embers of our great and united family of women'*. Emmeline emerged from Holloway on April 16th to a rapturous reception of a thousand people, a car in suffragette colours and a celebratory breakfast for 400 at The Criterion restaurant. The next day she and her niece, Freda Budgett, were led in a procession headed by a

Emmeline Pethick-Lawrence emerges from Holloway in April 1909 to a welcoming crowd of fellow campaigners. Mr Rapley is driving the car decked in suffrage flags. Whilst in prison Emmeline had continued to take care of her personal and WSPU affairs. On March 4th she told Fred that she had been denied a business meeting and instead must give him written instructions on the letting of the bungalow in Holmwood and for the bookings for the Esperance at The Sundial. She also sent instructions for redecorating The Mascot, getting Lutyens in to look at the rose garden, and for Mr Rapley to take care of the garden in Holmwood, as well as details of her forthcoming speaking engagements. She reports that outside the prison sympathisers are playing music and thanks Fred the tulips that he has anonymously sent from Holmwood. ((Heritage Image Partnership Ltd/Alamy Stock Photo)

supporter dressed as Joan of Arc and followed by her prison companions and the Esperance Girls Club from Hyde Park to the Aldwych Theatre. *'This movement absolutely absorbs me and gives me all I need and all I ever dreamed possible of inspiration and joy,'* she told Mary Neal. *'Nothing can ever be so worthwhile as to fight for the freeing of women from the age-long bondage in which they have lived.'*

The Esperance girls turned out in support of the suffrage cause again in May 1909 when they danced at the WSPU-organized Women's Exhibition at the Prince's Skating Rink in Knightsbridge. The organization of the week-long showcase of women's political, artistic and domestic talents had been taken over by Emmeline's sister, Marie, during her imprisonment.

Though the WSPU had initially drawn support from the labour movement, the middle-class women of London and the Home Counties, with their funds and free time, had become an excellent source of recruits. The ladies of Redhill were targeted by Mrs Pankhurst in May 1909 when she spoke for an hour at the market hall. But many of those attracted to the cause by militant tactics went not to the WSPU, but to local non-militant women's suffrage societies.

Emmeline Pethick-Lawrence (right, with rosette) marching alongside Mrs Pankhurst at the head of the Women's Coronation procession of 17th June 1911. Christabel Pankhurst, in her graduate's robes, walks behind the two Emmelines. Mrs Pethick-Lawrence customarily marched at the head of processions, and her name always followed Mrs Pankhurst's on headed paper and posters, above those of other campaigners. (LSE Library)

Suffragettes at The Mascot

Amongst the suffrage campaigners that FE Green met at The Mascot were Beatrice Sanders, Teresa Billington-Grieg and Henry Harben. Sanders (c1874-1932) was the WSPU's financial secretary who worked closely with treasurer Emmeline. Her connections to the couple were many as her husband was a Fabian Society lecturer and Independent Labour party member who had contributed to Fred's 'Labour Record and Review'.

Teresa Billington-Grieg (1877-1964) was a teacher, Independent Labour party activist and campaigner for equal pay in Manchester. One of the WSPU's first paid organisers, she had worked with Emmeline Pethick-Lawrence to set up the Clement's Inn headquarters. On Christabel's arrival in London she was sidelined and when Mrs Pankhurst dispensed with the WSPU's constitution she formed the Women's Freedom League with Charlotte Despard in 1907. She became a writer and lecturer on social, economic and political issues.

Henry Devenish Harben (1874-1967) was a reforming estate-owner. He was a member of the Fabian Society and the Men's Political Union for Women's Enfranchisement, and he resigned as a Liberal parliamentary candidate because of the party's lack of support for female suffrage. He offered refuge to imprisoned suffragettes at his Newlands Park estate in Buckinghamshire, acted as guarantor for Sylvia Pankhurst, and was close to Christabel Pankhurst. To an extent, he took Fred Pethick-Lawrence's place in the WSPU after the 1912 split as a contributor to funds and surety for suffragette activities. By 1914, however, he was disillusioned with the organisation's lack of organisation. His wife, Agnes, was a founder member and committee member of the United Suffragists where she worked alongside the Pethick-Lawrences in the years running up to the First World War. *Theresa Billington-Grieg from the collection of the family of Alice Hawkins, www.alicesuffragette.co.uk*

Mary Gawthorpe

Mary Gawthorpe (1881-1973) was a teacher from Leeds who became involved in the suffrage campaign through the Labour movement. A reader of Fred's 'Labour Record and Review', she went to hear the Pethick-Lawrences speak to the Leeds Women's Suffrage Society before it was known that Emmeline had joined the committee of the WSPU. She and her mother invited Fred and Emmeline to tea afterwards and they bonded when Emmeline spotted a copy of Cecil Sharp's collection of folk songs on the Gawthorpes' piano.

In August 1906 Emmeline invited Mary to the WSPU"s offices in London. She described her meeting at Emmeline's private apartment in Clement's Inn in almost religious terms: *'As I entered her apartment, Emmeline Pethick-Lawrence, writing at her desk, lifted her head and looked at me. She did not rise but drew me to a chair by her side. It was a full moment. Nothing was said but I knew I was nearing a great decision. I knew what the answer would be. I had written to Christabel less than nine months ago that I was ready to go to prison if that was necessary in order to win the vote. Now the tide of ineluctable choice had caught up with me and there could be no retreat.'*

Mary was with Emmeline on her first imprisonment in 1906 and later spent time recuperating in Holmwood where she was looked after by Mabel Tuke. She was amongst the group that accompanied Fred and Emmeline to Holmwood after the Hyde Park Demonstration in June 1908.

From the collection of the family of Alice Hawkins, www.alicesuffragette.co.uk

'Orderly means':
the non-militant campaign

"In great things Unity,
In small things Liberty,
In all things Charity."

LEITH HILL AND DISTRICT

Woman's Suffrage Society.

(Affiliated to the National Society of Women's Suffrage Societies).

PRESIDENT : MRS. FAWCETT.

MEMBERSHIP CARD.

Mrs Molyneux

Object.
To obtain the Franchise for Women on the same
terms as it is, or may be, granted to Men.

Methods.
Non-Party and Non-Militant.

"Women have not that voice they ought to
have in the ... tion of the representatives of the
English ... can conceive no argument by
wh...
The late Marquis of Salisbury.

...neve that the country would be made
...nd happier by the admission of Women to
...ne Franchise."—*Right Hon. H. J. Gladstone, M.P.*

Hon. Sec., MRS. JOCELYN BRAY,
Coast Bank, Westcott, Dorking.

Membership card of the Leith Hill and District Woman's Suffrage Society issued to Mrs Sarah Molyneux (nee Jones) of Dorking. (John Molyneux)

The publicity generated by the militant campaign brought as many supporters to non-militant, law-abiding groups as it did to the WSPU. Reports in the press of suffragette activities led to public debate at St Paul's Literary Society in Redhill in 1906, and an 'At Home' at the public halls in Reigate. The following year the Reigate Women's Suffrage Society was formed. In March 1907 Millicent Fawcett of the NUWSS came to speak at Reigate public halls and the society held its first public and drawing room meetings. Presided over by Helena Auerbach[5], the society covered an area that spread from Redhill to Dorking. In May 1908 a travelling group of suffragists visited Leatherhead with a women's suffrage van; they hosted an open-air meeting opposite the Bull Hotel and a meeting at Victoria Hall. And on 13th June 1908 members of the Reigate and Redhill WSS attended the great demonstration by non-militant groups in London. Thirty-four members from Reigate and fifteen from Redhill paraded behind the society's new banner. Designed by Muriel Woodhams, and worked in silk, the banner carried the arms of the borough, the letters RRWSS, and the motto '*Country and Liberty*'. A smaller blue and gold banner depicted the arms of the borough on one side, with the word '*Justice*' and the letters NUWSS, and the wording '*Women's Suffrage*' on the reverse. Margaret Crosfield and Mrs Taylor

---

[5] The Reigate (and subsequently Reigate and Redhill) WSS was lead successively by Ruth Pym (of Firle, the Way), Amy Klein (of Hathergrew, Reigate), Muriel Woodhams (of Twyford, Lynwood Road, Redhill) and then Margaret Crosfield with Miss Barnard of White Lodge, Deerings Road acting as treasurer. The mayoress, Mrs Lemon, hosted meetings at Wray Mill.

processed with a group of women from Cambridge colleges and Helena Auerbach presented a bouquet of orchids from the society to Millicent Fawcett. At the Albert Hall Lady Henry Somerset of Reigate Priory addressed the audience. Her attitude to the militants was ambivalent: she would not criticize WSPU tactics, she said, but she could not endorse them.

Reigate's Liberal MP, Sir Benjamin Brodie, was more negative. He had no doubt that change would come, he told a meeting of the Dorking Women's Liberal Association at Oddfellows Hall in November 1908; but those claiming the vote by force were harming the cause. He responded to Mrs Richmond's resignation as secretary of the Redhill and Reigate Women's Liberal Association on account of the violence meted out to the militants by a Liberal government, with a warning that many people who had been indifferent to the issue now opposed granting the vote to women on account of militant activity.

Over the course of 1908-9, when suffragette activities were being reported daily in the press, RRWSS membership increased from eighty-one members to 182. The society held garden fetes, open air meetings and drawing room gatherings. In February 1909 Lady Frances Balfour spoke at a meeting at Constitutional Hall in Horley and attended a suffrage 'At Home' with an orchestra and choir at Reigate's Colman Institute. In June fifty-three members processed through London and in July Mrs Richmond hosted an event at Fengates. Introducing the speaker, Alice Abadam, she refused to endorse criticism of the militants; women should not find fault with the methods of others, she said, unless they were working to the hilt themselves. At the society's annual general meeting at the Colman Institute members resolved to buy a permanent meeting place from which to conduct their educational and opinion-forming activities. They anticipated using their new headquarters

Letter to the Dorking and Leatherhead Advertiser from the committee of the Leith Hill and District Women's Suffrage Society seeking to distance the constitutional campaign from Mrs Pankhurst's WSPU, whilst simultaneously criticizing the government for its handling of the issue. (The Dorking Advertiser)

WOMAN'S SUFFRAGE.

[To THE EDITOR.]

Sir,—We, the committee of the Leith Hill and District Woman's Suffrage Society desire to point out that it is a branch of the National Union of Woman's Suffrage Societies, and does not use violent methods. The Society appeals to all who believe in the principle of woman's suffrage to come forward and strengthen the hands of those who are struggling by orderly means to gain this great and urgent social reform. At the same time the committee protests most earnestly against the manner in which the whole suffrage agitation has been handled by the Government.—We are, etc.,

SYLVIA DREW (Chairman Leith Hill and District Woman's Suffrage Society);
MADELINE E. BAKER;
ETHEL CHAPMAN;
GWENYDD CRUTTWELL;
LETITIA M. DIXON;
MARY DREW;
JOAN DREW;
ISOBEL HECHT;
MARIAN POLLOCK;
B. E. RAWLINGS;
JESSIE TOUCHE;
SANDRA BRAY (Hon. Secretary).
Westcott, Oct. 14th.

at 77 Station Road for educational purposes once the vote was won.

The relationship between the society and the militant campaigners remained contentious. At an afternoon meeting at Cravenhurst in January 1909 Edith Howe Martyn[6] and Miss Hodgson of the Women's Freedom League presented a duologue defending that organisation's use of militant tactics. And in October several committee members resigned over the society's statement in the 'Dorking Advertiser' *'strongly condemning the use of violence in political propaganda'*. Miss Quinton, Mrs Knight and Miss Wilson said that they had no authority to censure others who were acting according to their consciences. Such condemnation, they wrote to the paper, *'would involve a hardening of the heart and the closing of humane sympathy to those who face suffering and death for the cause'* and that would *'partake of the true nature of violence more than the symbolic acts of stone throwing at representative articles or institutions'*. They finished with a question: *'When the law ceases to become the ally of spirit of advancing righteousness, and is used rather to obstruct it, who shall condemn those who rise to resist it?'*

The Leith Hill and District Women's Suffrage Society held its first meeting in January 1909. Originally a subsidiary of the Reigate WSS, the original membership of 35 increased so rapidly in Dorking and the surrounding villages that the subsidiary almost immediately affiliated itself to the National Union as a separate branch. With Lord Farrer of Abinger as president, Sylvia Drew in the chair, and secretary Sandra Bray undertaking much of the organisation, it had attracted over eighty members by mid 1909.

National Union of Women's Suffrage Societies badge owned by Helen Gordon-Clark of the Leith Hill and District Women's Suffrage Society. The badge is in the NUWSS colours of red, white and green. (Courtesy of Sandra Wedgwood)

Lady Frances Balfour visited Dorking to promote the moderate campaign; on 31st March she spoke at a crowded meeting in the public halls chaired by Mary Drew. A letter of support was read out from Lord Farrer. Could the country which had passed the Married Women's Property Act, he asked, maintain that women were unfit to uphold the greatest doctrine of English liberty - the doctrine which won the Great Charter and the Bill of Rights: no Taxation without Representation? Frederick Leverton-Harris

---

[6] Edith Howe Martyn (1875-1964) was a physicist and mathematician who had been an early associate of Emmeline Pethick-Lawrence in the WSPU. She had been imprisoned in 1906 and formed the Women's Freedom League in 1907, in the belief that violent militancy would not advance the cause but that passive resistance would be effective.

MP (1864-1926) of Camilla Lacey in Westhumble wrote that he found militant suffragette tactics 'regrettable' and that instead the cause needed educational work.

A week later Marian Pollock (1855-1937) hosted an 'At Home' at The Old House in Mickleham with guest speakers Gertrude Baillie-Weaver (1855-1926) and Alys Russell nee Pearsall Smith (1867-1951), wife of Bertrand Russell. Mrs Heaton of Round Down in Gomshall, whose husband was the wealthy art collector Beresford Heaton, also hosted a meeting. By 1912 the Leith Hill WSS had 192 members and 178 'friends' and the villages of Brockham and Betchworth[7] had their own society.

In June 1909 the Leith Hill WSS hosted a week-long campaign of public meetings organised by the Drew sisters, (Mary, Sylvia and Joan), Sandra Bray, Bessie Rawlings, and Isobel Hecht. At Leatherhead's Victoria Hall Letitia Dixon of Cherkley Court took the chair. At Mickleham village hall Marian Pollock's husband, Archibald Gordon Pollock (1851-1937), presided and read a letter of support from Mr

Helen 'Nellie' Gordon Clark (1865-1952) was a member of LHDWSS from 1909. In 1912 she hosted two drawing room meetings at her home in Mickleham. The Gordon Clark family, like many others, was split on the issue of the vote. Helen's father-in-law, Gordon Wyatt Clark of Mickleham Hall, was opposed and her husband Henry's younger brother, Charles Gordon Clark, and his wife, Edith, who lived at Fetcham Lodge, were regular attendees at anti-suffrage meetings. In December 1911 Charles gave the vote of thanks at an anti-suffrage meeting and in April 1914 he chaired a debate between 'anti' Gladys Potts and 'pro' Lady Frances Balfour at Dorking Public Halls.

Helen's sister, Susan Lawrence (1871-1948), was more keenly and radically political. A member of the London County Council from 1910, she went to prison in 1921 as one of the Labour councillors in Poplar who refused to set a rate on the grounds that the poverty of the area meant that charging a rate would amount to taxing the poor to support the poor. In 1923 she became one of the first three women Labour MPs when she was elected to the seat of East Ham North. (Image of Helen Gordon Clark in later life courtesy of Sandra Wedgwood)

---

[7] Brockham and Betchworth's branch of the NUWSS was run by Paquerette Forester of Red Gables.

Leverton-Harris MP. At Holmbury St Mary school Miss Ayres of Peaslake took the chair. At Westcott's reading rooms Sylvia Drew chaired and prospective MP George Touche spoke. At the Norfolk Arms assembly room in Mid Holmwood Mary Drew presided on a platform decorated with plants loaned by sisters Anne and Eleanor Garrett of Holm Cottage. Meetings were also held at the Oddfellows' Hall in Dorking High Street. All the meetings commenced with a 'duologue', *Dare I tell her?'* written by Joan Drew and performed by herself and her sister, Mary, which culminated in the conversion of an 'anti'. The campaign brought 51 new members and £20 in donations. All meetings ended with a vote and reportedly only a dozen or so voted against the suffrage motion. Events continued into July with a public meeting at Abinger Hall, at which Eva Gore Booth and Maude Royden spoke, and a meeting in Shere village hall.

In July the Reigate and Redhill WSS hosted a series of open-air meetings. Freelance suffrage speaker Alice Abadam (1856-1940) was given a *'fairly patient hearing'* in Reigate market square, but subsequent speakers were interrupted. One male speaker accused hecklers of being *'little boys who should be in bed'*. Miss Abadam went on to speak at a garden fete held by Mrs Richmond at Fengates House in Redhill, but an event in a field in Horley had to be abandoned in favour of a school when it rained. Novelist Charlotte Despard (1844-1939) of the break-away Women's Freedom League spoke to a hundred guests in the garden at Stonifers on Reigate Hill in June 1909. In answer to the anti-suffragist argument that women knew little of some areas requiring legislation, Mrs Despard referred to the Children's Act and asked what men knew about babies – and working men's babies at that!

In November 1909 Cicely Corbett spoke at meetings in Shere and Dorking. The NUWSS journal, 'The Common Cause' reported that the Dorking meeting was well attended, with *'a goodly number of men of good standing in the town'* turning out to hear Dr Chapple, a member of the New Zealand House of Representatives, speak about the impact of granting women the vote there. In December Great Bookham held its first public suffrage meeting, featuring a play performed by a company from Brighton.

Millicent Fawcett herself spent a week campaigning in the Surrey Hills at the invitation of the Leith Hill WSS in May/June 1910. She spoke with Alice Abadam in Dorking, Leatherhead, Shere, Peaslake and Newdigate. Meetings were chaired by local supporters Colonel Pennycuick, Isobel Hecht, and prospective conservative MP (Sir) George Touche[8]. The Shere meeting went particularly well, demonstrating a change in attitude to the idea of women's suffrage over the course of a year: the previous year a meeting in the village had been beset by 'hooligans' who had made it impossible for speakers to be heard. All these events were reported for the 'Dorking Advertiser' by Isabella 'Isobel' Hecht nee Fitzroy (1861-1914) of Fitzroy Lodge in Westcott.

---

[8] Sir George Touche (1861-1935) founded the accountancy firm and was Conservative MP for Islington north from 1910-1918. He lived at Broomfield in Westcott.

Further afield, Godalming[9] had an active branch of the NUWSS supported by the garden designer, Gertrude Jekyll (1843-1932) and artist Mary Seton Watts nee Fraser (1849-1938), widow of the artist George Watts. But it was *'difficult to rouse Guildford to any interest let alone enthusiasm'* wrote Julie Chance to Lord Farrer in 1910. She attributed the lack of support to the town *'being largely inhabited by retired people whose lives are mostly over'*. When the WSPU's Helen Craggs and Marie Naylor spoke there in January 1911 large crowds attended and 200 copies of 'Votes for Women' were sold, but support was not sustained: William Chance resorted to staging a women's suffrage meeting with an all-male platform there in September 1913. Cranleigh was also slow to take up the cause; the Haslemere and Hindhead Women's Suffrage Society held an exploratory meeting there in 1910.

On 26th July 1913 women's suffrage 'pilgrims' marched from Brighton to London to take part in what was billed as a 'law-abiding' demonstration in Hyde Park. The marchers passed through Crawley and Horley on 23rd July. An open-air meeting at Earlswood was addressed by Bertrand Russell, followed by evensong at Reigate parish church. The marchers then assembled at the market hall in Redhill on 24th before marching on towards Croydon and London.

Opinion in the non-militant organisations remained divided as to WSPU tactics. With the rise of the WSPU the efficacy of their meetings, 'At Homes', and garden parties was up for discussion amongst members. Some were prepared to consider a change in tactics, but at the RRWSS annual general meeting in 1909 complaints were raised about WSPU publicity material having been sent out with RRWSS material. The committee was accused of being 'hand-in-hand' with the militants. And in January 1910 Sandra Bray of the LHWSS wrote to the paper to disassociate the society from a party of militant suffragettes who had driven through Dorking on a Monday afternoon in Mrs Pethick-Lawrence's car, calling to the crowd to *'Keep the Liberal Out'*. The LHWSS was not, she stressed *'in the very smallest degree responsible for anything that is done or said by Mrs Pethick-Lawrence's party'*. As time went on and the militant campaign veered towards property damage there was general reluctance amongst the constitutional campaigners to be associated with the militants. Bessie Rawlings told the 'Dorking Advertiser' that militants and non-militants were not all 'as one'. Opening speeches at meetings usually made clear that the suffrage societies were not connected to the WSPU; a meeting at Heathside in Tadworth in March 1912 took pains to disassociate supporters from *'all unseemly and mischievous proceedings'*. Many felt that suffragette activities were detrimental to the cause. WSPU members were, said Mrs James Powell (wife of a Reigate JP), *'doing so much harm to the cause of women's suffrage'*. But others transferred their allegiance from the non-militant societies to the WSPU. Mrs Richmond of Redhill, who had chaired Mrs Despard's visit to the RRWSS and hosted Alice Abadam at a

---

[9] The Godalming branch of the NUWSS was lead by Julia 'Julie' Chance nee Strachey of The Orchards.

meeting in her own garden, left the Society and became secretary of the Redhill branch of the WSPU. When the Church League for Women's Suffrage held a meeting in Dorking in 1913 one of their speakers was Joan Cather, another member of the Redhill branch of the WSPU, so the relationship between militants and non-militants was complex and shifting.

Gratifying as rises in membership of suffrage societies in these years may have been, government ministers were neither won over nor worn down by the argument that they represented such widespread support that the Government must introduce an enfranchisement bill. To many it seemed that the failure of such large demonstrations as the Hyde Park rally to persuade meant that all avenues of persuasion had now been exhausted.

Rather than peter out, however, the campaign intensified. And it was women of the Surrey hills who took the campaign in a new direction and onto a new level of intensity.

Bessie Rawlings and the illustrious Garrett family

Bessie Rawlings lived with her brother, Dr John Dunnell Rawlings, at Rose Hill House in Dorking. She sat on the committee of the Leith Hill and District Women's Suffrage Society, was a regular at local suffrage events, and wrote to the local press on suffrage issues. But her family surpassed even the Pankhursts in its contribution to the fight for women's freedom and equality.

Bessie's aunt (her mother's sister) was Louise Garrett (nee Dunnell) and her cousins were the formidable Garrett sisters: Elizabeth Garrett Anderson, Agnes Garrett and Millicent Garrett Fawcett. Bessie's cousin Elizabeth had been jointly responsible for initiating John Stuart Mill's first suffrage petition; she was England's first woman doctor, founded a women's hospital, and became the United Kingdom's first female mayor (in Aldeburgh). Originally involved in the non-militant NUWSS, she joined the WSPU in 1908.

Cousin Agnes Garrett was a suffrage-supporting interior designer and one of the first women to study for a qualification in architecture. The third sister, Millicent Garrett Fawcett, was a campaigner for women's education, co-founder of Newnham College, Cambridge, and the charismatic and fearsomely intelligent leader of the non-militant National Union of Women's Suffrage Societies. (Her daughter Philippa contributed to the cause of women's education when, in 1890, she became the first female student to attain top marks in the Cambridge mathematics examination, beating her male rivals by 13%, a feat which generated newspaper headlines around the world and some reconsideration of women's capabilities – though decades later women were still not eligible to take a degree at Cambridge.) Bessie Rawlings was closest in age to her cousin Millicent and the pair holidayed together. (Millicent's husband, the philosopher Henry Fawcett, was blind, and did not travel.)

Millicent Fawcett had been an associate of John Stuart Mill and Shere's Harriet Grote. In 1910 she undertook a speaking campaign in the villages around Dorking. The following year Rawlings welcomed her cousin back to the town in less happy circumstances. In July 1911 Dr John Rawlings, who had often attended suffrage meetings in the town, died at the age of 44. Millicent Fawcett attended the funeral with her niece, Louisa Garrett Anderson, (like her mother, Elizabeth, a doctor, an active member of the WSPU, and later co-founder of a women's military hospital during the First World War). The Rev Gerard Olivier, (father of the young Laurence), was amongst those who officiated.

Bessie Rawlings moved to 7 Rose Hill where she continued the family tradition of campaigning for women's freedom and equality by serving as secretary to the Leith Hill & District Women's Suffrage Society. Millicent Fawcett became close to the Pethick-Lawrences after they left the WSPU and worked with them through the United Suffragists. She spoke at their silver wedding anniversary dinner in 1926.

Image of Millicent Fawcett Library of Congress

The Drew Sisters

Amongst the most active suffrage campaigners in the LHDWSS were the Drew sisters of Rookery Farm, Westcott. Designer and embroiderer Joan Harvey Drew (1875-1961) produced postcards and a poster for the Artist's Suffrage League. With her sister, Mary, she performed a two-handed playlet on the conversion of an 'anti' at meetings in Dorking and the villages. The sisters were also involved with fellow suffrage supporter Evangeline Farrer in the Leith Hill Musical Festival. Sylvia conducted the Westcott choir and later the Blackheath and Abinger choirs; Joan designed and made many of the Festival's banners.

After the First World War Joan lived in the village of Blackheath and specialized in spectacular display embroideries for churches and public buildings. She was an early member of the Embroiderers' Guild, publishing books of embroidery design in the 1920s.

The Drew sisters feature on an embroidery by Blackheath Women's Institute.

Sandra Bray and a web of 'antis'

The Bray family had owned land in Shere for generations. Sir Reginald More Bray (1842-1923) was cousin to Augusta Spottiswoode with whom he founded Peaslake School and he inherited her cottages in Peaslake. He was also an associate of Harriet Grote, and of the Farrers of Abinger. Sir Reginald's socialist son Reginald 'Reggie' Arthur Bray (1869-1950) was a contemporary of Fred Pethick-Lawrence at Trinity College, Cambridge, and, like Fred, he was drawn into the settlement movement. He volunteered with the Cambridge University House Settlement which brought London children into the Surrey countryside. In 'The Town Child' (1907) and 'Boys, Labour and Apprenticeship' (1912), he explored similar social and labour issues to those which concerned Emmeline and FE Green. He was also involved in local issues and when Augusta Spottiswoode stood down from the Guildford Rural District Council in 1898 Reggie stood in her place on a platform of sewerage for the village of Shere.

Sandra Rose Dorothea Bray nee Onslow (1879-1966) married Reggie's brother, Jocelyn, in 1905. Born in British Honduras, she grew up in Western Australia where her father was chief justice. He and Jocelyn's father were friends and when the Onslow family was in England they spent time with the Brays and their Spottiswoode cousins. Sandra's sister, Elsie, was best friends with Jocelyn's sister, Olive, one of the lively Bray girls: Marjorie's passion was tennis, Lilian was an accomplished climber, and Olive was one of the first women to achieve a first class degree in literature at King's College, London.

From 1908 to 1911 Sandra and Jocelyn lived at Coast Bank in Westcott. As chairman and treasurer of the Leith Hill and District WSS she was determined to engage local anti-suffragists in debate. Other members of the family also attended meetings. Despite the birth of her son, Reynold, in 1911, Sandra continued with her suffrage activities. On one occasion when the 'antis' refused to debate, she drafted in her brother-in-law Francis Edmond Bray to debate on their behalf with Lord Lytton in Dorking. (A barrister, Francis later took on Netley Park and then Drydown, Augusta Spottiswoode's old home.)

The question of women's suffrage divided the extended family. Jocelyn Bray's mother, Emily nee Barclay, was the sister of Robert Barclay of Bury Hill near Dorking and Jocelyn managed the Barclays' estate. But Uncle Robert's wife, Laura (nee Wyvill), was President of the Dorking branch of the National League for Opposing Women's Suffrage. And one of Jocelyn's cousins on his father's side, Gerard Bray, was married to (Evelyn) Joan Broadwood, niece of Sandra's anti-suffrage adversary, Bertha Broadwood of Lyne House in Capel. In 1904 the two sides of the family came together when cousin Gerard and Joan Bray's daughter, Elsa, married Robert and Laura Barclay's son (and another of Jocelyn's cousins) Robert (known as 'Robin'). With these close-knit Broadwood and Barclay connections, Sandra can hardly have had the support of all her husband's family in her suffrage activities.

suffrage societies who wished to have his name on their headed paper. Julie Chance asked him to be vice-president on the formation of the Guildford Women's Suffrage Society and the Men's Liberal Suffrage Society also courted his favour.

In July 1910 'The Times' published a letter from the novelist, Mrs Humphrey Ward, proclaiming that the majority of women did not want the vote. Lord Farrer's response was published the following day. He had, he asserted, taken part in political gatherings where there was no argument more popular than that of making taxation and representation go together. Women in Surrey, he stated, had not forgotten that consent was necessary for taxation and he believed that at least half the women in the county earned their own living or owned property.

Lord Farrer was in regular correspondence with Millicent Fawcett and with Lady Constance Lytton's sister, Lady Betty Balfour, and brother, Lord Lytton. On behalf of the WSPU Mabel Tuke assured him that support by prominent men was of the utmost value. Despite disappointment and government intransigence, Lord Farrer and Evangeline remained constitutional suffragists. In commenting to her husband on Mrs Humphrey Ward's letter to 'The Times', Evangeline noted Mrs Fawcett's dignified response; her hope that *the other lot* would be the same suggests little fellow-feeling with Mrs Pethick-Lawrence's militants.

Lord Farrer's daughter, Frances 'Fanny' Farrer (1895-1977), went on to lead the Women's Institute. Too young to have campaigned for the vote, she became secretary of the Abinger WI when it was established in 1920. She was also responsible, with Ralph Vaughan Williams, for the establishment of Dorking Halls as a home for the Leith Hill Musical Festival. Appointed General Secretary of the Women's Institute in 1929, Fanny Farrer – later Dame Fanny – oversaw the wartime evacuation of WI headquarters from London to Abinger Hall in 1941. Abinger Hall has not survived.

Abinger Hall: Dorking Museum; Lord Farrer and Fanny Farrer reproduced by kind permission of the Farrer family

Evangeline, Lady Farrer, the Leith Hill Musical Competitions, and the War Hospital Supply Depot

Evangeline Knox (1871-1968) lived much of her youth abroad and spoke several languages. From 1888 to 1893 she studied piano, viola and composition at the Royal College of Music (where Ralph Vaughan Williams was also studying). After the death of his first wife, the second Lord Farrer's sister, Ida Darwin, engaged Eva to teach music to her brother's children at Abinger Hall. Eva married Lord Farrer in 1903.

Eva was a close associate of Margaret 'Meggie' Vaughan Williams, sister of the composer, who lived at Leith Hill Place. The two women established the Leith Hill Musical Competitions in 1904. Eva chaired and Meggie acted as secretary to the organisation, cycling between Leith Hill Place and Abinger Hall for meetings. The first competition was held at Dorking Public Halls on 10th May 1905. Eight choirs from villages within a ten mile radius of Abinger Hall competed in six classes. The evening concert was conducted by Vaughan Williams. The competitions were held annually and were very popular in the town and villages with crowds having to be turned away in the early years. Vaughan Williams attracted some of the most distinguished musicians of the day to participate, including the composer, Gustav Holst, and Hubert Parry. Vaughan Williams was devoted to the festival. He took village choir practices and inspired members to achieve difficult pieces.

During the First World War members of the Leith Hill and District Women's Suffrage Society ran a waste paper depot to provide funds for the Dorking Hospital War Supply depot which Eva had founded at Nower Lodge. Eva and her husband were non-militant women's suffrage supporters.

Drawing by Charles Geoffroy-Dechaume reproduced by kind permission of the Farrer family

Lady Katherine Somerset, Lady Henry Somerset, and the Duxhurst Colony for Inebriate Women

Lady Henry Somerset *Library of Congress*

Lady Katherine Somerset was a prominent supporter of the Reigate and Redhill WSS. She officiated at meetings and hosted speakers at Reigate Priory. Born Katherine de Vere Beauclerk, daughter of the Duke of St Albans, she was related to fellow RRWSS member Isobel Hecht. Unlike many in the non-militant movement, however, she was sympathetic to the militant WSPU and its tactics. On arrival in New York in November 1911, she was met with headlines about the hundreds of women held in custody following a window-breaking raid; asked for an opinion, she proclaimed herself *'in sympathy with them, and I think they have been treated very badly by Mr Asquith who has not kept his promises to them'*. On the subject of window-smashing, she told 'The New York Times': *'But what else could they do, poor things, after the way they had been treated? It was necessary to attract the attention of the public to their wrongs.'*

Lady Katherine had links with Emmeline Pethick-Lawrence through her mother-in-law, social reformer and temperance campaigner, Lady Henry Somerset. Born Isabella Somers-Cocks (1851-1921), Lady Henry was an heiress whose family owned Reigate Priory and Eastnor Castle. She had separated from her husband shortly after their marriage in the 1870s. That Lord Henry was homosexual was unmentionable in polite company; therefore Isabella was socially ostracized when she and her young son, (also named Henry), returned to Reigate. She spent the rest of her life working for social reform. Persuaded of the iniquities of drink through her experiences with the poor on her estates and through the White Ribbon Settlement that she ran in Bow, she became chairman of the British Women's Temperance Association.

Lady Henry established Reigate's 180-acre Duxhurst Colony in 1895 to rehabilitate alcoholic women. Thatched cottages grouped around a green provided living accommodation with a chapel and a sanatorium. A pottery was established for therapeutic purposes by Mary Watts (wife of the artist, George Watts). Residents' children were cared for in The Nest, a purpose-built children's block. Lady Henry kept a cottage at the Colony and spent much of her time there.

Like her daughter-in-law, Lady Henry was a suffrage supporter. She spoke at a suffrage rally at the Albert Hall in 1908 and corresponded with the Pethick-Lawrences' friend, the novelist and WSPU committee member, Elizabeth Robins. But unlike her daughter-in-law, she had little sympathy for militancy: *'it makes me miserable because I do firmly believe in their cause but women are such despairingly stupid creatures at times'* she wrote to a cousin after a suffragette bit a policeman.

During the First World War the Duxhurst Colony took in abandoned babies; many were the children of unmarried mothers and soldiers who never returned from the war. The manager of the Duxhurst children's unit was Emmeline Pethick-Lawrence's friend Kathleen Fitzpatrick, an associate from her time in youth work who often holidayed with Emmeline in Cornwall.

Lady Henry Somerset distributing cabbages to children at Duxhurst, 1913. Library of Congress

Helena Auerbach and the early Women's Institute

Helena Auerbach nee Joshua (1872-1955) led the Reigate and Redhill WSS. Millicent Fawcett and Israel Zangwill both spoke at events at her home, Hethersett in Reigate. An all-day garden party in July 1911 saw attendance in the hundreds; 'The Common Cause' was sold alongside cakes and books, lucky tubs and tombolas, and the town band played for dancing in the evening.

Helena Auerbach grew up in a wealthy Jewish family. She married at 19 and was a keen driver. Although not a great speaker, she spoke at the first meeting of the Jewish League for Women's Suffrage and was recruited onto the committee of the NUWSS where she played a similar role to Emmeline Pethick-Lawrence at the WSPU, as honorary treasurer. Completely untrained, her first act on taking the post was to buy a book-keeping primer. She was supported by her husband, Julius, and commuted to London for meetings.

During the First World War she sat on the Women's War Agricultural Committee which established the UK's first Women's Institutes. Originating in Canada, the WI in Britain grew out of the suffrage movement and the experience of war, both of which saw women re-assessing their relationships with society. Many of the WI's early leaders had a background in the campaign for the vote and saw the organization as a way of encouraging women to become active citizens. Auerbach oversaw the establishment of the WI in Surrey and in 1919 she became treasurer of its National Federation. It is largely due to her financial acumen that the WI had the stable footing that enabled it to spread all over the country. She later served as deputy chair of the WI's national committee. On her death Helena Auerbach left a trust which enabled the WI to purchase premises in Guildford.

'*Oh the joy!*': Mackie's Hill and the hunger strike

The hunger strike caught the public imagination to such an extent that it has become forever associated with the suffragette movement. That it did so is largely the legacy of two women who successively occupied a house in the Surrey village of Peaslake. The hunger strike was not a tactic adopted under direction from the Clement's Inn leadership; it was initiated by Marion Wallace Dunlop. The government's horrifying response was then publicized in a semi-autobiographical novel by Helen Gordon Liddle.

By the early twentieth century Peaslake was home to a number of *'ladies of very advanced views'*, according to Edwin Waterhouse[10] of Feldemore in Holmbury St Mary. There was, he claimed in 1912, a *'nest of suffragettes'* in the village. Dunlop and Liddle were amongst a number of artists resident there. Artists played a significant role in the WSPU and the suffrage movement generally. Such women had a degree of autonomy that made them very useful to the organization. Not only did they earn their own money rather than relying on their, (perhaps unsympathetic), husbands or fathers, but as freelancers they were not hampered in their activities, as were other working women, by employers' opinions or the fear of losing their jobs. They contributed hugely to the image of the suffrage movement and to the WSPU's merchandising and events. Many of the WSPU's artist supporters were recruited through contact with Sylvia Pankhurst and her London studio or through her associates. Some of the most prominent, like Dunlop and the Brackenbury sisters, lived in the Surrey hills; others retreated to the area for periods of the year.

Marion Wallace Dunlop (1865-1942) was a Scottish-born sculptor and illustrator who claimed to be descended from William Wallace. She studied at the Slade School of Fine Art and exhibited at the Royal Academy. Her 'Fairies, Elves and Flower Babies' and 'The Magic Fruit Garden' were published in 1899. With Sylvia Pankhurst and Edith Elizabeth Downing she designed many of the WSPU's spectacular themed processions at her Kensington studio. Costumes were made at the nearby studios of the Brackenbury sisters whose country home, Brackenside, was in the heart of Peaslake.

Dunlop was a member of the Weybridge WSPU when she was arrested for stamping a quotation from the Bill of Rights onto the wall of St Stephen's Hall at the House of Commons in June 1909. It asserted the right of subjects to present petitions to their king, a right that was being denied the women. She was sentenced to a month

---

[10] Waterhouse was the founder of the well-known accountancy firm.

in Holloway. She demanded to be treated as a political prisoner rather than as a common criminal, as were men convicted of political offences, particularly those campaigning for Home Rule in Ireland. When she was refused Dunlop commenced a hunger strike. She was released after 91 hours.

'Votes for Women' swiftly acclaimed her action: Dunlop, it asserted, possessed the *'resourcefulness and energy in the face of difficulties that marked the true Suffragette'*. Her ingenuity was enthusiastically embraced and the WSPU took up the hunger strike as a tactic. A group of stone-throwers who had been arrested on a deputation to Parliament from Caxton Hall a week after Dunlop's action were next to adopt the fast. Within weeks it was common practice. Throughout the summer of 1909 early releases undermined the effect of long sentences. Faced with an epidemic of hunger strikes in prisons and cells all over the country the Home Office instigated force feeding that autumn.

The process of force feeding was brutal, degrading and often excruciatingly painful. It seldom worked; many women still had to be released early as a result of the devastating effect on their health. Some suffered strokes, others developed infections as food entered their lungs. Their faces were bruised, their teeth broken and their lips cut as their mouths were forced open with steel bands. Many never recovered. Nor was the feeding equipment always cleaned after use, risking serious infection. In 1914 Emmeline Pethick-Lawrence's sister, Dorothy Pethick, described her experience of force feeding to the 'New York Times' as *'exquisite torture'*. Three doctors and six policemen had held her down, she said, and no medical examination had been conducted beforehand.

One of the fullest accounts of force-feeding was written by Helen Gordon Liddle (?-1952). Another of Emmeline Pethick-Lawrence's recruits, she had been living at Loseley Farm in Ewhurst and then at Mackie's Hill in Peaslake. Her interest in the fight for the vote had been aroused when she heard of Emmeline's arrest and found Emmeline's description in the press unrecognizable as the woman she had met in Surrey.

Fabian Society member Marion Wallace Dunlop acquired Mackie's Hill in Peaslake from fellow suffragette Helen Gordon Liddle at the height of the suffrage campaign. In later years she kept chickens and goats and was often to be seen painting on the common nearby. (Image: Wallace Dunlop Private Archive-London

By 1910 it was Liberal party policy to exclude women from meetings so that they could not raise questions or protest. On finding herself excluded from a public meeting, Liddle threw a stone at a Post Office in protest. The Post Office was government property and therefore an anti-government target. She was sentenced to a month's hard labour in Strangeways. She duly went on hunger strike. After three days she was gagged and fed by nasal and throat tube. So disturbed was she by the experience that she was unable to speak afterwards and attendant wardresses had to go outside because they were feeling faint. Her novel, 'The Prisoner' (1911), is a thinly fictionalized account of her ordeal, ending with a late night return to Mackie's Hill. *'Oh the joy,"* she wrote, *'of waking up with the bare bough of an apple tree swinging in the dark morning blue, before the garden window, dancing on a stray golden leaf.'*

Mackie's Hill in Peaslake is a 16th century house. It was renovated in the early 20th century, with the addition of a studio by CR Ashbee. Helen Gordon Liddle moved out soon after her imprisonment. She probably knew Marion Wallace Dunlop through her close association with the Brackenbury sisters who lived in the same village, but the two women were not close. Liddle moved into Dorking, from where she later ran the Dorking and Holmwood campaign with Charlotte Marsh. Mackie's Hill is secluded and remote, reached down a winding lane; it was a perfect place of retreat. (Dorking Museum)

There was much discomfort from all political parties once details of the realities of force-feeding became known. Questions were raised in the House of Commons and a deputation of doctors petitioned Asquith. In January 1910 Edwin Richmond resigned as treasurer of the Redhill and Meadvale Liberal Association over the issue. He told the 'Dorking Advertiser' that he found the Liberal government's treatment of women so unjust and unwise that, though he agreed whole-heartedly with the government's social reform programme, he was severing his links with the party. He regretted that the denial of full rights of citizenship to women, together with these 'ruthless measures', had made his response necessary[11]. The furore served to confirm many women's sense of injustice and many were inspired to join the WSPU in anger at its use. Injustice and inequality within the criminal justice system went even deeper, however, and it was another of Emmeline Pethick-Lawrence's recruits who determined to reveal that.

Emmeline's involvement with the Esperance Club had been affected by her involvement with the WSPU, but Mary Neal and the girls had carried on dancing. They had made regular appearances at suffragette events, like the Knightsbridge women's exhibition, and continued to holiday in Littlehampton and in Holmwood. They had also brought to the cause a woman who was able to enlist not just personal determination and courage, but powerful political influence.

Lady Constance Georgina Lytton (1869-1923) was the daughter of an ex-Viceroy of India, the late Lord Lytton. Her sister Betty Balfour, was married to the brother of the leader of the Conservative party. Her sister Emily's husband was the architect Sir Edwin Lutyens (who had worked for Fred and Emmeline on the billiard room at The Mascot). Her brother Victor, the 2nd Earl of Lytton, sat in the House of Lords.

Lady Constance was interested in the Morris dance revival. Another brother, the war artist Neville Bulwer Lytton (1879-1951), was also interested in the dance revival and was a correspondent of Cecil Sharp. When she received an inheritance, he suggested that she donate it to the Esperance Club. It was a decision which she later said marked the beginning of her spiritual life. After watching the girls perform she arranged for one of them to visit her family home at Knebworth to teach the villagers there to dance. She was drawn into the activities of the club and Mary Neal asked her to accompany the girls to Littlehampton to play piano for the dancers. In the late summer of 1908, Lady Constance Lytton met Emmeline Pethick-Lawrence and Annie Kenney at The Green Lady.

Lady Constance had no idea when she volunteered with the Esperance Club that its founders were suffragettes, and one of them of its leadership. But she was impressed with them: '*I realised at once that I was face to face with women of strong personality*', she wrote in her autobiography 'Prisons and Prisoners', '*and I felt, at*

---

[11] His wife was an active member of the non-militant Reigate and Redhill WSS. She had resigned from the Redhill and Reigate Women's Liberal Association and later defected to the WSPU.

first vaguely, that they represented something more than themselves, a force greater than their own seemed behind them. Their remarkable individual powers seemed illumined and enhanced by a light that was apart from them as are the colours and patterns of a stained glass window by the sun shining through it.'

It was only when Annie Kenney's sister, Jessie (1887-1985), (who was working as Mrs Pethick-Lawrence's secretary), came to talk to the girls about her time in Holloway that Lady Constance realised that she had fallen amongst suffragettes. By her account she was not pleased at the discovery, but she had a long talk with Emmeline, whom she described as *'lovable and sympathetic'*, whilst out on a motoring expedition. She volunteered to take song classes at the Esperance during Hugh MacIlwaine's illness. On her return she wrote to a friend from the waiting room at Kings Cross station that she had *'got knotted up with suffragettes.'* And on October 14th she visited the WSPU's offices to offer her services. On October 28th Emmeline Pethick-Lawrence wrote a characteristically effusive letter welcoming Lady Constance to the cause. Emmeline knew, she said, that in due course Lady Constance would play her part *'whatever that part may be'*. Her involvement was a matter of destiny just as Emmeline and her husband had been brought together to accomplish this work.

WSPU postcard of Lady Constance Lytton (From the collection of Ann Lewis and Mike Sponder)

In November Lady Constance spoke at a meeting in Cobham near her Aunt Theresa's home. When the Pankhursts were released from prison in December she walked to the breakfast celebrations alongside the Brackenbury sisters from Peaslake. Despite life-long ill-health, she then determined upon active campaigning. In February 1909 she took part in her first delegation to Parliament. She lunched beforehand with the Pankhursts, Emmeline Pethick-Lawrence and Mary Neal at Clement's Inn. Marching alongside Emmeline Pethick-Lawrence, she was arrested for refusing to be turned back by the police. On refusal to be bound over to keep the peace, she was sentenced to a month in Holloway. Lady Constance served her sentence alongside Mrs Pethick-Lawrence. Though Emmeline spoke at her release breakfast of prison clothes removing all marks of social distinction, such was not Lady Constance's experience: because of her status, and with the officers of the law aware of her powerful friends, she was treated leniently and released early. In April she joined Emmeline on a speaking tour of the West Country and visited Emmeline's family in Weston-super-Mare.

Lady Constance endeavoured to get herself arrested for a second time in October 1909 by throwing a stone wrapped in a slogan at Lloyd George's car in Newcastle. She was again given preferential treatment; she received a medical examination and was released without force-feeding when she went on hunger strike.

High profile campaigners like Pethick-Lawrences and Lady Constance received much publicity. But newspaper reports did not adequately represent the suffering, both mental and physical, endured by the majority of those arrested who were of lower social status. Determined to expose the brutality repeatedly endured by ordinary women in the cells, Lady Constance cut her hair and dressed herself as a working-class girl before demonstrating outside Liverpool's Walton prison in January 1910. On her arrest she gave her name as Jane Warton. This time none of the niceties were observed; there was no medical examination and she was force-fed eight times before her identity was discovered. Her account, published in 'The Times' and in 'Votes for Women', exposed the government to furious correspondence in the papers.

After suffering a series of strokes in 1912 which left her partly paralysed - blamed by her family on the effects of force-feeding - Lady Constance's activities were severely curtailed. She wrote her memoir with her left hand. The Mascot and her Aunt Theresa's home in Cobham were amongst the few places that she was able to visit. In March 1914 The Mascot provided her with a place of respite and refuge. Housekeeper May Start was instructed by Emmeline Pethick-Lawrence to send a car to meet Lady Constance. May, Emmeline assured, would *'do everything to show (you) how much we love you'*. Lady Constance later recalled that she and Nurse Oram had been *'showered with kindness'* by Fred and Emmeline. Lady Constance remained an invalid until her early death.

Lady Constance's revelations coincided with the general election of January 1910, precipitated by the rejection of Lloyd George's 'pensions' budget by the House of Lords. Despite some misgivings the WSPU held to its position of campaigning vigorously against Liberal candidates throughout the campaign. The NUWSS opposed candidates only if they were anti-suffrage and supported pro-suffrage candidates of whatever party, including Joseph Clayton, who stood against anti-suffrage Hillaire Belloc in South Salford, and Walter McClaren (who had a home in Holmwood and had spoken to the Reigate Women's Liberal Association at the public halls in November 1910), in Crewe. In Dorking suffragettes drove through the streets in Emmeline Pethick-Lawrence's car, shouting *'Keep the Liberal Out!'* The government was returned to power, but with a reduced majority. The women hoped that the government would now be more open to negotiation as it would be reliant on minor party support. And Prime Minister Asquith had stated during campaigning that should a reform bill be introduced, the subject of a women's suffrage amendment would be a matter not of the party whip but of a free vote. In the hope of progress, the WSPU called a truce.

Lady Constance's brother, Lord Lytton, chaired the committee which sought to take advantage of this apparent softening in government policy. With support from MPs of all parties, the committee drew up a bill to give the vote to a limited number of female householders. The so-called Conciliation Bill was introduced by a private member in June 1910. In great hope the women of the WSPU processed with the break-away Women's Freedom League to a large meeting at the Albert Hall. Carnival floats designed by Marion Wallace Dunlop and Edith Downing processed with former prisoners who marched in suffragette colours carrying prison banners and wearing their prison medals. Demonstrations of support were held in cities all over the nation. In July another procession to Hyde Park ended with forty speakers addressing large crowds. When the bill passed a second reading with a large majority it seemed that the vote had been won.

But Prime Minister Asquith would not allocate time for the bill to complete the parliamentary process before the summer recess. In effect he imposed a veto. The WSPU held fire when Parliament reconvened in the autumn of 1910, hoping that the Conciliation Bill might be resurrected. But in November stalemate was reached between Lords and Commons over Lloyd George's budget once again. Asquith announced the dissolution of Parliament with the business of women's suffrage unfinished. It was the impact of this disappointment, together with the events of Black Friday, which precipitated the WSPU into all-out warfare and made the Surrey village of Holmwood a battleground.

Crowds watch the procession through London on 17th June 1911. Women dressed in period costume to represent women's achievements throughout history. (Library of Congress)

The Election Campaign of January 1910

During the election campaign of January 1910 the Leith Hill and District WSS rented 43 High Street in Dorking as their campaign headquarters and committee rooms. Large banners and posters outside invited members of the public to come in and sign a petition calling on Parliament to grant an extension of the franchise to women on the same terms as men. The Reigate and Redhill WSS opened a committee room at 33 Bell Street in Reigate and a shop window at 90 Station Road in Redhill. The RRWSS's Helena Auerbach reported to a meeting at the public halls that both candidates, the sitting Liberal MP, Sir Benjamin Brodie, and the challenging Conservative, Colonel Rawson, had put women's suffrage onto their election programmes and pledged their support. She called upon voters to show their support by signing the national suffrage petition.

'The Common Cause' - the magazine of the National Union of Women's Suffrage Societies - reported that signatures to the petition had come in from many local tradespeople in the constituency and that the Conservative and Liberal agents had both signed. The NUWSS claimed to have collected 280,000 signatures across the country during the election period. The petition from Dorking, Redhill and Reigate was presented to the victorious Conservative candidate, Colonel Rawson, at Conservative Association headquarters in Redhill in February by Mr and Mrs Auerbach, Miss Crosfield, Mrs Lemon, Miss Hecht, Miss Drew, Miss Aston, Bessie Rawlings and Miss Molyneux. 3,315 signatures had been collected in the towns and surrounding villages; the greatest number came from Dorking (642), Reigate (437) and Redhill (305).

The militants took over Carlton Hall in Redhill for the 1910 election campaign. The WSPU organiser in Redhill and Reigate was Catherine 'Kitty' Sydney Louisa Margesson (1887-1939). A Cambridge graduate, (though as a woman she was not formally able to take a degree), she was the 23 year-old daughter of Sir Mortimer Margesson and Lady Isabel Augusta nee Hobart-Hampden (1863-1946), a prominent WSPU speaker. In March 1912 Lady Isabel wrote in 'The Standard' that *'we suffragettes'* had been forced by the government into militant tactics and that for those like herself who were unable to join in the fight there would be undying regret as well as shame that they had not had the honour of suffering with those brave women who counted liberty worth any sacrifice.

Lady Isabel's daughter Catherine was based in Reading and conducted the election campaign from the home of Mrs Richmond at Fengates House in Redhill. It was standard practice for both the WSPU and the NUWSS to parachute experienced organisers into small towns to organise events or campaigns. In later years Catherine's mother served with Reigate's WSS leader Helena Auerbach on the management committee of the newly-formed Women's Institute with which Catherine was also involved.

Postcard of the campaign headquarters of the Leith Hill and District WSS. The back reads: 'Dear Sis, didn't we have plenty of placards up. The Misses Drew went to ask the photographer to sign the petition and he would not, did not believe in it etc. Of course they talked a lot to him, and strange to say he came to the rooms to beg their pardon for being rather rude to them, on the morning after, and signed the petition and offered to take photographs of the building for them, so they were set up they had converted him to their way of thinking. I was pleased to hear Mr P is interested in our cause.' It is not known who the suffrage supporting writer was. The Misses Drew referred to are sisters Mary, Sylvia and Joan Drew of Westcott. (Dorking Museum)

The Lytton family

Lady Constance's family was pro-suffrage. Her father was Robert Bulwer Lytton, 1st Earl of Lytton (1831-1891), ex-viceroy of India. Her mother, Edith (?-1936), her sister Lady Elizabeth 'Betty' Balfour (1867-1942), and her brother Victor, the 2nd Earl (1876-1947), were all active non-militant campaigners. Her maternal aunt, Maria Theresa Villiers (?-1925), author of 'A Surrey Pot Pourri', worked with Gertrude Jekyll (1843-1932), who designed the Godalming WSS banner. Her sister-in-law, Lady Frances Balfour (1858-1931) was president of the London Society for Women's Suffrage and sat on the executive of the NUWSS.

Another sister, Lady Emily Lutyens (1874-1904), was an early supporter of the WSPU. Her husband, who designed The Mascot, was opposed to the militant campaign. In 1908 he described Lady Constance's new comrades as *'a crew of notorious rioters'* and Mrs Pethick-Lawrence as *'so very very second rate.'* Lady Emily left the WSPU in 1909 but later worked with Emmeline in the United Suffragists.

Who was at The Mascot on the night of the 1911 census?

The 1911 census was carried out on the night of 2nd April. Campaigners argued that as women did not 'count' in electoral terms, they should refuse to be counted for census purposes. Many suffrage supporters made their point by frustrating government enumerators. Emily Davison hid in a broom cupboard at the House of Commons so that if she had to be recorded it would be in a symbolic location. Others stayed out all night so that they would not appear at any address. To this end the WSPU hosted an all-night roller skating session at the Aldwych skating rink backing on to Clement's Inn. It was claimed that 500 women and 70 men attended.

Fred Pethick-Lawrence filled in the form for The Mascot. He listed himself and a visitor, Sidney Dillon Shallord, a journalist. On signing the declaration that the schedule was filled to the best of his knowledge he annotated: *so far as the males are concerned. The women in the house being suffragists have requested me not to include them and I have accordingly not done so.'*

The enumerator added, in different handwriting, *'Mrs Lawrence, wife, about 35'.* It seems he did not know Emmeline's name or age but estimated from Fred's given age of 39. He also added a *'servant'.* This may have been May Start, the Pethick-Lawrences' housekeeper. The enumerator was able to fill in nothing but an estimate of her age (40). Some accounts suggest that Emmeline was present at the Aldwych Skating Rink, but the enumerator's inclusion of Emmeline and May would suggest that the two women were present for at least part of the night but refused to be logged or to answer questions.

Dora, the daughter of tea merchant Arthur Brooke of Leylands in Wotton, and his wife Alice, was another census refusenik. In 1904 she had married her younger brothers' language tutor and moved with him to Bedales School where he took a job as art master. A progressive co-educational boarding school near Petersfield, Bedales was founded by socialists John and Amy Bradley. Dora's husband appears on the census, at Byways Cottage with a cook and a housemaid, but Dora does not. An annotation refers to the return for the Bedales Staff House, where Amy Bradley has written: '*No Vote. No Census – Government must rest upon the consent of the people'*. Below Amy's signature is that of Dora Hooper, with the hand-written comment: '*Dora Hooper age 36 Wife of Art Master at Bedales School – entered here by Registrar General's instruction'.*

In Little Bookham, Leith Hill and District WSS committee member Gwenydd Cruttwell does not appear on the census return for Bayfield House. Her servants, Louisa Lacey, Frances Monk, Lilly Peerless and Winifred Summers appear but without details of age or place of birth. They must have shared their employer's commitment to the vote, as Gwenydd's husband annotated the form to explain that they would not give their details for as long as the vote was withheld from women.

'Female faddists' and 'really superior women':
anti-suffragism in the Surrey Hills

Campaigners, whether militant or not, were often subject to verbal and physical attack. In May 1908 members of the Women's Freedom League were heckled by a crowd outside The Old Bull in Leatherhead where they were speaking from a horse-drawn wagon as part of a tour of southern England. Their scheduled meeting at the Victoria Hall there was cancelled when a mob pursued them. The event was later reconvened with Letitia Dixon of Cherkley Court in the chair.

Such events often represented knee-jerk misogyny rather than reasoned opposition. But there were plenty of arguments to be levelled at campaigners by those opposing the female vote. Some asserted that men and women had different responsibilities in life and that as women took no part in major spheres of activity - warfare, mining, shipping or finance - they were in no position to have an opinion on such matters. (Though their lack of experience in numerous matters relating to women's lives did not prevent men believing

An anti-suffrage poster contrasts the full-figured and serene anti-suffragist woman in her classical drapes with the scrawny, ill-dressed, hammer-wielding militant suffragette behind her. Anti-suffrage posters depicted suffrage supporting women as unattractive, often masculine, and aggressive, with squalid homes and neglected children. Depictions of men in suits holding babies suggested that women wished to overturn the established social order, whilst depictions of the Parliament of the future, where women nursed crying babies and did their knitting, mocked the idea of women's participation in political life. (From the collection of Ann Lewis and Mike Sponder) that they had the expertise to legislate in those areas.) A vote in local elections, where women might influence politics within their local spheres on poor relief and education, was argued to be sufficient. Some feared that giving the vote to women would introduce politics into the home, coming between a man and his wife. Others contended that the majority of women did not want the responsibility of the vote. Still others argued that the situation might arise whereby there were more female voters than male, raising the unthinkable prospect of the country being notionally controlled by women.

Probably the Surrey Hills' most high profile 'anti' was Bertha Broadwood (1846-1935) of Lyne House in Capel, just south of Dorking. She had an interest in politics and in the 1870s she had gone to listen to debates at the House of Commons with suffragist Margaret Pennington of Broome Hall. Pennington did not manage to convert her to the cause, however.

A member of the Broadwood piano-manufacturing family, Bertha was confident, energetic and community-spirited. Educated conventionally at home, she was said to have been *'the very ditto of her father'*, which perplexed her family. Her older sister, Katherine puzzled that she was *'born a young woman and not a man for some inscrutable reason.'* The *'necessary feminine conventionalities'* were a clog to her *'ardent, aspiring nature'*. Bertha turned these energies to the benefit of the local community. She established the village institute in Rusper, supported schools in Capel, Rusper and Newdigate, and promoted the work of the Free Rural Readers Union and the Popular Lecture Association. In 1883 she founded the Cottage Benefit Nursing Association which trained working-class nurses in the Holt-Ockley method (named after the nearby village). Nurses were employed to go into the homes of impoverished village women in Capel and Holmwood and to live with them, attending, not just to medical care, but to domestic duties which enabled the patients to rest. To have set up such a system indicates that Bertha had an understanding of the lives of women less privileged than herself, and a desire to improve conditions for women and their children. One of her collaborators in the Holt-Ockley project was Rosa Spottiswoode, sister of suffrage supporter, Augusta. The organisation was successful and Bertha developed it as a model for a national organization with a national committee, nationwide branches, and a London training scheme.

Bertha Broadwood in 1903. (Image courtesy of Broadwood by Appointment by David Wainwright)

As her parents aged Bertha took on much of the running of the family estate at

Lyne. She also involved herself in the management of the family piano-making firm, (not always to the benefit of the business). And she adopted the orphaned children of her brother, James. Bertha was warm, generous with her time, and devoted to her family, her religion and her country. Unlike others involved in social welfare initiatives, however, she did not question the framework of her society. She was vigorously opposed to socialism, trades unionism and to women's suffrage.

Bertha Broadwood may have dallied with the cause in the campaign's early days; in 1874 she was asked to collect signatures for a petition in support of a suffrage bill. But in the event she penned a draft paper setting out the argument against. By the 1890s she was attending meetings of the National League for Opposing Women's Suffrage in Dorking with her friend, Margaret Malden. The wife of the Surrey historian Henry Eliot Malden, Margaret Malden (1852-1919) was very much of Broadwood's social milieu. Her family lived at Kitlands near Coldharbour with Margaret's wealthy uncle, Douglas Denon Heath, and Margaret's cousin, Ada Heath, was married to Bertha's brother. When the Maldens moved to 17 Rose Hill in Dorking, Bertha went to anti-suffrage meetings at the Public Halls with Margaret's daughter, Anne, taking tea with the family first and dining with them afterwards.

Bertha Broadwood's sister, Mary Shearme, who lived at the vicarage in Oakwoodhill, was also an anti-suffragist. She collected signatures in the village for anti-suffrage petitions and she and Bertha regularly exchanged opinions in correspondence. Bertha described those who chained themselves to railings as *'female faddists'* who lacked the experience necessary for cool, calm, clear-headed decisions. In letters to the 'Dorking Advertiser' she exhorted readers not to be carried away in admiration for the likes of *'really superior women'* such as Dr Elizabeth Garrett Anderson because, she said: *'as a rule women are unfitted to political power by their natural excitability, impulsiveness and variety (which arises out of the very qualities which fit them for their special duties) and want of that practical knowledge which men of all classes gain by after painful experience of their rougher training and harder work. As the nature of women cannot be changed the exceptions to this rule, produced by education, will probably always remain few enough to prove the rule.'* One can only assume that Bertha considered herself one of these few 'superior' women. We would explain such pronouncements now as internalised misogyny.

As the campaign for the vote grew more intense Bertha's opposition became more vehement. She mocked those who demanded the vote in verse, claiming that the only women who were interested were those who were 'unwinsome' (and therefore wanted men to pay them attention for their votes since they were never going to attract attention for their looks), or those who were not fully occupied in womanly duties and so sought to satisfy their vanity in public life. Such 'superfluous' women, she suggested, might be sent to the colonies, leaving work and husbands for those who remained.

Anti-suffragists like Bertha Broadwood began to organize themselves nationally in the early years of the twentieth century. In March 1907 Ermine Taylor announced the creation of the National Women's Anti-Suffrage League, and called for representatives from each town to come forward to sit on its committee and to collect signatures for an anti-suffrage petition in their locality. Local committee members were drawn from the wealthy families occupying the grand mansions that surrounded the Dorking: the Harrowbys and Ryders of High Ashurst on Box Hill, the Barclays of Bury Hill, the Salomons of Norbury Park, the Powells of Goodwyns, the Broadwoods of Lyne House, and the Aggs of Pippbrook. In February 1909 Bertha Broadwood and her associates took the argument into Pethick-Lawrence territory. The East Surrey branch of the Women's National Anti-Suffrage League staged an anti-suffrage meeting at Holmwood village hall where the assembled company was addressed by barrister Mr FJ Newman. Retired naval officer Captain St John Hornby of The Oaks presided. Bertha attended with Cuthbert Heath of Anstie Grange and his wife. Accompanying Bertha and the Heaths was Colonel Henry H Helsham Jones of Redlands. Other well-to-do members included Henry Lee-Steere of Jayes Park, near

Cuthbert Heath (1859-1939), his wife (Sarah) Caroline nee Gambier (1859-1944), and Colonel Henry H Helsham Jones (1839-1920). Heath was the hugely wealthy insurer who transformed Lloyds of London from a shipping insurer into a world-wide, multi-faceted insurance business. The Broadwoods and the Heaths had grown up together and Cuthbert's sister, Ada, was married to Bertha's brother, Harry. When the Broadwood family piano business got into trouble Heath had been instrumental in turning its fortunes, converting it into limited company - of which Bertha was a director. One of the investors was William Spottiswoode, nephew of Augusta. Colonel Helsham Jones' daughter, Constance, had married one of Cuthbert Heath's brothers. All were regular attenders at anti-suffrage events. (Images courtesy of JJ Heath-Caldwell)

Ockley, and his wife, and the Hargreaves-Brown family of Broome Hall. Newman argued that Britain was not like Norway or Finland - nations which had already granted the vote to women - on account of its empire. The governance of one of the greatest empires the world had known was no business for women, he said, for the empire had been built on force and it was maintained by force. The country could not continue to hold its own, he said, if the vote was granted to people who could not be called upon to fight for it. And if foreigners thought that the empire was ruled by women, they would seek to wrest it away.

The 'antis' liked to meet in private. Insistence on the wearing of membership badges ensured that those who were not of a like mind could be excluded. But a few pro-suffragists infiltrated the meeting. Sandra Bray, one of the Drew sisters, and Constance Aston of Sondes Place all put questions to the speakers. When Sandra Bray said that she wanted equality Newman dismissed her with the assertion that women occupied a more special place: *'My dear young lady! You don't realise that we men have certain ideals, and that we want you to occupy that elevated pedestal.'* When Miss Drew asked if it was right that men should legislate on milk supply, cradles and fire-guards, Bertha Broadwood asserted that women should seek reform of society in other ways than through Parliament, as she had done. She reminded people that she had sat before a parliamentary committee and been listened to. Those attending were overwhelmingly opposed and when barrister Alfred Percival Perceval Keep (of The Hut - now Bentleys - in Mid Holmwood) proposed a vote against women's suffrage, he was seconded by Colonel Helsham Jones and the motion was carried with only six dissenting votes.

The Epsom branch of the Women's National Anti-Suffrage League held a meeting at Victoria Hall in Leatherhead the following month. The meeting was chaired by Edith Gordon-Clark of Fetcham Lodge. Amongst the concerns expressed was the fear that giving the vote to women would lead to the spread of socialism.

The 'antis' reluctance to engage in debate was the subject of an amused letter to the 'Dorking Advertiser' by Conrad Schmidt of Highgate. Of no particular allegiance, he attended a meeting of the Church League for Women's Suffrage in the Westcott reading room in 1909. Men were always saying that they did not understand women, joked Joan Cather of Redhill, so how could they presume to legislate for them? Miss Pringle, in the chair, put the question to debate and the resolution in favour passed. By contrast the organisers of a meeting by anti-suffragists which he attended took care to ensure that only 'antis' were admitted. There followed, Schmidt reported, *'absurd proceedings'* by the 'antis' who *'seemed to have convened a meeting which they knew quite well beforehand would consist of nothing but people who were of their own way of thinking and in which they knew there would be absolutely no opposition. Such a meeting strikes the disinterested person as very humorous, with its spectacle of everybody solemnly assembled and looking rather like an amateur mothers' meeting, with speakers getting up and saying what an excellent lot of people they were, and what a bad lot the other side were, knowing full well that nobody was likely to differ from their opinions'.*

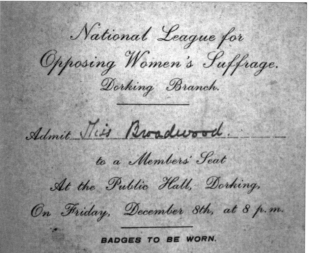

National League for Opposing Women's Suffrage.

Friday, December 8th, 1911.

⚛ PROGRAMME. ⚛

PIANOFORTE SOLO, ...
MRS. CAREY DRUCE.

SONG, ..."The Soul's Awakening."
MRS. COWIE.

SONG, ... "Mary."
DR. MAW.

SONG, ... "Stay in your own Back-yard."
MISS HARRISON.

PIANOFORTE SOLO, ... "Valse in E-minor" (Chopin).
MISS M. LOUGHBOROUGH.

SONG, ... "Daddy."
MRS. COWIE.

SONG, ... "Down in the Forest."
MISS HARRISON.

SONG, ... "Oh promise me."
DR. MAW.

⚛ "WOMAN'S WRONGS." ⚛

CHARACTERS:

HAROLD WOODLEAF ... MR. HAROLD CARLILE
MARGARET WOODLEAF (his wife)
      MRS. HAROLD CARLILE
MRS. PERCY (Harold's sister)
      MISS DOROTHEA POWELL
PARLOURMAID... ... ... MISS HARRISON

Time—The Present.
Scene—Drawing Room in Woodleaf's House.

Above left: Bertha Broadwood's invitation to an anti-suffrage event in Dorking. Local anti-suffrage publicity usually requires 'Badges to be worn' so that members can be identified. (By permission of Surrey History Centre ref 2185/BMB/7/1/26)

Left: The programme and running order for an anti-suffrage event in Dorking. (Surrey History Centre ref 2185/BMB/7/1)

Above right: The Badge of the National League for Opposing Women's Suffrage depicts the national symbols of the English rose, the Scottish thistle and the Irish shamrock growing from the same stem. The design originated as the emblem of the Women's National Anti-Suffrage League and was then adopted by the National League for Opposing Women's Suffrage. (LSE Library)

In March 1910 Sandra Bray of the Leith Hill WSS made an attempt to stage a formal debate between pro- and anti-suffrage speakers. She asked Bertha

B⸻ representative of the Dorking branch of the Women's National Anti-
su⸻ e (WNASL), to speak for the 'antis' in response to an unnamed
'e⸻ er'. (This was later revealed to be Millicent Fawcett.) Though she
di⸻ ı, Broadwood ultimately declined to participate, resulting in taunts in
th⸻ from Isobel Hecht. Reigate anti-suffagists took the same stance. On
b⸻ participate the following month, the branch took advice from head
o⸻ ormed members that the organization did not consider there to be any
u⸻ ı having debates. The committee then announced to the press that the
b⸻ *ıake it a practice never to debate'.* There was, a member told the
l⸻ *ıch behind the feminist movement which cannot be discussed in*
p⸻

L⸻ ıe Women's National Anti-Suffrage League merged with the Men's
⸻ ısing Woman Suffrage to form the National League for Opposing
y⸻ ge. The new organization was active in Dorking and the following
I⸻ tried again to engage the 'antis' in debate, this time against Lord
N⸻ ıntis' would put up neither speaker nor chair for the debate on 15th
⸻ was forced to draft in her brother-in-law, Francis Bray (1882-
s⸻ or them instead. He described himself as an 'independent anti-
'⸻ iliated to any group. Lord Farrer chaired in the absence of a willing
t⸻ ıge of the stand-off was orchestrated by the pro-suffragists. Forced
⸻ antis' claimed that their refusal to participate was because an
⸻ vould not attract an intelligent audience but that most of those
⸻ o so for the sport. It was not the general public's derision that they
⸻ pro-suffragists. Alfred Keep, chairman of the Dorking branch,
⸻ a debate would be a dishonest one in front of a meeting packed
⸻ orters. Isobel Hecht refuted the suggestion, pointing out that the
⸻ vas open to all. In the event the motion in favour of the women's
⸻ d by 85 votes to 41. Taking into account the high 'pro' turnout
⸻ 'anti' to speak, this suggests that the disinterested bystanders of
⸻ verwhelmingly persuaded of the cause.
⸻ ave been reluctant to engage in debate but Broadwood and the
⸻ al local support. The hills about the town attracted the liberal,
⸻ and Pethick-Lawrences and the artists of Peaslake, but it was
⸻ the mansions of a wealthy conservative elite. Before the
⸻ r, the Dorking branch of the Women's National Anti-Suffrage
⸻ sided over by Laura Barclay nee Wyvill, who was married to
⸻ ry Hill. The dowager Countess Harrowby (Susan Juliana Maria
Dent) of High Ashurst on Box Hill, sat on the committee with
⸻ Margaret (1860-1932), Lady Constance (1871-1950) and Lady
⸻ ı-1956). Other committee members included the Countess's
⸻ mons of Norbury Park; the daughter of George MacAndrew,

another neighbour of the Ryders at Juniper Hall in Mickleham; Bertha Broadwood; Mrs Carey Druce of Rokefield in Westcott[12]; Anne Aggs, mother of the banker Henry Aggs of Pippbrook in Dorking; Mrs Harman Grisewood of Little Dudley House; Mrs Powell, wife of the stockbroker Thomas Edmund Powell of Goodwyns Place, and her daughters, Margaret and Dorothea; Miss Edith Corderoy who was well-known for her fundraising for the Dorking British School; Mrs RH Wilson of the Old Croft in Holmwood, and Mrs Lascelles Batson.

In May 1911 the writer Hillaire Belloc (1870-1953) came to speak against the vote at Dorking's Oddfellows Hall. On giving the vote of thanks Bertha Broadwood alleged that the suffrage movement was being engineered by socialists - though those involved, she claimed, did not know it. Fear of the spread of socialism should women get the vote was a common concern: it had been raised at an anti-suffrage meeting in Leatherhead, and a member of the Reigate branch of the WNASL had accused pro-suffragists in the press of having *'immoral and Socialistic principles'*. They wished to get into Parliament, it was claimed, in order to spread the doctrine of free love!

Anti-suffrage events followed a social format with piano recitals, solo song performances from members, and humorous short plays on the folly of calls for women's rights. At a NLOWS event of December 1911, Mrs Carey Druce performed at the piano and Dorothea Powell featured in the playlet 'Women's Wrongs'. A similar event on 23rd January 1912 at Holmwood Village Hall featured a comedy entitled 'As You Were' written by Mr and Miss Loughborough. The speaker at that event, Gwladys Gladstone Solomon, was the daughter-in-law and sister-in-law of two of Emmeline Pethick-Lawrence's closest (suffrage-supporting) friends so the occasion was very much an assault in enemy territory. Several of the

Annie Salomons of Norbury Park sat on the committee of the Dorking branch of the Women's National Anti-Suffrage League. Her husband was the financier Leopold Salomons who gave Box Hill to the nation in 1914. (By permission of Surrey History Centre ref 6529/19)

---

[12] Mrs Carey Druce was vice-president of the Leith Hill Musical Festival. She conducted the Westcott choir and chaired the committee when Evangeline Farrer was indisposed. She played piano at anti-suffrage events.

Pethick-Lawrences' Holmwood neighbours were active in promoting and organising the event[13]. If all women got the vote, Mrs Gladstone Solomon told the audience, there would be more female voters than male - which was clearly a ridiculous proposition.

In March 1912 Colonel Rawson, the MP for Reigate, (which constituency included Dorking), received a deputation from members of the Redhill and Reigate and Dorking NLOWS branches, including Bertha Broadwood, Henry Lee Steere and Mrs Wilfred Ward. The party expressed regret at Rawson's voting on the Conciliation Bill and urged him to change his opinion in view of recent 'extremist' violence. Rawson told them that he had believed the Conciliation Bill to have been a good measure, and that he had stated in his election manifesto that he was in favour of women's suffrage. But he had changed his view on account of the violence of the militants. He told the deputation that he now believed that the suffrage movement had 'socialistic' designs; he would not vote for women's suffrage again, but nor would he vote against it.

In April the Redhill, Reigate and District branch of the NLOWS held a public meeting at Reigate market hall, which was decorated with anti-suffrage posters. At a meeting in Great Bookham the speaker told the Effingham branch that the extension of the franchise to the women would be hostile to their own welfare and to the welfare of the state. Henrietta Keswick of Eastwood Park, widow of William Keswick, formerly MP for Epsom, was in the audience. Bigger guns in the anti-suffrage movement appeared in Redhill in September 1912 when the local branch of

the NLOWS hosted a visit from Lord Robert Cecil. (A previous anti-suffrage meeting at the market hall on November 25th 1911 had attracted a large attendance.) And the debate was carried on even in the villages: in November of the same year Mrs Harold Norris spoke at the League's meeting in Bookham, Helen Page from central office spoke at the Westcott Reading Room, and

The writer Hilaire Belloc came to Dorking to speak against women's suffrage at the invitation of the local branch of the National League for Opposing Women's Suffrage. His sister lived in the town. (Library of Congress)

[13] Alfred Keep chaired; Fanny St John Hornby of The Oaks was responsible for seat reservations; and Mrs RH Wilson of The Old Croft was on the League's committee. Lady Laura Hampton, who lived across the road from the Pethick-Lawrences at Oakdale, provided the flowers.

the ex-MP for Reigate, Sir Benjamin Brodie, presided at a meeting in Brockham School where Mrs Norris told the company that the suffrage movement was restricted to female artists, actresses, writers and other 'unimportant people'. In the 'Dorking Advertiser' Isobel Hecht questioned how Mrs Norris could speak so contemptuously of women writers in the presence of fellow anti-suffragist Mrs Wilfrid Ward, who had given the world a series of successful novels! The novelist Mrs Humphrey Ward spoke at a meeting of the Redhill, Reigate and District NLOWS in January 1913, and at a large meeting at The Old House in Westcott in July 1913, Mabel Smith from NLOWS central office told the assembled company that there was no connection between women's low wages and their lack of political representation. With so few occupations open to women, she argued, it was inevitable that the labour market in those jobs open to women was oversubscribed, and this kept wages low. In March 1914 Gladys Potts told a large meeting of the Redhill and Reigate branch of the League that granting the vote to women would not be in their own interests or that of the community. The branch resolved to call upon Colonel Rawson to vote against all forms of female suffrage.

Bertha Broadwood and her supporters no doubt felt vindicated when the militant WSPU's campaign turned increasingly violent. *'The papers are full now of tragedy and comedy. The suffragettes providing the latter'*, wrote her friend, Mary Whitemore Jones after the WSPU window-smashing raid and the arrest in early March 1912, on charges of conspiracy, of the Pethick-Lawrences. *'I hope Pethick-Lawrence will get penal servitude'*, she wrote. And pondering Emmeline's publicised breakdown on an earlier imprisonment, she wondered: *'whether it occurs to these good people (who say) that women are equal to men in all things that a man would not have cried because his cell was cold! I think and sincerely hope that the fools have killed their own movement'*.

Not all in the Broadwood family felt as Bertha, however. Like many families, the Broadwoods were divided on the issue of female suffrage. Bertha's niece, Jean Todhunter nee Forsyth (daughter of Bertha's sister, Evelyn Forsyth) was, reported Mary Shearme in March 1912, *'involved with her Pethick-Pankhurst friends'*. While her aunts sought to prevent women getting the vote, young Jean spoke

Jean 'Jeanie' Forsyth, Bertha Broadwood's suffragette niece, at Sevres, France, in December 1914. (By permission of Surrey History Centre 2185/LEB/9/22)

for the militant WSPU. *'I heard last night from Mr Churchill at Jayes that a friend of his was at Mrs Fuller Maitland's[14] meeting when some suffragettes were present,'* wrote Mary Shearme to her sister, *'and that Jean's speech was not at all convincing. It is just as well to hear the opinion of more than one person who heard her.'*

The antis would be on the wrong side of history, proclaimed Lady Frances Balfour, at a meeting of the Leith Hill and District WSS at Dorking Halls in February 1914. And they would be judged severely, *'as those who stood against the emancipation of slaves'*. But families and communities were divided on the matter.

Edith Corderoy, the Powell family, and the Dorking British School

Women's National Anti-suffrage League committee member, Edith Mary Corderoy stood for election in 1893 as a member of the Board of Guardians for the Poor. In 1896 she raised funds for the Dorking British School with wealthy stockbroker Thomas Edmund Powell of Goodwyns Place; the school is now known as the Powell Corderoy School. She was involved in the management of the school for many years.

Members of the Powell family were also active anti-suffrage campaigners: Mrs Powell sat on the WNASL committee, her daughter Margaret was its secretary, and the League met at Goodwyns Place. In December 1911 her daughter, Dorothea, acted in an anti-suffrage playlet, *'Women's Wrongs'*.

---

[14] The Fuller-Maitlands were closely related to the Broadwoods.

Gwladys Gladstone Solomon – a family split

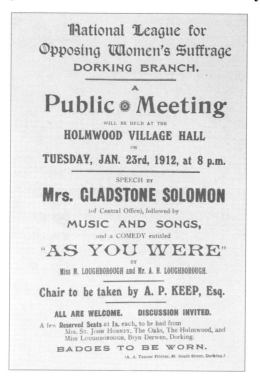

National League for Opposing Women's Suffrage
DORKING BRANCH.

A

Public Meeting

WILL BE HELD AT THE

HOLMWOOD VILLAGE HALL

ON

TUESDAY, JAN. 23rd, 1912, at 8 p.m.

SPEECH BY

Mrs. GLADSTONE SOLOMON

(of Central Office), followed by

MUSIC AND SONGS,

and a COMEDY entitled

"AS YOU WERE"

BY

Miss M. LOUGHBOROUGH and Mr. A. H. LOUGHBOROUGH.

Chair to be taken by A. P. KEEP, Esq.

ALL ARE WELCOME.   DISCUSSION INVITED.

A few Reserved Seats at 1s. each, to be had from
Mrs. St. John Hornby, The Oaks, The Holmwood, and
Miss Loughborough, Bryn Derwen, Dorking.

BADGES TO BE WORN.

(A. A. Tanner Printer, 43, South Street, Dorking.)

In January 1912 anti-suffrage campaigner Gwladys Gladstone Solomon spoke for the NLOWS in Holmwood. Her family had close connections with the Pethick-Lawrences, perhaps explaining why she elected to visit.

Gwladys was an artist. She was married to fellow artist, William Ewart Gladstone Solomon (1880-1965). Her husband's mother, Georgiana Margaret Solomon nee Thomson (1844-1933), was the widow of newspaper proprietor and Cape Colony politician, Saul Solomon. Georgiana and her daughter Daisy, (Gwladys' sister-in-law), were committed members of the WSPU.

In February 1909 Daisy Solomon served two months in prison with Emmeline Pethick-Lawrence after leading a deputation to Parliament with Lady Constance Lytton. Georgiana Solomon claimed in a letter to 'The Times' to have been seriously assaulted by police officers on Black Friday (see p117) when she was grabbed by the breast, thrown to the ground and crushed. Close to the Pethick-Lawrences, the Solomons left the WSPU on the split with the Pankhursts and joined the United Suffragists; Daisy served as joint secretary in the Hampstead branch with Emmeline's sister, Dorothy. She went on to campaign for Fred when he eventually stood for Parliament. Georgiana remained one of Emmeline's closest correspondents for the rest of her life. Gwladys, however, waged a strenuous campaign against her in-laws' cause.

Lead by Lords Curzon and Cromer, the NLOWS had a mixed membership though its leadership was male. Most of its speakers were male, reflecting the organisation's ambivalence towards women engaging in public debate. As one of the League's most prominent female speakers Gwladys Gladstone Solomon undertook numerous speaking campaigns; she was one of the few female speakers who would participate in outdoor speaking events for working men.

She was, she wrote to Lloyd George in 1912, a ratepayer and taxpayer and as such she exhorted men, with their broader shoulders, to maintain the burdens of Empire, of army and navy, trade, mining and shipping. She paid her taxes, willingly, she claimed, in return for such protection, allowing her to take care of her home and child. She was, she claimed, 'unfortunately' - and her relationship with her husband and his family may have had some bearing on her attitude to the vote - in the position of having to earn a living as well as to perform her duties as a mother, so why, she asked, should she be obliged to add to those responsibilities consideration of matters of Empire and state? The majority of women, she claimed, felt the same way.

Though she warned Lloyd George against giving the vote to property-owning women, (which would have benefited the Conservatives), she also travelled the country addressing audiences of working women who, she asserted, were at best indifferent to the vote, if not repulsed by the thought of it. In response to such activities the NUWSS campaigned to educate working women, who were, wrote Julie Chance of Godalming to Lord Farrer, *ignorant and fall prey to the 'antis' who say it isn't nice or womanly to want to vote'.*
Handbill for Gwladys Gladstone Solomon's event in Holmwood. (By permission of Surrey History Centre ref 2185/BMB/7/1/37)

Mrs Wilfrid Ward

Anti-suffrage campaigner Josephine Mary Ward nee Hope-Scott (1864-1932) accompanied Bertha Broadwood on a deputation to Reigate MP Colonel Rawson in March 1912. Later that year she was present at an anti-suffrage meeting in Brockham where the speaker dismissed suffrage supporters as artists, actresses, writers and other 'unimportant' people. In the 'Dorking Advertiser' Isobel Hecht of the Leith Hill and Dorking WSS pointed out that Mrs Wilfrid Ward did not think the Married Women's Property Act was necessary, yet without it everything the novelist earned would have belonged to her husband.

Ward's husband was a leading Catholic thinker. Published under the name Mrs Wilfrid Ward, her own novels were conservative, dealing with the moral choices arising from the conflict between religious principles and personal desire, and defending the sanctity of marriage.

The remarkable Flora Shaw

One of the more surprising local anti-suffragists was Flora Shaw (1852-1929) of Abinger. Grand-daughter of an Irish MP and daughter of a general, like many girls of her time, Shaw was virtually self-educated. She grew up nursing her sick mother and taking care of younger siblings, but as a teenager was adopted as a protégé by family friend John Ruskin, who encouraged her to write. At the age of twenty she went to work for the family of Colonel Charles Brackenbury, a distant relation. She became house-keeper/governess to his daughters. The Brackenbury sisters later became militant WSPU supporters and it was their relationship with Shaw that brought them to Peaslake.

Colonel Brackenbury was 'The Times' correspondent on the Franco-Prussian War. Like Ruskin, he encouraged Shaw's writing, and sent her first novel for comment to his friend, George Meredith of Box Hill. Shaw went on to write a series of novels, the most popular of which was 'Castle Blair' (1877).

In 1883 the illness of a friend's baby brought her to Abinger, which was to become her life-long home. She rented Parkhurst Cottages and entertained numerous friends there, including Brackenbury, now a general, who recuperated in the village after a heart attack; he later brought his family to live in Peaslake. Shaw often walked over to Box Hill to visit mutual friend Meredith, who suggested that she try journalism. Whilst on a visit to Egypt in 1886 she filed reports for the 'Manchester Guardian', using the byline 'F. Shaw'. In 1892 'The Times' sent her to South Africa, its first female permanent staff member. The following year she was appointed Colonial Editor, a post that she held until 1900, making her the highest paid female journalist of her day. She was convinced of the benefits of Empire, to colonizer and colonized alike.

Flora Shaw travelled up to London from Abinger, where she lived with her sister, Lulu, via the station at Gomshall. In 1902 she married Sir Frederick Lugard, whom she had met when he came to Abinger to discuss a review of his book. She gave up journalism and travelled with her colonial governor husband to Nigeria and Hong Kong. But life as a governor's wife did not suit her; illness and depression brought her back to Abinger where she remodeled the cottages into a grander house, Little Parkhurst.

Out of the country for much of the suffragette agitation in which her former Brackenbury pupils were so involved, one might have expected Shaw to have had sympathy with the charges of her youth. Despite her groundbreaking career, however, she did not support the vote for women, deeming it incompatible with the natural order of empire. And like many pioneering women, she distanced herself from wider moves to emancipate women. Perhaps she feared that negative feelings towards women stirred up by the suffrage campaign might undermine the position of women like herself. Unlike Bertha Broadwood, however, she was passive in her opposition, her commitment limited to signing a statement put out by the National League for Opposing Women's Suffrage in 1910.

After the First World War Shaw, (now Lady Lugard), was awarded the DBE for her work housing displaced Belgian refugees. Returning to Abinger with her husband, she rented farmland at Wotton and sold vegetables to Covent Garden. Her visitors in Abinger included Joe Chamberlain and Winston Churchill. *(National Portrait Gallery, London)*

A Sketch, an Appeal, A solution – a poem by Bertha Broadwood

Unwinsome Widows!
Maidens whom none will wed!
Feel unimportant.
And would be wooed instead
For votes:… by Men!!!

Impulsive women!
Girding at slow reform,
In sheer impatience,
Seek power of magic form
In votes: like men.

Surer reformers,
Trusting to silent growth,
And ripe experience,
Deem but a form of slowth
Voting like men!

With steady workers rare
Will not their sisters share
Some of the toil?
Must all their thousands go
Towards Meeting speeches,
Clamour and broil?

Women superfluous here
Send those thousand where
Colonies need them
Those who remain behind, far
Better work would find
And husbands to feed them!!

'The purpose for which we were born':
the great conspiracy trial

The 18th of November 1910 became known to the suffragettes as Black Friday and it is generally regarded as a turning point in campaign tactics. Women marched from Caxton Hall to Parliament in protest at the lack of any announcement as to the fate of the Conciliation Bill on the dissolution of Parliament. Marchers set out for Westminster in groups of 12 as the law prohibited gatherings of more than 12 people within a mile of Parliament. Rather than being arrested in the usual manner, they were confronted by policemen who had been bussed in from the East End. Aggressive policing caused deliberate injury and members of the public stepped in to protect women from beatings. At least three are claimed to have died as a result of treatment received on that day. Mrs Pankhurst's sister, Mary Clarke, succumbed on Christmas Day 1910, shortly after having been released from prison where she underwent force-feeding. She was proclaimed the movement's first martyr. Her obituary in 'Votes for Women' was written by Emmeline Pethick-Lawrence.

In the wake of Black Friday Asquith refused to give anything more than the vague assurance that should the Liberals be elected at the forthcoming election, they would introduce a suffrage bill that might be amended to include women's suffrage. It seemed to many that peaceable persuasion had failed to convince and, given the actions of the police on Black Friday, was increasingly foolhardy. The campaign took its notorious turn towards property damage. Better to throw a stone and be arrested quickly, some women reasoned, than to march peacefully and risk a beating from the police. When women marched on Downing Street in the wake of Asquith's announcement stones were thrown and windows smashed and scores of women were arrested on charges of assault and causing damage to property.

Further property damage was not immediate. The dissolution of Parliament lead to yet another general election in December 1910 and the WSPU held to an uneasy truce whilst assessing the intentions of the newly-constituted government. During these months the WSPU worked with non-militant suffrage organisations on joint events and Mrs Pankhurst and Emmeline Pethick-Lawrence shared platforms with NUWSS speakers. The truce held even when yet another private member's bill designed to enfranchise women was dismissed after two readings for lack of time in May 1911. Asquith assured Lord Lytton that the government would allot time to the completion of the bill's passage in the next session. Once again it appeared that the battle had been won.

The WSPU held its truce throughout the celebrations for the coronation of George V. There was a large turnout from local branches of the WSPU and from local non-militant suffrage societies at the Coronation Procession and Albert Hall rally on 18th June 1911. A hundred and seventy suffrage supporters joined a train chartered by the Brighton branch of the WSPU at Redhill. The Redhill and Reigate WSS marched behind the Leith Hill and District WSS, accompanied by the Reigate town band. Muriel Woodhams carried the Society's embroidered banner and Miss Judd and Maud Brown carried the Reigate Women's Liberal banner. Members Margaret Crosfield and Amy Klein acted as stewards on the route. The women of the Redhill branch of the WSPU marched behind their own banner, carrying pennants. Several branch members took part in the WSPU's historical pageant which celebrated women's achievements: Mrs Richmond represented Lady Russell and Grace Gillespie Hardy, Eleanor de Bohun, both of them accompanied by numerous attendants, indicating the militant organisation's strength in the town. Buses took women back to Reigate from Redhill station when the return train got in at nearly midnight. It was the women's fervent hope that a new reign and a new session of Parliament would at last see a women's suffrage bill becoming law.

It was a bitter disappointment, when, on Parliament reconvening in the autumn, Asquith announced that he proposed nothing more than a government-sponsored manhood suffrage bill to which he held out only the hope that an amendment might be made to include women. Mrs Pankhurst was away on a speaking tour of the United States when the announcement was made. Emmeline Pethick-Lawrence, Christabel Pankhurst, Annie Kenney, Lady Constance Lytton, Mabel Tuke and the actress and novelist Elizabeth Robins (1862-1952) formed a joint deputation to the Prime Minister with the leaders of the Women's Freedom League. Asquith received them on November 17th 1911. It was a heated and unproductive meeting. Four days later, as Emmeline Pethick-Lawrence lead another deputation to the House of Commons, (during the course of which she was arrested and sentenced to another month's imprisonment), hundreds of women set about breaking the windows of shops, business premises and government buildings.

Stone-throwing had occurred before on a sporadic and individually motivated basis. Now it became an 'official' tactic. It was, to an extent, incited by the comments of male MPs - and particularly those of Bristol East MP Sir Charles Hobhouse (1862-1941) - to the effect that had there been any real support for women's suffrage there would have been riots and arson attacks such as had persuaded previous governments to extend the franchise to men. Such comments were interpreted as a challenge to women to demonstrate their resolution. Emmeline Pethick-Lawrence commented in 'Votes for Women' that holding up to women the violence of men as an example made Hobhouse guilty of incitement to serious forms of violence *'in comparison with which Mrs Pankhurst's exhortation is mildness itself.'* For many, stronger measures seemed not only justified but provoked.

Taking a prominent role in the new tactics of window-breaking, stone-throwing, letterbox-burning and petty arson were the Brackenbury sisters. Their country home, Brackenside, was in the heart of Peaslake village. It would soon eclipse The Mascot as the WSPU's second home, and their London home at 2 Campden Hill Square would become as celebrated as the Pethick-Lawrences' Clement's Inn apartment. On 1st March 1912 the sisters were joined by their mother, Hilda, on a window-smashing campaign that saw hammers taken to 270 windows in Regents Street, Oxford Street, Piccadilly, Bond Street and The Strand. Three days later windows were broken in Whitehall.

Christabel Pankhurst was now the driving force in the WSPU. There is no evidence of Emmeline Pethick-Lawrence having cast a stone or having used a hammer, but nor did she stand against such actions. And Fred recalled going with Christabel one dark evening to a country lane to select a bag of 'suitable missiles'. As a leader of the organization Emmeline was responsible for the actions of the membership in the eyes of the government. Whether she was responsible in the eyes of the law was now the issue.

Two days after the coordinated window breaking of March 1912 Emmeline and Fred were arrested at Clement's Inn. *'This is their hour,'* whispered Fred, *'and the power of darkness.'*

Evelyn Sharp happened to call into the WSPU offices as the police arrived. As he was arrested, and before he was hand-cuffed, Fred managed to hand her a cheque transferring the WSPU's funds into the account of physicist Hertha Ayrton. He and Emmeline were then taken to Bow Street police station where they remained overnight. Mrs Pankhurst and Mabel Tuke had already been arrested but Christabel was away from the office; tipped off by Sharp, she fled to Paris. Her whereabouts were not revealed for months, requiring the police to follow up reports of sightings all over the country.

From the police station Emmeline Pethick-Lawrence sent word to Mary Neal, who collected nightwear from Clement's Inn and brought it to the cells. Unable to find a siphon of soda water for finickity Fred, she called at the nearby Savoy Hotel. She was barred from entry when the taxi-driver mentioned where she was headed but the management had a siphon brought out to her. When she reached the cells Fred handed her a cheque for £200 to cover her expenses to travel down to Holmwood to pay the staff wages and to keep the household at The Mascot running. It was two weeks before Fred and Emmeline were bailed.

Held in separate prisons, Fred and Emmeline wrote to one another. Fred was visited in Brixton by a succession of people seeking his instructions: Emmeline's brother-in-law Mortimer Budgett, who managed all her financial affairs, and his wife Nance; his own secretary, Shepherd; Mr Sayers, the WSPU accountant; Evelyn Sharp, who took over as editor of 'Votes for Women'; and Mary Neal who was taking care of The Mascot and the couple's other Holmwood affairs. When not dealing with business matters, he began learning Italian.

Above: Drawing by court artist William Hartley of Mabel Tuke, Emmeline Pankhurst, Emmeline and Fred in the dock at the preliminary hearing in 1912. The case against Mabel Tuke was later dropped. (The Crime Museum, Gresham College) Below: The cover of 'Votes for Women' points out the irony of the Pethick-Lawrences' arrest on a charge of conspiracy to commit criminal damage, when such actions were incited by the comments of such as Sir Charles Hobhouse. (The Master and Fellows of Trinity College, Cambridge);

SHOPWALKER: Please take Mr. Hobhouse in charge; it is he who has incited the women to violence.

Charges against Mabel Tuke were dropped but Fred, Emmeline and Mrs Pankhurst were charged with *'conspiracy to incite persons to commit malicious damage'* and bailed. The trial was set for May 1912. In mid-April Mrs Pankhurst told Lady Constance Lytton that she intended to spend a weekend with the Pethick-Lawrences in Holmwood; she was, she said, looking forward to talks with her *'fellow conspirators'*. At The Mascot the three planned their court appearances and the manipulation of press interest for maximum effect.

The trial began on Thursday 15th May 1912. It lasted six days and at the weekend the couple retreated to Holmwood where the roses were in bloom. The defendants' days in court were orchestrated by Fred and Mrs Pankhurst to great effect. The press reported in detail what the women wore, who was in attendance, the flowers that were delivered to them, and the looks that passed between them. Fred and Mrs Pankhurst represented themselves, Emmeline was represented by Tim Healy KC, a leading Irish politician. Knowing that he would be found guilty, Fred concentrated his efforts on inducing the jury to qualify their verdict. He was, he

Emmeline and Fred Pethick-Lawrence arriving at The Old Bailey. The uniformed driver is Vera 'Jack' Holme who had been a singer with the D'Oyly Carte Company. (Women's Library, LSE)

argued, an instinctively law-abiding person, but the suffragettes were outside the constitution. As they had no vote by which to make their voices heard, he argued, they had been forced to find unconstitutional means of being heard.

'*Beloved,*' wrote Fred to Emmeline on the eve of the verdict: '*we are very near to a great day, the greatest that we have seen in our lives. To me it seems that an honour such as is conferred only on a few in many centuries is about to be conferred on us. We are to stand where the great and noble have stood before us all down the ages. We are to be linked with those who have won the everlasting homage of the whole human race. If next week you and I were to be crowned King and Queen in the presence of an adulating people, how paltry would be the honour in comparison. It is supreme joy that you and I will stand there together.*' Joint imprisonment, was, she responded: '*the purpose for which we were born and for which we were mated*'.

Fred also paid tribute to Mrs Pankhurst, according her a heroic mythical status in the manner so often fashioned by his wife: '*It is good that we shall have by our side that great woman who is our friend, who of all women in the world we would wish to have with us in that hour.*'

The three were found guilty on 22nd May. On giving the verdict the jury handed a note to the judge: they unanimously hoped that: '*taking into consideration*

Fred, Emmeline and Mrs Pankhurst surrounded by crowds outside court. (LSE Library)

the undoubtedly pure motives that underlie the agitation... you will be pleased to exercise the utmost clemency and leniency.'

The judge was not so motivated. He sentenced them to nine months. Fred and Mrs Pankhurst were also ordered to pay the costs of the trial under a new sanction for conspiracy. Protests came in from around the world, including from female Nobel laureates Marie Curie and Selma Lagerlof.

On arrival in Holloway the two Emmelines were greeted by other suffragette prisoners with a performance of scenes from Shakespeare. They were allotted adjoining cells. The outraged jurors petitioned the Home Secretary. Pressure was brought to bear to give the leaders political status as prisoners. Though he eventually did so - entitling the prisoners their own clothes, bedding, towels, food and reading materials - the three promptly went on hunger strike when it was discovered that this applied only to themselves and not to any of the other women serving time in various gaols. In order to keep their leaders' spirits up, suffragette supporters marched each day to Holloway and stood outside, singing.

According to Mrs Pankhurst the most dreadful moment of her imprisonment came when, lying weak in bed she heard *'a sudden scream from Mrs Lawrence's*

WSPU postcard of the imprisoned leaders. Fred is acknowledged as one of the 'suffragist' leaders despite not being eligible to join the all-women WSPU. (The Women's Library. LSE)

cell, then the sound of a prolonged and violent struggle and I knew that they had come to carry their brutal business to our doors. I sprang out of bed and, shaking with weakness and with anger, I set my back against the wall and waited for what might come.' When the door opened she demanded to go to Emmeline Pethick-Lawrence's cell where she found her companion *'in a desperate state. She is a strong woman and a very determined one and it had required the united strength of nine wardresses to overcome her. They had rushed into her cell without any warning, and had seized her unawares, else they might not have succeeded at all. As it was she resisted so violently that the doctors could not apply the stethoscope and they had great difficulty in getting the tube down. After the wretched affair was over Mrs Lawrence fainted and for hours afterwards she was very ill'*. Afterwards the matron and one of the wardresses reportedly came in tears to apologise for what they had been forced to do. Mary Neal, meanwhile, claimed that she had had a *'chill feeling'* of union with Emmeline and had been unable to swallow whilst her friend was being force-fed.

Emmeline underwent forcible feeding just the once. Fred was subjected to it twice a day for a period. Both were visited in prison by the Unitarian chaplain Fred Hankinson, a long-time friend of Emmeline's family. He was able to bring each news of the other. Emmeline's sisters also acted as go-betweens. Before their conviction they had come to an agreement with one another not to write too often, since letters were rationed and to receive too many letters from one another would have meant no news from other friends or of the outside world. In her bi-weekly letter Emmeline

---

Fred Hankinson

The Reverend Fred Hankinson (1875-1960) became a lifelong friend of Fred Pethick-Lawrence. He was born into a Unitarian family with a strong commitment to equality and inspired by Christabel Pankhurst and Annie Kenney's imprisonment to join the Men's League for Women's Suffrage. When his sister was imprisoned for the cause he began visiting suffrage prisoners who claimed to be of non Church of England persuasion. As their spiritual advisor Hankinson was left alone with the women and was able to receive and transmit confidential information. Christabel Pankhurst encouraged him to visit Marion Wallace Dunlop when she went on hunger strike, even though she was not religious, probably so that information might be conveyed between the two. He also visited Charlotte Marsh. He was described by one woman as the *'brickiest of bricks'*. Eventually the authorities concluded that he had gone further than his ministerial duties allowed and he was barred from visiting.

Hankinson joined the United Suffragists on its formation in 1914. During the First World War he organised Fred's employment in Sussex in satisfaction of the requirement that he do work of national importance. Hankinson remained close to Fred all his life, taking fishing holidays with him on a regular basis.

described her state of mind and her cell with its vaulted ceiling and view of the prison garden which made her feel close to 'Mother Earth'; she could hear the birds singing in the mornings. The day was spent learning Italian, and with Mrs Pankhurst in the prison garden where they worked embroidery; Sylvia Pankhurst, she reported on one occasion, was designing a banner for each of them to work on so that there would be a memorial to the events of 1912. She used her letters to assure Fred that her spirits remained high, despite at first feeling like crying, and concluded one letter proclaiming the two of them *the happiest, luckiest people in the world'*. In more prosaic mood, they pondered whether to ask Lutyens to re-design the rose garden at The Mascot (and decided instead to ask Arnold Dunbar Smith.)

Meanwhile Emmeline's associates lead the prison governor a merry dance, demanding visits and instructions. Whether their claims to need to see her were legitimate or simply nuisances is hard to tell: Mary Neal had Esperance Club business to discuss and Arnold Dunbar Smith needed instructions in order to draw up plans for the rose garden. Housekeeper May Start, who divided her time between London and Holmwood, complained that poor Mrs Pethick-Lawrence had three establishments to run, to which the exasperated prison governor replied that *'people who have three establishments to run ought to take care not to find themselves in prison.'*

Neither the Pethick-Lawrences nor Mrs Pankhurst served their full sentences. Emmeline was released on medical grounds two days after her force-feeding. Her recovery in Holmwood was overseen by Dr Chapman and her sister, Dr Marie Pethick. Fred remained incarcerated, studying French and Italian between force feedings. He was transferred from Wormwood Scrubs to Brixton and released in a weakened state on June 27th. On leaving he fancied that he heard the warders cheer his departure, though this sounds more a romantic notion, in keeping with his sense of destiny, than an accurate recollection. He was met by Dr Marie Pethick who accompanied him in the car to Holmwood. *'It was a lovely June evening,'* he wrote. *'As I drove up the long hill from Dorking to Holmwood, I saw the last of the wild roses at the roadside in bloom.'* Prison, he said, making light of the experience, had been like prep school; but to the end of his life he wore his WSPU imprisonment medal.

Mrs Pankhurst went to recuperate with Ethel Smyth in Woking. The close working relationship between the Pankhursts and the Pethick-Lawrences, the cosy visits to Holmwood and the scheming in the Surrey hills were, however, about to come to an unexpected end.

Prominent speakers in Redhill and Reigate

On March 19th 1911 two prominent non-militant NUWSS speakers appeared at the parish hall in Lesbourne Road, Reigate. Selina Cooper nee Coombe (1864-1946) was a paid NUWSS organizer who worked with the Surrey, Sussex and Hampshire Federation of the NUWSS. She had begun life as a textile worker in the mills of Lancashire at the age of twelve, and came to the campaign via the trades union and labour movements. Educated through the Women's Cooperative Guild, she was the first working-class woman to be elected to the position of Poor Law Guardian. A powerful speaker, she was much admired by Millicent Fawcett. She spoke alongside Maude Royden, a woman from a very different background, who had already spoken in Dorking in 1909.

(Agnes) Maude Royden (1876-1956) was the daughter of a Liverpool ship-owner. Educated at Cheltenham Ladies' College and Oxford, like Emmeline Pethick-Lawrence, she came to campaigning through work in the Settlement movement. She was one of the NUWSS's best speakers, was elected to its executive committee and edited 'The Common Cause' in 1913/14. During the First World War she was a supporter of the Non-Conscription Fellowship and left the NUWSS on account of its support of the war effort to join Emmeline in the Women's International League for Peace and Freedom. She was the first woman to be awarded a doctorate in divinity and began campaigning for the ordination of women in the 1920s in the hope of being ordained herself. Turning down an invitation to stand for Parliament for Labour, she devoted much of her life working to promote the cause of peace. *(Image by permission of John Royden)*

The Brackenburys of Peaslake

The Brackenbury family lived at Brackenside in Peaslake. They were drawn to the area by close friends George Meredith and Flora Shaw. Canadian-born Hilda Brackenbury nee Campbell (1832-1918) was a widowed mother of nine who hated 'housekeeping'. She had employed Shaw when her children were young. In her youth she had designed a skating outfit of bloomers and tunic to allow women hampered by crinolines to take to the ice. She was also a talented singer and writer of songs. She was in her 70s when she joined the WSPU.

Georgina Agnes Brackenbury (1865-1949) was a portrait painter; her portrait of Mrs Pankhurst in later life is amongst the best known images of the suffragette leader. With Sylvia Pankhurst, Marion Wallace Dunlop and Edith Elizabeth Downing, she designed processions and tableaux for the WSPU. Costumes for these events were made up at the studio that she shared with her sister at 2 New Road, Campden Hill, by volunteers from the Artists' Suffrage League. Classes for WSPU speakers were also held at the studios with neighbouring Peaslake artist, Marion Wallace Dunlop.

Georgina was one of the movement's most eloquent speakers. She was selected by Emmeline Pethick-Lawrence to speak at the Hyde Park Rally. A fluent German speaker, she undertook a speaking tour of Germany with her mother and sister. She also contributed poems to 'Votes for Women'. In February 1908 Georgina Brackenbury organized the Pantechnicon Raid with Sylvia Pankhurst, during the course of which twenty women stormed the House of Commons from a removal lorry. The sisters subsequently served six weeks in Holloway where they modelled animals out of squeezed bread and presented them to prison officers. The Brackenburys, wrote Emmeline Pethick-Lawrence had inherited their father's valour and military spirit.

Mary 'Marie' Venetia Brackenbury (1866-1946) was a landscape painter. Like her sister a veteran of provincial by-elections, she was something of a daredevil. In Northampton she climbed a forty-foot scaffold to address a husting, encouraging voters to hoot at Winston Churchill. On another occasion she was called as a defence witness by Christabel Pankhurst to expose government interference with the judiciary. Marie claimed that after the Pantechnicon Raid she had met the magistrate who had sentenced her at a dinner party where he admitted that in giving her a stiff sentence for the minor offence of obstruction he had been acting on Home Office instructions – in breach of the convention that the judiciary should operate independently of the executive.

'The truth for a penny! The truth for a penny!' she would cry when selling 'Votes for Women'. Receiving the response of *'No thank you'* on one occasion, she asked: *'What, don't you like the truth?'* *'Certainly not!'* replied the woman.

Marie became inured, she claimed, to the abuse of the streets, to being spat at and told that she ought to be dragged around Trafalgar Square by her hair for the offence of handing out leaflets. But *'nothing mattered except faithfulness to the cause. We were raised,'* she said, *'to throw aside all conventions and cost what it might to break down the barriers of false prejudice and false conceptions of the ideal woman.'* And aid came from unexpected quarters: a provincial mayor offered to smuggle her into a meeting, policemen apologized for having to carry out arrests, and passing old gentlemen wished her well.

In March 1912 all three Brackenburys were in prison together. At the age of 79 Hilda joined a window-smashing sortie. She put a hammer in her muff and broke a window at the United Services Institution. The target was a symbolic one: as the widow of a general she had lost two sons to military service. Hilda thanked the policeman who arrested her and refused the option to go to the prison infirmary, (thought suitable on account of her age). She told the doctor that if he tried to take her there she would cling to the bars of the cell. Arrested at the same time, Marie refused to be bound over to keep the peace: *'I cannot bind myself in any way. I am a soldier in this great cause,'* she said. Georgina was not initially arrested. She was brought into Bow Street police station injured and asked to see her mother and sister. On being refused she was thrown out. She promptly threatened the officer with a charge of assault, whereupon she was arrested too.

In court Hilda claimed to have been acting in response to Mr Hobhouse's provocation and in protest at the *'oppression, suppression and repression of women'*. She would, she claimed, be willing to give her life to the cause. She served 14 days and on her release addressed a large crowd at the London Pavilion. *Images: left: Georgina Brackenbury from the collection of Alice Hawkins wwwalicesuffragette.co.uk; right: Marie Brackenbury by permission of the Women's Library, LSE*

'Government burglary': the Dorking and Holmwood campaign of 1912

The Director of Public Prosecutions v. F. W. Pethick Lawrence.

"The Mascot,"

HOLMWOOD, SURREY,

NEAR DORKING.

G. M. FRIEAKE

Will Sell by Auction, as above, on
THURSDAY, OCTOBER 31st, 1912,
At ONE o'clock precisely,

THE CONTENTS
OF THE ABOVE

WELL-FURNISHED RESIDENCE
IN EARLY ENGLISH STYLE,
INCLUDING

OAK & ENAMELLED BEDROOM SUITES
And Bedsteads,
DRAWING & DINING ROOM FURNITURE
Chesterfield Settee, Lounge and Easy Chairs,
FULL-COMPASS PIANO BY BECHSTEIN,
Small Library of Books, Pictures, Ornaments,
QUANTITY OF A.1. PLATE,
Linen, China, Glass, Copper Culinary Utensils & other effects

May be Viewed Day Prior and Morning of Sale. Catalogues
8g, **CHANCERY LANE, W.C.**

Poster advertising the sale of the contents of The Mascot by order of the Director of Public Prosecutions. 'Dorking Advertiser'

The story goes that the Pethick-Lawrences' expulsion from the WSPU came as a complete surprise to them. The truth is rather more complicated.

After leaving prison the couple spent some time in Holmwood. Then they planned to convalesce in Switzerland. They were invited by Mrs Pankhurst to break their journey in Boulogne where she and Christabel would meet them to discuss the future of the campaign. On 10th July 1912 the Pethick-Lawrences arrived at the Hotel de Paris in Boulogne. The Pankhursts travelled from Paris under the names of Mrs Richards and Amy. The Pethick-Lawrences were, wrote Mrs Pankhurst to a friend, *'still rather weak and shaky'* after their prison ordeals.

The foursome took a walk along the cliffs between the town and Wimereux; Fred and Christabel went ahead, with the two Emmelines following. As they walked Christabel outlined to Fred her plans for an autumn campaign of increasing damage to property aimed at forcing the government to concede the vote. Fred told Christabel that he thought the window-smashing had aroused considerable opposition as it was targeted at private, rather than public, property. He argued that the public would need convincing of its necessity. Fearing that the sympathy and goodwill that the conspiracy trial had engendered would be squandered, he proposed instead that Christabel return to London from Paris. She would receive a hero's welcome and the government would be forced either to proceed with her trial for conspiracy, or to drop the charges, risking accusations of capitulation. With her attractiveness, eloquence and notoriety she would generate huge amounts of newspaper coverage, sympathy and support for the movement. Christabel declined the suggestion. There was always, she said, opposition to new methods but the campaign would be intensified and she would remain at large to direct it.

At this point the two Emmelines caught up with Fred and Christabel. Not only did Mrs Pankhurst agree with her daughter's proposal; she was disgruntled that Fred should have questioned Christabel's judgement. Emmeline Pethick-Lawrence took Fred's part but the Pankhursts were not to be dissuaded. Nonetheless, when the Pethick-Lawrences left for Switzerland the following morning it was apparently on good terms with the Pankhursts.

The discussions were taking place in a highly charged atmosphere, however. Soon events back in England that could not have been anticipated on the cliff-top in Boulogne came to influence Mrs Pankhurst's attitudes to her comrades. The meeting coincided with a serious attempt at arson when in July 1912 Helen Craggs was arrested trying to set fire to Nuneham Courtney, the Oxfordshire home of cabinet minister Lewis Harcourt. A note found at the scene stated that she had taken part in every peaceful method and petition in support of the vote, but on realizing that such actions were useless, she had *'accepted Mr Hobhouse's challenge'* and *'done something drastic'*. The action, like Marion Wallace Dunlop's hunger strike, was taken on her own initiative and without the fore-knowledge of the leadership. None condemned the action, however, and Mrs Pankhurst stated that she stood by anyone who took action on behalf of the cause. A stepping-up of the campaign against property was already under way.

This policy put the Pethick-Lawrences' wealth, until now an asset to the organisation, in jeopardy. The judge in the conspiracy trial had ordered Fred and Mrs Pankhurst to pay the costs of the trial. Mrs Pankhurst had no assets and was not worth pursuing, but Fred was a wealthy man. When he refused to pay, the Director of Public Prosecutions initiated proceedings against him to recover the money. Owners of property that had been damaged also gave notice of their intention to sue him. It must have been immediately apparent to both the Pankhursts and to Fred and Emmeline that a campaign of property damage would see Fred become the target of multiple such civil cases.

From Switzerland Emmeline confided to Georgiana Solomon a feeling of inertia: *'which I suppose most ex-prisoners experience when the first wild exuberance of release has worn off.'* She and Fred decided to extend their convalescence. In early August they visited Emmeline's sister Annie, and her husband, Mortimer Budgett, in Lyme Regis and her parents in Weston-super-Mare. They then crossed the Atlantic to visit to her brother Harold in Vancouver Island in western Canada. But Fred was already anticipating action being taken to recover the costs of their trial and for damages, either from his bank account or by proceedings against The Mascot. Before he and Emmeline sailed he wrote to Christabel Pankhurst in Paris, expressing disappointment that the authorities had not allowed them time to recover their health before taking action against them, and urging her to publicize any government action in this respect. He similarly instructed Evelyn Sharp to give a good account of any such legal action in 'Votes for Women' in the hope that if the general public realised that he and Emmeline were being punished unduly, public sympathy would result in increased support for the cause. The question of whether the WSPU could, or should, refund his losses from its campaign funds was already on his mind. He drafted a letter to Christabel before sailing, instructing her not to make any decision on the matter in his absence, but then crossed out reference to it.

From Canada Emmeline corresponded with Mrs Pankhurst on the intricacies of their position. On 8th September Mrs Pankhurst wrote a letter to Emmeline; it was, she made clear, a business letter, though *in our hearts are feelings which are very deep and real but which it would be out of place to express here'*. What followed was an analysis of the Pethick-Lawrences' situation. It was clear, she said, that the government and the insurers of damaged property intended to attack Fred for 'profit' and thereby to weaken the movement. If he was to be the target of court action for damages every time a woman took militant action against property, then only the cessation of the militant campaign or their financial ruin would bring an end to the situation. In one night hundreds of militant acts might cause thousands of pounds worth of damage, and, save for the imprisonment of the perpetrators, the only people to suffer would be Fred and Emmeline. Mrs Pankhurst intended to address a meeting at the Albert Hall in the autumn; her militant speech, she said, would lead to reprisals from the authorities, and another prosecution for conspiracy. Since she had no funds the government were unlikely to pursue her, but would scapegoat the Pethick-Lawrences again as they had the funds which government could claim to offset the costs of the trial. Fred would become a weapon with which to damage the movement as ruining him would weaken it. What, she asked rhetorically, was to be done?

Mrs Pankhurst suggested that rather than returning to the United Kingdom, the couple remove their assets to safety in Canada and lead the movement for the vote there. She reported that she had met with Mabel Tuke, Annie Kenney and Christabel in Boulogne, and all approved this proposal. *'You can do this work,'* she assured Emmeline, in a tone positive and affectionate, urging her to spread the movement throughout the Empire. From the Waldorf-Astoria in New York, Emmeline Pethick-Lawrence declined the proposal.

In later years Emmeline admitted that she had not seen the differences between herself and Fred and the Pankhursts as a chasm, for to do so would have meant the end of her passionate dream. *'It seems a miracle,'* she wrote in her autobiography, *'that for six years there could have existed a four-fold partnership like ours in which each member played a unique and important part.'* That dynamic partnership, of four people working in harmony for a cause in which they believed, was not just a matter of pride and satisfaction, but a romantic notion of the dignity of humanity which meant so much to her. It seems she was unwilling to see that collaboration end, even if to continue meant setting aside her reservations as to policy.

On September 27th a telegram was received at Clement's Inn. It read: *'Greetings to all: returning on Campania ready for the fight: no surrender; unitedly – Pethick Lawrence'*. The couple arrived back in the country on 2nd October. They were met by a friend, (probably their housekeeper, May Start), who gave them the news that there was no further place for them in the WSPU. In their absence the organization had moved offices from Clement's Inn to Lincoln's Inn House on Kingsway. (Clement's Inn had been repossessed by the landlord.) On arrival there the couple discovered that no office space had been made available to them. They were greeted with embarrassed silence by Mabel Tuke and Annie Kenney. Emmeline Pankhurst then informed them that their association with the WSPU was at an end. The Pethick-Lawrences were surprised and shattered by the news. Initially they refused to accept the situation and Christabel was forced to slip into the country incognito to confirm the decision.

On October 14th the situation was explained to the WSPU's national committee. There was no point in the Pethick-Lawrences appealing for a reasoned vote there: the organization had never been democratic, the Pankhursts and Pethick-Lawrences being responsible both for policy and for appointing members to a committee which seldom met[15]. Emmeline implored Elizabeth Robins, with whom she spent, according to Robins *'a strange and moving hour'*, to attend. Mary Neal was also there. Neither the Pankhursts nor Mabel Tuke or Annie Kenney would shake the couple's hands when they assembled. Mrs Pankhurst announced that where confidence no longer existed, working together was impossible. Fred attempted to speak but was told that as he was not a member of the committee he had no right to speak. Following a heated discussion Fred and Emmeline were asked to leave. When Elizabeth Robins and Mary Neal protested they were told that they had rarely attended meetings and ought to have better informed themselves of the facts. The Pethick-Lawrences then walked out. Elizabeth Robins resigned, followed by Mary Neal. The terms of the split, whereby 'Votes for Women' went with the Pethick-Lawrences whilst the WSPU kept the Women's Press and Fred was reimbursed for his loans to the organization, were thrashed out at another meeting in Boulogne. A statement was prepared for the coming Albert Hall meeting at which the split would be announced to the membership.

It is usually suggested that, unable to acquiesce in the stepping up of attacks on property, (and of arson in particular), the Pethick-Lawrences departed from the WSPU on a point of principle. Both suggest this to be the case in their autobiographies. The announcement that went out in 'Votes for Women' and 'The

---

[15] The WSPU had split over the issue of democracy within it in 1907, at which point the Pethick-Lawrences had acquiesced in the Pankhursts' autocracy on matters of policy. That split lead to the formation of the Women's Freedom League lead by former WSPU members Charlotte Despard, Edith How Martyn, Teresa Billington-Grieg and Margaret Nevinson.

Suffragette' was to that effect: *'At the first reunion of the leaders after their enforced holiday Mrs and Miss Pankhurst outlined a new militant policy which Mr and Mrs Pethick-Lawrence found themselves altogether unable to approve.'* But that is a half-truth that has served the reputation of the Pethick-Lawrences well.

While it is true that the Pethick-Lawrences had misgivings about the efficacy of a stepping up of property damage, particularly against private rather than public targets, it is not true that they had been unwilling to acquiesce in the Pankhursts' decision. They had been willing to do so even to their own detriment. Mrs Pankhurst had written to them outlining the danger to Fred's wealth *'So long as Mr Lawrence can be connected with the movement's actions... they will make him pay. They see Mr Lawrence as a potent weapon against the movement and they mean to use it... They also intend, if they can, to divert our funds. If suffragists... raised a fund to recoup Mr Lawrence it would mean that our members' money would go finally into the coffers of the enemy and the fighting fund would be depleted or ended. It would also reduce militancy to a farce for the damage we did with one hand would be repaired with the other.'* It was for that reason that she had advised them to stay in Canada. The couple's response on 22nd July 1912: *'We shall continue to be jointly responsible with you in the future as we have been in the past, and that though we are menaced... we will fight until victory is won.. with regard to militancy – we have never for a single instant allowed our individual interests to stand in the way of any necessary action on policy to be pursued by the Union, and we never shall'* was hardly a rejection of the policy of intensified property damage.

Events taking place in Holmwood simultaneously could not but have confirmed to Mrs Pankhurst the correctness of her analysis. Whilst the Pethick-Lawrences were in Canada the Director of Public Prosecutions, pursuant to the order of the court, had taken steps to recover the costs of the prosecution from them.

Though he could simply have written a cheque, (which would have been considerably cheaper than forcing the government to sue for its money), Fred refused to do so. He had, he wrote in 'Votes for Women', staked his health and life in support of the cause of human equality and he could not renounce it because of the risk to property. *'The warfare between us and the government has now been carried on to the financial plane,'* he wrote, *'and the only course consistent with my principles is to fight every inch of the way. I take identically the same view of the present situation that I took of my personal position when I refused to abandon the hunger strike, though threatened with forcible feeding.'*

To prevent The Mascot falling into the hands of his creditors it was sold. The buyer, Thomas Mortimer 'Mort' Budgett of Lyme Regis, was married to Emmeline's sister, Annie (known as Nancy). Fred's golf partner and a regular visitor to The Mascot, Budgett was a long-term women's suffrage supporter. He had been arrested for the cause and was a founder of the Mens' League for Women's Suffrage. He had also visited Fred in prison.

Unable to sell The Mascot, the Director of Public Prosecutions ordered a sale of its contents. When Fred and Emmeline arrived back from Canada the bailiffs were in occupation to prevent the removal of items of value. 'Burglary' Fred called it in 'Votes for Women'. In retaliation - and whilst the leadership wrangled about the terms of the Pethick-Lawrences' departure from the organization - the WSPU launched the 'Dorking and Holmwood Campaign'.

Throughout September and October 1912 rallies were held in Holmwood: at The Norfolk Arms and in the open air on the common. Meetings were held in Ockley, Westcott and Bookham and every night for weeks in Dorking, outside The White Horse or at the Rotunda, on Flint Hill, and at the public halls. The campaign was run by Charlotte Marsh and Helen Gordon Liddle from 43 Howard Road in Dorking.

Charlotte Marsh was an experienced campaign organizer. She had recently served six months for window-smashing on The Strand and Dorking shopkeepers feared that if the sale went ahead women would go on the rampage. But at a meeting in early October in Dorking's public halls Marsh gave assurances that this would not

THE GOVERNMENT'S POUND OF FLESH

The Mascot, Holmwood, the Country House of Mr. and Mrs. Pethick Lawrence
(*Where the Government are threatening a sale of the furniture to pay the costs of the recent trial.*)

The Mascot in 1912. The figures standing outside are probably Emmeline Pethick-Lawrence and her housekeeper, May Start. The bailiffs were in occupation for many weeks and the cost of their wages and sustenance was charged to the Pethick-Lawrences. The two men quarrelled at the beginning of their assignment and thereafter they sat in separate rooms, ignoring one another. ('Votes for Women' reproduced by permission of the British Library)

133

happen. The WSPU only wished to convert the people of Dorking to the cause and to arouse indignation at the government's treatment of the Pethick-Lawrences, she said, before reading out a letter of support from the couple's friend, George Lansbury. She was followed onto the platform by Annie Kenney and Welsh organiser Rachel Barratt (1875-1953). Unbeknownst to the Pethick-Lawrences, Christabel Pankhurst had delegated to Barratt the task of launching a rival paper to 'Votes for Women' to appear as soon as the split between the leaders was announced. On release from hunger-strike under the 'Cat and Mouse Act' the following year, Barratt went to recuperate with the Brackenburys.

The date of the auction was announced for October 31st 1912. Many with local connections and others who had enjoyed the hospitality of The Mascot appeared to speak over the six-week period of the campaign, including Georgina and Marie Brackenbury, Marion Wallace Dunlop, Helen Gordon Liddle, Sylvia Pankhurst and Annie Kenney. Joan Cather and Grace Gillespie Hardy of the Redhill WSPU came to speak, and Grace Cameron Swan from Croydon.

With Charlotte Marsh presiding, two or three public meetings a day passed off in an orderly manner. She finished meetings by calling on those present to join the WSPU in protest. Correspondence kept events in the local press and Marsh reported signs of sympathy in good donations to funds and excellent sales of 'Votes for Women'. (Whether this is true is difficult to gauge, however, for Marsh was hardly likely to admit to any failure to galvanise local opinion.)

Adverts in the suffragette press and posters in the town and villages urged supporters to attend the auction in a show of sympathy. On the day large crowds arrived at Dorking and Holmwood stations, many wearing suffragette colours and wearing their prison badges. The 'Dorking Advertiser' estimated the attendance as between three and four thousand. Most did not go inside to view the couple's possessions, which were assembled for viewing like a jumble-sale.

43 Howard Road in Dorking was the headquarters of the six week Dorking and Holmwood campaign. It was the home of suffragette hunger-striker, Helen Gordon Liddle.

134

GOVERNMENT'S HIGH-HANDED ACTION AT HOLMWOOD

Bailiffs in Possession of Mr. & Mrs. Pethick Lawrence's Home

As we stated briefly last week, the Sheriff's Officers levied an execution on Monday, August 19, on the country home of Mr. and Mrs. Pethick Lawrence at Holmwood, Surrey, under a Treasury order for the costs of the prosecution in the Conspiracy Trial. The following statement was at once issued by the Women's Social and Political Union:—

"Great indignation is felt by members of the Women's Social and Political Union at the Government's latest action. In the absence of Mr. and Mrs. Pethick Lawrence, who are now in Canada paying a visit to Mrs. Lawrence's brother, the Government have ordered that their country home in Surrey be entered, and their furniture seized and sold in payment of the costs of the recent prosecution for conspiracy.

"The order to pay costs was in itself an act of persecution, the object of which was to impose a heavy fine in addition to the sentence of nine months' imprisonment. The costs include a sum of nearly £350 payable to the Attorney-General, a member of the Cabinet. The injustice of this order to pay costs is apparent when it is remembered that the broken windows were replaced by the insurance companies, and that these companies secured thereby an advertisement which has brought them in a great deal of new business.

"The promoters of the coal strike, which caused an infinitely greater loss to traders and to the community at large, have not been required to suffer either in pocket or in person, yet the motives were no purer than the jury declared the motives of the Suffragist leaders to be. To order the payment of costs is in itself an injustice, while to compel payment by invading a house and seizing furniture in the absence of the owners is a highly disgraceful proceeding."

What a Member of the Public Thinks

Similar indignation at this vindictive action on the part of the Government is expressed in the following letter which appeared in the *Standard* ("Woman's Platform") last Monday:—

"Sir:—I have read with amazement the statement that the Treasury have seized Mr. Pethick Lawrence's goods at Holmwood, Surrey, and entered into possession of his house. The fact that the whole of the costs of the conspiracy trial will fall upon him, whose connection with the window-breaking was of the thinnest description, should surely entitle him to some sympathy and consideration! When one reflects upon his honourable career, both at the university and as a professional man, his work among the poor in East London, and his other claims to public gratitude, the conduct of the authorities appears little short of disgraceful. He is away in Canada; the bill of costs can only very recently have been delivered to him, and his solicitor is without instructions.

"The Treasury cannot wait until his return, which is expected in October, but they must subject him to this unnecessary suffering and indignity—and that during the long vacation, when the public find it impossible to secure the transaction of any useful legal business! One can only hope that such arbitrary procedure will not pass unnoticed, but that the action of the Treasury will be another nail in the coffin of this 'Liberal' Government.

"INDIGNANT."

Further Developments

Further developments have been awaited with interest, the indignation and amazement aroused having been widespread. On Monday evening a report was circulated in the London Press to the effect that the bailiffs had been withdrawn from the house. This was at once denied by the W.S.P.U., the bailiffs having remained in possession since they entered last Monday week; though they had taken no further action, and proceedings were kept in suspension until Wednesday morning in this week.

On Wednesday morning we were informed that the Treasury had decided to suspend proceedings for another fourteen days. Meanwhile, however, it must be remembered that the Sheriff's officers are still in possession of the house, and are being kept at Mr. Pethick Lawrence's expense. Thus do the Government fight their battles with an enemy who is too far off to retaliate!

Article in 'Votes for Women' about the occupation of The Mascot by bailiffs on the orders of the Attorney General. The piece quotes a letter of support in 'The Standard'. Given the anonymous 'Indignant's' knowledge of Fred's whereabouts and the state of play between Fred and his solicitor, the writer was probably close to Fred and Emmeline. (Reproduced with permission of the British Library)

Twenty constables were present, many in plain clothes, under the command of Superintendent Coleman and there was, reported the paper: *'a feeling of excitement and expectancy quite foreign to the usual quiet and serene atmosphere of the village'*.

Just before one in the afternoon Fred and Emmeline walked up to the house from The Sundial. Fred spoke to the crowd in the back garden. The bailiffs, he said, were soldiers fighting under the government banner and he was entitled to make their job as unpleasant as possible. He had chosen not to do so because he recognised them as unfortunates doing their duty even if they were acting for the enemy. He had therefore treated them with courtesy. Emmeline was cheered and waved as she thanked friends and neighbours. Things that she treasured were to be sold, she said, but there was a greater prize and treasure for which they were bidding. *'O liberty! thou choicest treasure!'* she said, adding that such a treasure did cost dear.

The crowd was generally sympathetic, and many goods were purchased by *'those who could appreciate the single-mindedness of Mr and Mrs Pethick-Lawrence who had risked so much in both health and pocket for the cause they had at heart,'* wrote FE Green. Ruth Cavendish-Bentinck organised for friends and supporters to buy back the couple's possessions. (Mortimer Budgett returned the grandfather clock that he had bought as a wedding present.) Even the auctioneer, who had expressed his appreciation for the courtesy Fred had shown his men, got caught up in the spirit of the day and bought an item which he returned to the couple. Thanking Mrs Cavendish-Bentinck a few days later Emmeline commented that the presence of so many supporters had *'made the occasion one of rejoicing rather than one of regret.'* She would, she continued, have a tablet put up in the hallway of The Mascot commemorating the day. Still in the house, the tablet reads: *'O Liberty thou choicest treasure! Oct 31 1912'.* The idea for the wording came from the piece of embroidery that Sylvia Pankhurst designed for her mother to work on when she was in prison with Emmeline Pethick-Lawrence.

Forcing government and creditors to sue him cost Fred more in terms of fees and other expenses than would have been the case had he agreed to pay at the outset. The auction raised £300, insufficient to cover the costs of the trial, the bailiffs and the auction. He also faced civil actions from the owners of businesses whose windows had been broken. These he also refused to pay, arguing that the stone throwing had not been incited by him but by the government, and in particular, by Mr Hobhouse. The Director of Public Prosecutions had him declared bankrupt so that the outstanding monies could be recovered from his accounts. Since he had the money to pay, the bankruptcy was only technical. But he was expelled from the Reform Club as a consequence. It was a difficult time *'but hand in hand we are stronger than tempests and avalanches and all the forces of evil'*, he wrote to Emmeline, adding that her voice was music and her eyes were like the sentinels of heaven. *'Thus he underwent every variation of the sacrifice demanded for the*

THE GOVERNMENT'S POUND OF FLESH

Mr. and Mrs. Pethick Lawrence are expected to be in England by the middle of next week. Unless notice of sale is given at once, they will return to find their country home in the possession of the bailiffs. As we have already pointed out, the order to pay costs in the Conspiracy Case was made for the purpose of striking at Mr. Pethick Lawrence, and was an act of revenge for his championship of the woman's movement. It is indeed one of a long list of discreditable Anti-Suffrage Government methods.

Miss Marsh and Miss Liddle, who are in charge of a special campaign of protest against the Government's vindictive action in seeking to get back the cost of the Conspiracy Trial by such methods, report excellent meetings and a good reception everywhere.

Open-air meetings have been held in Ockley, Flint Hill, Holmwood, Westcott, and Dorking. VOTES FOR WOMEN sells well, and collections are good. Thanks to the Misses Brackenbury, Miss West, Mrs. Cameron Swan, Mrs. Cather, Miss Naylor, and Miss Hardy for help as speakers. Also to Miss Pym, Miss Pringle, and Miss Holah for help in working up meetings. A by-law prevents a stall in Dorking Market on Thursdays, but pamphlets and papers are being sold, and a meeting held for the farmers.

Contributions are needed to pay expenses: Gratefully acknowledged: Miss Johnson, £2 2s.; Mrs. Bamfield, 4s.; Miss Kanaar, 2s 6d. Meetings will be held as follows: To-day (Friday) and to-morrow (Saturday) at Dorking at 6.30 p.m.; Monday, September 30, at Holmwood at 6.30 p.m.; Tuesday, October 1, at Bookham at 6.30 p.m.; Wednesday, October 2, at Dorking at 6.30 p.m. Organisers, Miss C. A. L. Marsh and Miss H. Gordon Liddle, 43, Howard Road, Dorking.

Above and below left: reports on the Holmwood Campaign; Fred and Emmeline surrounded by their possessions on the lawn. Below right: Fred addressing the crowd. ('Votes for Women' reproduced by permission of the British Library)

DORKING AND HOLMWOOD CAMPAIGN
Organisers: Miss C. A. L. Marsh and Miss H. Gordon Liddle, 43, Howard Road, Dorking

The special campaign to protest against the threatened sale of the furniture at The Mascot, Holmwood, by the Government to pay the costs of the prosecution in the Conspiracy Trial, is now in huge swing. Two or three meetings are being held daily. The date of the sale is not yet announced, but much indignation is felt locally at the action of the Treasury in seizing the house during the absence of Mr. and Mrs. Pethick Lawrence. The campaign opened with a very successful meeting on Tuesday evening in Dorking, when Mrs. Cameron Swan and Mrs. Cather were the speakers. A meeting will be held every evening at 6.30 in Dorking, opposite the "White Horse." The loan of a motorcar would be much appreciated, as there is a great deal of ground to cover. Contributions towards the expenses are needed, and should be sent to the above address. Gratefully acknowledged: The Misses Sotheran, £1 4s.

Meetings Arranged

Thursday, Sept. 19, Holmwood, 6.30 p.m., Miss West, Miss M. Brackenbury; **Dorking**, 6.30 p.m., Miss Brackenbury, Miss Marsh.

Friday, Sept. 29, Flint Hill, 6.30 p.m., Miss Hardy, Mrs. Cather; **Ockley**, 6.30 p.m., Mrs. Cameron Swan, Miss Marsh; **Dorking**, 6.30 p.m., Miss Liddle, Miss Hicks, M.A.

Saturday, Sept. 21, Westcott, 6.30 p.m., Miss M. Brackenbury, Miss West; **Dorking**, 6.30 p.m., Miss Brackenbury.

Monday, Sept. 23, Holmwood, 6.30 p.m., Miss Marsh; **Dorking**, 6.30 p.m., Miss Naylor.

Tuesday, Sept. 23, Dorking, 6.30 p.m., Miss Naylor.

Wednesday, Sept. 24, Dorking, 6.30 p.m., Miss Liddle, Mrs. Cather.

freedom of women – imprisonment, hunger strike, forcible feeding, bankruptcy, loss of financial substance and expulsion from his club,' wrote Emmeline in her autobiography.

Had the Pethick-Lawrences remained central to the WSPU it is probable that the events of October 31st 1912 would have been repeated over and again. And in the coming campaign of property damage Fred's wealth would have proved less an asset to the WSPU than a weakness, inhibiting women from taking action in case he was sued for the consequences. (Indeed the following year Fred and Emmeline, and the absent Christabel, were sued by West End Clothiers Co and 92 other business for damages for windows broken in November 1911 and March 1912; judgment was entered against them for £1,423 plus costs.) Fred conceded this in his memoirs, and it is as much the reason for their ousting from the organization as their lack of enthusiasm for stone-throwing and arson.

There were other factors at play in the split with the Pankhursts. Eyewitnesses claimed that Mrs Pankhurst had never been fond of Fred, that he was infatuated with Christabel, and that Mrs Pankhurst was jealous of Emmeline's motherly relationship with her daughter. Others recalled that Christabel, isolated in Paris, was fearful that her position in the WSPU would be eclipsed should the Fred and Emmeline take her

Emmeline's portrait from a report in the 'Dorking Advertiser' of The Mascot sale. It was unusual in the period for local papers to carry photographs of personalities so the appearance Emmeline's photograph indicates a level of celebrity. The image was taken from an official WSPU postcard. ('Dorking Advertiser')

place in the day-to-day running of campaigns. (Her suspicions in this respect would later fall upon her sister, Sylvia, and on Emmeline's friend, Evelyn Sharp.) In ousting the Pethick-Lawrences Mrs Pankhurst regained her favourite daughter and control over the organization that she had founded. Christabel also felt increasingly that the campaign should be fought by women alone, whereas Fred and Emmeline attracted a wide circle of supporters, both male and female, to whom they had figurehead status as the couple at the centre of the WSPU. Fred's friend, the journalist Henry Nevinson, suggests further complexities in his diary. On walking with Fred in Holmwood Fred told him that the relationship between the two men and their other male associates was part of the problem: *'It seems the origin was my work for the paper when they were all arrested,'* wrote Nevinson. *'I was supposed to be an* intimate friend of Brailsford whom I seldom saw at that time, and he of Lloyd George. So this silliness went on.' With Nevinson's partner (of sorts) Evelyn Sharp jointly editing 'Votes for Women', it may have seemed to Christabel that male associates of the Pethick-Lawrences were moving to prominence within the organisation, a prominence that she - suspicious of the duplicity of politicians, and particularly of Lloyd George - feared might compromise the campaign.

The announcement of a significant policy divide over forthcoming campaign tactics denied the government the publicity value of victory in having forced out the WSPU's major financial backers. It masked internal and personal issues within the leadership from supporter and critic alike. The fact that there was no real disagreement explains why, though Fred and Emmeline sought to dissuade the Pankhursts from an arson campaign, they never sought to split the WSPU when they failed. Though they had their misgivings, they were prepared to defer to the Pankhursts. Their ousting was at Mrs Pankhurst's behest and can be attributed as much to personal and financial issues as to questions of policy.

The Pankhursts were, Fred reflected years later with magnanimity, a force of destiny and therefore not to be judged by ordinary standards. *'Those who run up against them must not complain of the treatment they receive,'* he wrote. It had taken many years to reach this state of equanimity; Henry Nevinson recorded in his diary a trip to Holmwood in July 1914, some two years after the split: *'Sunday: at Holmwood. Walked with Lawrence through the woods the talk again of the shameful behaviour of Mrs Pankhurst at the time of the split, which had been carefully prepared long before... His contempt for her meanness and hatred of her 'play act' for sympathy are very violent; almost an obsession.'* The ousting may have had justification in terms of practicality but the way in

DAMAGES FOR BROKEN WINDOWS.

Ninety-three plaintiffs whose shop windows were smashed by suffragettes during a West End raid were awarded damages on Monday against Mr. and Mrs. Pethick Lawrence, Mrs. Pankhurst, and Miss Christabel Pankhurst.

The case of the West End Clothiers' Company, whose windows were broken on Nov. 21, 1911, and March 4, 1912, was before Mr. Justice Coleridge, and Mr. Ernest Pollock, K.C. (for the plaintiffs), said there were ninety-two other plaintiffs, and he asked for judgment in their favour for damages amounting altogether to £1,423 and costs, and also for an injunction restraining the defendants from repeating or continuing the acts complained of.

Mr. and Mrs. Pethick Lawrence had agreed to allow judgment to pass against them on terms agreed, and he asked for judgment against them in favour of all the ninety-three plaintiffs, with costs, and also for a certificate for three counsel.

With regard to Mrs. and Miss Pankhurst, he asked for judgment in the action for all the plaintiffs, with costs, and also an injunction against them, with liberty to apply as to ascertaining the amount of damage against these defendants. He added that the amount that had been claimed in the case was £1,600.

Mr. Henle (for Mr. and Mrs. Pethick Lawrence) said in view of the result of a recent case of Robinson and Cleaver against the same defendants, his clients felt that they would not be justified in allowing the public time to be taken up by investigating a similar case. In the circumstances they were prepared to submit to judgment as stated.

Mr. Justice Coleridge : Very well.

Fred was sued by the owners of property whose windows had been smashed. The sums involved were considerable; in 1914 a large detached house with 6 acres of garden and a staff cottage was on sale in Holmwood for £1,500. ('Dorking Advertiser') which it had been manoeuvred in secret in their absence amounted to a betrayal of the couple's personal relationship with their long-time collaborators, particularly with Christabel who had for so long lived in their home. It was the underhand and pre-planned nature of their dismissal which hurt Fred so deeply. The fact that Mrs Pankhurst was immediately able to send out a subscription form for the new 'Suffragette' magazine (which Christabel would edit from Paris) to members with notice of the split only brought home to him the extent to which all had been planned meticulously in his absence in Canada. Overcome when speaking of the breach, Fred told George Lansbury that being asked to leave the organisation to which he had contributed his life blood was like a mother being asked to part from her small child. He was, wrote Henry Nevinson, *'bitterly hurt especially at the long underground preparation and sudden explosion upon their innocence.'*

Emmeline reflected later that there was something quite ruthless about Mrs Pankhurst: *'The break was final and complete. From that time forward I never heard from Mrs. Pankhurst again, and Christabel, who had shared our family life, became a complete stranger.'* *'Thus'*, wrote Fred, *'ended our personal association with two of the most memorable people I have ever known.'*

Fred and Emmeline never spoke publicly of the split, nor did they call upon others to leave the WSPU. Many with personal connections to the couple, Dorothy Pethick, Nellie Crocker and Mary Neal amongst them, did leave. Their mindfulness of the effect that any public rancour would provoke in their enemies was justified for many predicted a fatal split that would render the organisation ineffective. Punch magazine published a cartoon by E.H. Shepherd[16] depicting one budding suffragette asking another 'with intensity' if she was a 'Peth' or a 'Pank'. In November 1912 Isabel Hecht of the non-militant Leith Hill and District WSS wrote a column on the subject for the 'Dorking Advertiser' supposing that WSPU members were in astonishment at the breach and accusing Mrs Pankhurst – justifiably - of autocracy. *'It is not an edifying spectacle to anybody,'* she wrote, *'when heroic, if mistaken, devotees of a great cause dissolve partnership without apparent regret or expressions of respect'*. She predicted civil war within the organization and took the Pethick-Lawrences' part in the anticipated 'tug of war'. *'Might Mrs Pankhurst and her daughters be left high and dry?'* she asked.

That no great schism came to pass is largely due to the stoic discretion of Fred and Emmeline who continued to work with suffrage supporters of all kinds, even those, like Evelyn Sharp, whose loyalties were torn. *'Those who know me and my husband will understand how our only thought in taking the action that we have is for the good and welfare of the movement to which we dedicated all that we had in life or fortune six years ago,'* maintained Emmeline, refusing to be drawn into criticism of the Pankhursts in a letter to Vera Holme. *'We leave it for the same*

---

[16] Ernest Howard Shepherd (1879-1976) is best known for his illustrations for 'The Wind in the Willows' and 'Winnie the Pooh'.

reason that we entered it - to serve it without regard to our own interests.' That letter would also seem to suggest a residual loyalty to the WSPU, and a sense of self-exile for the good of the organisation.

The Pethick-Lawrences may have felt that there were other routes open to the movement than the campaign of arson which followed, but they did not condemn stone-throwing or window-smashing. Dorothy Pethick told the New York press in 1913 that her sister believed arson to be unnecessary when there were plentiful windows still intact. And Emmeline makes much in her autobiography of the fact that there was never any physical injury to any person despite the violence often meted out to the suffragettes or the pain suffered during the hunger strikes.

The Pethick-Lawrences did not form any formal rival organization, but a more moderate grouping formed around them, largely a result of family and personal relationships and as a consequence of their inclusiveness of men. Free of their obligations to the WSPU and notwithstanding the fact that they had been willing to bow to the judgement of the Pankhursts, the Pethick-Lawrences sought to distance themselves from the policy of arson as the WSPU's campaign intensified. That they raised their voices in a call for moderation served their reputations well as questions began to arise as to the efficacy of escalating property damage in the later years of the campaign. And that reputation has served them well since. For this reason, perhaps, the depth of their opposition to the arson campaign is a matter that neither Fred nor Emmeline probed too deeply in their respective autobiographies.

Friends and Confidantes – Evelyn Sharp and Henry Nevinson

Emmeline's closest friend in the suffrage movement was Evelyn Jane Sharp (1869-1955), the sister of Mary Neal's collaborator, Cecil Sharp. As a young woman she had moved out of the family home and supported herself by writing novels and fairy tales. She also contributed to 'The Yellow Book'. Sharp became involved in the cause after hearing Millicent Fawcett speak at a working women's conference that she was covering for the 'Manchester Guardian'. Originally a member of the NUWSS and the Women Writers' Suffrage League, she joined the Kensington WSPU; her sister Bertha became its secretary. But she did not take militant action until she was able to overcome her mother's opposition.

Henry Nevinson described Sharp as *'the very best speaker of the suffragettes'*. After hearing her at the Brackenburys' studio, he wrote that she deployed *'every sort of wit and eloquence and surprise and insight'*. She also wrote for 'Votes for Women'; on one occasion Emmeline congratulated her on *'a perfectly delicious little article... the sweetest you have written'*.

Sharp was instrumental in keeping the WSPU funds out of the hands of the authorities when the Pethick-Lawences were arrested, and in Christabel's escape. Fred passed the editorship of 'Votes for Women' to Sharp when he was in prison and she continued as joint editor after his release. She also published 'Rebel

Women', stories of suffragette life. Sharp remained with the WSPU when the Pethick-Lawrences were ousted. But Christabel was concerned that Sharp's presence in London (while she was exiled in Paris) threatened her position and Sharp was sidelined. She followed Nevinson to the newly-formed United Suffragists with Fred and Emmeline in early 1914.

Sharp tried to join Emmeline at the Women's International Peace Congress in The Hague in 1915 but was unable to obtain a passport. Throughout the First World War she refused to pay tax on the grounds that she had no vote on whether her taxes were used to wage a war that she did not support, and therefore she ought not to have any liability to pay tax to fund it. In February 1918 tax office bailiffs auctioned her possessions to recover unpaid tax. She became involved with the Women's International League and after the war she worked for the Society of Friends (Quakers) in Germany, and in famine-stricken Russia.

On 6th February 1918 Sharp and Nevinson were present with Bertha Brewster, (secretary of the United Suffraists), in the House of Commons when the act giving women over 30 the right to vote received royal assent. At the organization's victory celebration at Caxton Hall she was presented with a book containing the signatures of many members, Emmeline and Fred amongst them

Sharp's partner for many years was the campaigning journalist and war correspondent, Henry Woodd Nevinson (1856-1941). He was a close friend of Fred Pethick-Lawrence and a regular visitor to The Mascot and Fourways. He was present in court throughout the conspiracy trial and it was to Nevinson that Fed confessed his feelings on the split from the Pankhursts during walks in Holmwood.

Nevinson was the son of a solicitor. He came to radical politics after teaching the poor in London's East End. As a war correspondent he reported from Turkey, South Africa, Russia, India the Balkans and the Middle East. Women's suffrage was just one of the radical causes which he supported. He also organized relief work in Macedonia and Albania, worked for the Friends' Ambulance Service during the First World War, and campaigned against bonded servitude in the Angolan cocoa plantations. Wounded whilst covering the Dardanelles campaign, he was motored down with his nurse to recuperate at The Mascot in 1917.

Nevinson became involved with the WSPU with his wife, Margaret Wynne Nevinson nee Jones (1858-1932). He continued to speak for the WSPU and to march with it even after she left to form the Women's Freedom League. He resigned his post at 'The Daily News' (with Henry Brailsford) in protest at the paper's refusal to condemn force-feeding. (He later claimed that this action had lost him all prospect of regular work for the daily papers in Britain.) A founder member of the Men's League for women's Suffrage, he considered that organization insufficiently radical and went on to found the militant Men's Political Union for Women's Enfranchisement.

Nevinson was estranged from his wife and maintained a long relationship with Evelyn Sharp. His involvement (and that of Brailsford) in the production of 'Votes for Women' under Sharp's editorship during Fred and Emmeline's imprisonment seem to have contributed to Christabel Pankhurst's decision to oust the couple from the WSPU. Nevinson regarded this split as highly detrimental and continued to support Sylvia Pankhurst in her breakaway East End campaign, writing for her 'Women's Dreadnought' magazine. It was with regret at the failings of the WSPU that - with Fred and Emmeline - he became a founder member of the United Suffragists.

Sharp and Nevinson were life-long confidants of the Pethick-Lawrences. They both joined Emmeline in the Kibbo Kift movement. And despite their friendship with Mary Neal, they were also involved with Cecil Sharp's endeavours; Evelyn Sharp wrote a history of English folk dance and played a part in the establishment of Cecil Sharp House, home of the English Folk Song and Dance Society.

The couple were regular visitors to Holmwood and to Peaslake; they were also friends with Fred and Emmeline's neighbours, the Roden-Buxtons. In 1933, at the age of 66, Evelyn Sharp was finally able to marry the 75 year-old Henry Nevinson, on the death of his wife. When Nevinson died Fred acted as his executor and Sharp recalled in her diary the joy of their walks together between Clandon and Shere. She continued to correspond with Fred and Emmeline for the rest of her life, visiting them into the 1940s and proof-reading Fred's autobiography.

Evelyn Sharp by EA Walton reproduced from 'The Yellow Book' by permission of Hamlyn Octopus Publishing; Henry Nevinson (Library of Congress.)

Ruth Cavendish-Bentinck and the Holmwood 'buy-back'

The woman who organised the buy-back of Fred and Emmeline's possessions was typical of the well-to-do women that Emmeline was so good at attracting to the WSPU. Ruth Cavendish-Bentinck (1867-1953) was the illegitimate daughter of Earl St Maur. Her mother was a maid, but she had been adopted by her father's parents, the Duke and Duchess of Somerset. Her beauty, wit and the fortune left to her by the Duke compensated for the stigma of her origins, and she married wealthy barrister (William George) Frederick Cavendish-Bentinck, descendent of the Duke of Portland. The couple received the castle on Brownsea Island as a wedding present.

Ruth Cavendish-Bentinck came to socialism via William Morris and wrote for the Fabian Society. Like Emmeline, she was involved in social work with young women. She joined the WSPU in 1909 and set up a suffragist lending library so that women could borrow books that they might not otherwise be able to get hold of, including censored volumes. (It is now the Cavendish-Bentinck Library at the Women's Library.) She supported the WSPU with money, articles and letters to the press, but never took militant action. She left the WSPU for the non-militant NUWSS in 1912 and organised its Election Fighting Fund which raised money to assist Labour candidates at by-elections in their campaigns against non-suffrage supporting Liberals. She later joined Fred and Emmeline in the United Suffragists and wrote on women and labour issues for 'Votes for Women'. *(Image EM Habben Jansen)*

'Charlie' Marsh – leader of the Dorking & Holmwood Campaign

Charlotte 'Charlie' Augusta Leopoldine Marsh (1887-1961) was born in Alnmouth near Newcastle-upon-Tyne. Appalled at what she learned of ordinary women's lives through her work as one of the first female sanitary inspectors, she determined to give women a voice public affairs and became a paid organizer with the WSPU. She headed the processions in support of the Conciliation Bill in 1910 and in celebration of the Coronation in 1911. Her femininity concealed an unshakeable will and huge reserves of courage.

In 1908 she spent a month in Holloway. In September 1909 she and Mary Leigh staged a roof-top protest in Birmingham where they bombarded Bingley Hall, where Asquith was speaking, with slates. Sentenced to three months hard labour, she was in Winson Green prison when Marion Wallace Dunlop began her hunger strike and became one of the first women to undergo force-feeding. At Winson Green she endured the experience nearly 150 times. In 1912 the experience was repeated at Aylesbury prison over a four-month period following window-smashing in the West End. It was her zest for life, as much as her extraordinary resilience that was an inspiration to others: in prison she invited others to join her at golf with a stone and stick.

Marsh stayed with the WSPU when the Pethick-Lawrences departed and was the cross-bearer at Emily Davison's funeral procession in 1913. In 1914 she trained as a mechanic and became Lloyd George's driver. (He suggested that to do so would further the suffrage cause.) By the end of the war she had joined the Pethick-Lawrences in the peace movement and was on the staff of the Women's International League for Peace and Freedom. She remained close to Emmeline Pethick-Lawrence and stayed at Fourways in Peaslake. Emmeline left money to Marsh in her will and in tribute Fred recalled that it was impossible not to be captivated by the charm and personality of this *'bonny fighter'*, whose outstanding characteristic was her kindness. (*WSPU postcard from the collection of Ann Lewis and Mike Sponder*)

Local speakers at the Dorking and Holmwood campaign

On 22nd and 23rd September Marie Isabel Naylor (1866-1940) addressed crowds in support of the Pethick-Lawrences in Dorking. She was a veteran of the Pantechnicon raid and a speaker at the Hyde Park rally. An associate of the Brackenbury sisters of Peaslake, she was an artist who had exhibited in Paris and at the Royal Academy.

On 20th September Grace Cameron Swan came to lend support, giving a speech in Ockley. She and her husband, Donald lived at Craig Bhan in Mayfield Road in Sanderstead; both were suffrage campaigners with connections to the Pethick-Lawrences. Grace Swan nee Williamson (1879-?) was the organising secretary of the Croydon WSPU and had been imprisoned for the cause. Donald was organising secretary of the Men's Political Union for Women's Enfranchisement and sat on its committee with Fred's close friend, Henry Nevinson. Like the WSPU, the MPUWE was a militant organisation; many of its members, including Swan, were imprisoned in support of the women's cause.

Donald Cameron Swan (1863-1951) was the son of Sir Joseph Swan who had obtained the first patent for an electric light bulb before going into business with Edison to form the Ediswan company. Donald managed the photographic reproduction business which was founded to take advantage of his father's innovations in photographic processing.

In the 1920s the Cameron Swans emigrated to South Africa. When the Pethick-Lawrences visited in 1930, Grace Cameron Swan hosted a reception in Emmeline's honour at the Cape Town social club. It was '*a real suffragette meeting in spirit and warmth*', wrote Emmeline. During the Second World War Grace, now in her sixties, was responsible for the mobilisation of the women of South Africa as an inspector for female labour. *Left: Marie Naylor ('Votes for Women' reproduced by permission of the British Library); right: Donald Cameron Swan (The Women's Library, LSE)*

Militancy and 'Mouse Castle': Brackenside

Post-boxes were set alight, flower-beds attacked, telephone wires cut, and paintings damaged. Amongst those taking part in the escalating campaign of property damage of 1913 and early 1914 were a number of women with close connections to Peaslake.

One of the organisers of the window-smashing campaigns was Edith Elizabeth Downing (1857-1931). She was a sculptor who had exhibited in Paris and at the Royal Academy. She felt that it was degrading to be in a position of inferiority and joined the Chelsea branch of the WSPU in frustration at the failure of peaceful campaigning in 1908. She put her skills to use selling statuettes of Christabel Pankhurst and Annie Kenney and worked on some of the WSPU's great spectacles, designing tableaux, processions and pageants at her Tite Street studio. Many of her designs were executed at the Brackenbury sisters' studio. With Marion Wallace Dunlop and Sylvia Pankhurst, she designed the procession for the Conciliation Bill, and she worked on the Coronation procession of 1911 with the Brackenbury sisters.

Downing was a close friend of Marion Wallace Dunlop, and a regular visitor to Peaslake. London-based demonstrators were directed to Tite Street to collect stones which had been collected on motor trips to country lanes outside the capital. It is not unlikely that some were collected on trips to Marion Wallace Dunlop's Peaslake home, and Edith Downing lived in the village in later life.

The Brackenburys also stayed loyal to the WSPU. Their London home at 2 Campden Hill Square provided a place of refuge to released women as the government trialled a new tactic to bring the movement under control. The Prisoners (Temporary Discharge for Ill Health) Act 1913 allowed hunger-striking women to be released when dangerously ill and rearrested to finish their sentences when sufficiently recovered. Its purpose was to break the hunger strikes without forcible feeding. Its effect was a game of 'cat and mouse'. It was Fred Pethick-Lawrence who coined the term 'Cat and Mouse Act', by which it became known, in 'Votes for Women' which he continued to edit with Evelyn Sharp, independent of any organization. The WSPU took the term and created visuals depicting a suffragette mouse dead in the jaws of the Liberal cat.

The Act was widely deplored; Emmeline Pethick-Lawrence and Evelyn Sharp protested at its use in the summer of 1913 and Emmeline served her last prison sentence for doing so. With characteristic aplomb, their old comrades in the WSPU turned outwitting the authorities into a game of ingenuity. Released women disappeared to evade re-arrest, often to reappear in prominent locations, at hustings or on-stage at rallies. The Brackenburys' home became known as 'Mouse Castle' for its role in sheltering released women. When Mrs Pankhurst took up residence there it was placed under constant surveillance. But many escaped from its walls whilst on temporary release; on one occasion Annie Kenney donned black tights, swimsuit, bathing hat and mask to climb over the garden wall in the dark. On 10th February 1914 Mrs Pankhurst disappeared from the house when police arrested the wrong woman after she had spoken from a front balcony.

Two more suffragette friends of Marion Wallace Dunlop were semi-resident on the borders of Peaslake. Cecily Bertha Hale (1884-1981) and Elizabeth Gordon shared a house in London and rented a cottage in nearby Gomshall. Hale was a GP's daughter who had spent her childhood summers at The Hermitage in Holmwood. She worked in the information department of the WSPU, providing quotes and information to the press and to WSPU speakers. Her role became more significant when the printer of 'The Suffragette', (the magazine launched by Christabel Pankhurst to replace 'Votes for Women'), was imprisoned and the presses seized. Overnight Hale learned to typeset and not long afterwards, when the WSPU's offices were raided, she went undercover, producing the magazine in secret. She moved production from house to house to evade discovery, creeping in from the presses at dawn with papers stuffed down her blouse. Elizabeth Gordon was another artist. Hale and Gordon came down by train to Gomshall each weekend and walked the two miles into Peaslake to visit Marion Wallace Dunlop[17].

Window-smashing and the hunger strike were now accompanied by sporadic arson attacks. Though there were no reports of suffragettes causing damage in

Brackenside in Peaslake, home of the Brackenburys, and a place of refuge for hunger strikers. (Dorking Museum)

[17] In later life Cecily Hale wrote an autobiography. It was typed by Esther Knowles, Fred Pethick-Lawrence's secretary. After the First World War Hale trained as a health visitor. For many years she wrote the 'Baby Circle' column for 'Women's Own' magazine. She worked for the Girl Guiding association from 1947 to 1968.

Holmwood or Peaslake, there was anxiety at the presence of known militants in the villages. In April 1913 Sandra Bray's father-in-law, Sir Reginald Bray, urged vigilance. Suffragettes, he wrote in private correspondence, were known to be active in Shere and Peaslake and he had heard tell of them being seen near sixteenth-century High House in Shere at night. As the property was unoccupied, and therefore a possible target, he suggested keeping watch.

His fears were to some extent justified. By 1913 targets were no longer confined to prominent city buildings. On 19th February 1913 the empty home of Chancellor of the Exchequer, David Lloyd George, at Walton-on-the-Hill between Dorking and Reigate, was fire-bombed. Those responsible struck in the early hours of the morning. A car was spotted by local policeman heading towards Walton at 2.50am and returning towards London at 5am. Nearby residents heard the car, and the landlady of The Chequers Inn heard a car stop and voices in the nearby lane. Those responsible entered the house through a small window and set two home-made bombs. These were simple devices: a tin can full of gunpowder and nails bound with cord, with a parafin-soaked rag leading to a lit candle acting as a fuse. At 6 in the morning an explosion rattled windows at The Blue Ball pub. When the foreman of the works, James Gray, arrived for work he found ceilings wrecked and walls cracked. One bomb had detonated in a bedroom; the second, set up in a cupboard, had failed to go off when its candle was blown out by the blast from the first. Superintendent Coleman of Dorking police station called Special Branch.

Lloyd George's house at Walton-on-the-Hill was still under construction and unoccupied when it was targeted by suffragettes. Many theories have been put forward but it has never been possible to establish who was responsible. (Leatherhead Museum)

Speaking in Cardiff Mrs Pankhurst announced that her supporters had committed the act to awaken the Chancellor and that she would take responsibility for any such act that women felt driven to commit. Though she had had no personal involvement in the action, and probably knew nothing of it in advance, she claimed that she had advised, incited and conspired. The authorities need not look for the women who had actually planted the devices, she said, as she accepted responsibility. She was arrested on 24th February. She was brought to Leatherhead's Kingston Road police station, questioned, and detained overnight in the local police inspector's house. From Leatherhead she was driven to Epsom Police Court the following morning. (She was the first person to be conveyed to court in a car by the Surrey Constabulary.) The police turned out in large numbers to prevent any demonstration outside the court.

Mrs Pankhurst was charged with incitement to commit offences under the Malicious Injuries to Property Act 1861 and committed for trial at Guildford Assizes. Asked if she would apply for bail, she said that she could not give the necessary undertaking. She vowed to go on hunger strike if she were to be remanded in prison. If she was tried at the summer assizes it would be as a dying woman, she said. Though she claimed there was no evidence to implicate suffragettes, she was found guilty in April and sentenced to three years.

Shortly after the attack on Lloyd George's house, suffragettes set fire to Trevethan, home of Lady White, in Englefield Green. Two women on bikes were seen leaving the scene and papers left in the rockery read: *'Votes for Women'* and *'By kind permission of Mr Hobhouse'.* A bomb at Oxted Station in April 1913 was (probably erroneously) attributed to suffragettes. The partly-exploded device was found in the gentlemens' lavatory. It was a more sophisticated device than that used at Walton-on-the-Hill. A man's felt hat and pistol were also found at the scene. Investigations lead to a woman WSPU member in Battersea, but

GOLF LINKS DAMAGED AND HAY-STACKS SET ON FIRE.

Suffragettes visited the new Betchworth Park golf links at Dorking yesterday morning and damaged two greens by cutting the letters V.W. on them.

A haystack in the vicinity, belonging to a local farmer, was also set on fire and was practically destroyed before the fire brigade had extinguished the flames. A fireman says he saw three women disappearing as he arrived on the scene. The links were new ones, and were to have been opened next Saturday.

A stack of hay on the farm of one of Lord Derby's tenants, at Knowsley, near Liverpool, was also set on fire early yesterday morning. A message was left which read:—"This is the result of the Cat and Mouse Act."

Newspaper cutting reporting the vandalism of the newly opened Betchworth Golf Club by supporters of votes for women. Golf courses were considered legitimate targets as they generally excluded women. It is unknown who perpetrated the attack. (Dorking Museum)

150

Above: The police hold back crowds on Mrs Pankhurst's appearance in Epsom.
Below: Mrs Pankhurst leaving Epsom court (Leatherhead Museum)

local police had stopped a male cyclist and two young men claiming to be on night hikes early that morning, and they suspected that the young men had been disturbed as they planted the bomb. Theories abound: that the attack was a protest at Mrs Pankhurst's being imprisoned, perhaps carried out by male supporters; that it was carried out by men who wished to discredit women; and that it was totally unconnected with the campaign for the vote, but the work of anarchists.

In June 1913 an arson attack destroyed a stand at Hurst Park in West Molesey, and in August of that year the new Betchworth golf links near Dorking were attacked. A large 'V' and 'W' were carved into two of the greens and a nearby haystack was set alight. Three women were seen leaving the scene by firemen in the early hours of the morning. In June the following year there was an attempted arson attack at Chipstead Church near Reigate.

As a result of these activities, Brackenside in Peaslake came under surveillance in early 1914. Mrs Pankhurst had been in and out of prison since her conviction in relation to the attack on Lloyd George's house. After a stint in Dartmoor she was temporarily released in a fragile physical state and brought to convalesce in the village. The police kept watch on Brackenside from neighbouring houses, intent on preventing her from absconding.

If window-smashing caused unease in the general public, arson brought an even more mixed response, putting off as many supporters as it attracted. As the Pethick-Lawrences had predicted, increasingly violent attacks on property provoked hostility. They also served to entrench the government's position, as it could not be seen to give in to violence. Dismayed non-militants such as Millicent Fawcett regarded arson as being as much an obstacle to women getting the vote as Prime Minister Asquith. Non-militant suffrage groups took increasing pains to differentiate themselves from the WSPU.

Without the Pethick-Lawrences' steadying influence and with Christabel out of touch, both with the mood of the nation and with her own supporters, moderate campaigners were replaced by extremists. Damage escalated – to golf links, paintings, grandstands, churches and private residences. From Paris Christabel demanded sacrifice; but with women now serving out their sentences under the 'Cat and Mouse Act', the hunger strikes had lost effectiveness. The days of joyous rallies and spectacular processions were over.

Operationally things grew more difficult for the WSPU: landlords terminated leases on rented premises, venues declined bookings for meetings, and the police refused permission for rallies. The printer of 'The Suffragette' was arrested and the police occupied Lincoln's Inn House. The organization was being driven underground. Huge efforts were put into hunger strikes and evasion of the police, but less attention was paid to the business organization and fund-raising that had been Emmeline's Pethick-Lawrence's forte. Donations dropped; the WSPU cut back on paid organizers and office girls worried about their employment. And as the infrastructure of the organization disintegrated, action became more sporadic, unpredictable and personal in nature.

Emmeline Pethick-Lawrence's sister, Dorothy Pethick, made headlines on a visit to New York in early 1914. A WSPU organizer, she had travelled to the United States with Mrs Pankhurst on a speaking tour in 1909. Despite having left the WSPU with her sister, Dorothy, like Emmeline, stressed the ties of sympathy between suffrage supporters in a speech to the Equal Franchise Society. *'Let the women die'*, she said of those in prison in England, claiming that the hunger-strikers had embraced martyrdom. For a decade women had been fighting with not a drop of blood spilt but their own. But Black Friday had been a turning point. In allowing such atrocities men had shown no reverence for the women that they professed to cherish and protect, and women would no longer allow the fight to be conducted on their own bodies. From that point, she said, violence had been directed at the property that was the real object of male reverence.

Of the rift between her sister and Mrs Pankhurst, Dorothy does not admit much disparity of opinion: *'Mrs Pankhurst believes in arson and Mrs Pethick-Lawrence does not. She simply does not believe that it is advisable; that the time is not ripe for it.'* She did believe, claimed Dorothy, that there was still *'a very large and healthy amount of window-smashing to be done.'*

In Holmwood Fred and Emmeline continued to publish 'Votes for Women'. It became a forum where suffrage supporters of all hues, militant or otherwise, might spread the suffrage message. In November 1912 they had set

LET MILITANTS DIE, SAYS MISS PETHICK

They Are Willing to Sacrifice Their Lives, Mrs. Pankhurst's Friend Declares.

DIVIDED ONLY ON METHODS

Mrs. Pethick-Lawrence Holds That Arson Is Not Proper Just Now with So Many Windows Left.

Headline in 'The New York Times' on Dorothy Pethick's visit to the United States. Dorothy Pethick (1881-1970) was educated at Cheltenham Ladies' College. Like her older sister, she had taken up social work, (at the Women's University Settlement in Blackfriars), and had worked at a girls' club in Nottingham before becoming a WSPU organizer in 1907. In 1909 she organized a programme of WSPU events in Cornwall, at which her sister was a speaker. She went on to organize campaigns in Leicester, Reading and Oxford. She was imprisoned twice and underwent force-feeding. During the First World War she joined the Women's Auxiliary Service, serving as a police officer. In later life she became secretary of the progressive Steiner School in London.

153

up the Votes for Women Fellowship to promote it, and they found themselves at the centre of a loose group of suffragists who, for one reason or another, were not part of the WSPU: men, family and close associates, those who had always been opposed to militancy, those who had become uncomfortable at the escalation in property damage, and those who could not separate the women's campaign from socialism in general. The couple provided a base around which left-leaning suffragists and social reformers coalesced. By early 1914 Henry Nevinson, observing the strained relationship between WSPU headquarters and its supporters, felt that the organization's strength was slipping away. He was instrumental in forming the United Suffragists in February 1914. Evelyn Sharp joined its first committee. With many of their associates, including Mary Neal, transferring their allegiance, Fred and Emmeline dissolved the Votes for Women Fellowship and joined the new organisation. The United Suffragists adopted purple as one of its colours, alongside gold and white, and the motto *'Usque ad finem'*: 'until the end'. In August Fred and Emmeline gave 'Votes for Women' to the US as its house journal. Evelyn Sharp continued as its editor. Emmeline accepted a place on the organisation's committee and planned a suffrage tour of the world.

Though she was also expelled from the WSPU, Sylvia Pankhurst did not join the United Suffragists but continued to campaign with her East London Federation of the WSPU which integrated the campaign for the vote with action on wider socialist issues.

With the founding of the United Suffragists the WSPU lost the services of such influential men as Nevinson and George Lansbury, who had provided funds, advice and publicity. Finances were in disarray. Headquarters was forced to move from private house to private house, the police on its tail. (The Brackenbury residence became home to the WSPU in June 1914; it was raided by police after a few days.) And with women serving their sentences as a result of the Cat and Mouse Act, the Government largely had the organisation under control.

Relieved of their all-encompassing role in the fight for the vote, Fred and Emmeline turned their attention to other causes. During 1913 a lock-out of striking workers at the Jacob's biscuit factory in Dublin reduced families to destitution. Emmeline sent Mary Neal out to offer a home at The Sundial to malnourished children. Neal met with resistance from Catholic labour leaders, fearful of attempts to convert the children to Protestantism. She telegraphed Emmeline asking if the children might be accompanied by a mother and Emmeline persuaded the Irish peer, Lord Ashbourne, who lived nearby at Moorhurst, to allow the priest attached to his residence to minister to the spiritual needs of the children. On arrival in Holmwood the children were so ridden with lice that a farm labourer who doubled as the village barber cut their hair and burned it. Six of the children attended school in South Holmwood for three months. In January 1914 Emmeline addressed a suffrage rally in Dublin; the front row was occupied by the children, all dressed in green caps and jerseys donated in Holmwood by Emmeline's sister, and their mothers.

In May 1914 the South African suffragist, pacifist and writer on socialism and gender and racial equality, Olive Schreiner (1855-1920) stayed with the Pethick-Lawrences at The Mascot. Not many months later it was Belgian refugees that Emmeline was bringing to Holmwood.

Marguerite Douglas of Lawbrook

Lawbrook, a grand mansion and small farm between Gomshall and Shere, was the birthplace of Marguerite 'Margot' Laura Douglas (1885-1963), honorary secretary of the WSPU in Worthing. It had previously been the home of Arthur Pooley Onslow, grandfather of Sandra Bray. Marguerite Douglas was the daughter of the painter of portraits, animals and country scenes, Edwin Douglas. She painted but had no career in art. Nor did she marry, though as a girl she had fallen in love with a stable boy, keeping a gift of the dressing-table set that he had given her all her life. She returned to campaigning in 1938 when she was instrumental in preventing the urban creep of Worthing onto the downland at High Salvington in Sussex.

Lord Ashbourne of Moorhurst and the woman who shot Mussolini

When Emmeline needed to find a Catholic place of worship for the Irish children being brought to The Sundial in Holmwood in 1913, she turned to near neighbour, William Gibson, Lord Ashbourne (1869-1942). He lived nearby at Moorhurst. He was the son of Edward Gibson, 1st Lord Ashbourne, the former Irish Chancellor.

The 2nd Lord Ashbourne came from an aristocratic Protestant family but he had converted to Catholicism. He was known for parading around Holmwood in Irish national dress, including a kilt and sporran in which he allegedly kept a turtle. Succeeding to the title at about the time of the children's stay in Holmwood, Lord Ashbourne was virtually disinherited by his father because of his Irish nationalism. His sister, Violet Gibson, gained notoriety when she shot the Italian Fascist leader, Benito Mussolini, in 1926.

War, Peace and the Vote

Crowds gathered to see the Dorking company of Territorials off from the station on August 5th 1914, the day after war was declared. (Dorking Museum)

Fred and Emmeline were in the garden at The Mascot when they heard of the assassination of Archduke Franz Ferdinand on 28th June 1914. On the outbreak of war six weeks later Mrs Pankhurst and Christabel announced that the WSPU would abandon the struggle for the vote, to the astonished outrage of many of their supporters. Victory, they said, must take precedence over women's enfranchisement, and they turned their energies to recruiting men for the army. The National Union of Women's Suffrage Societies also announced the suspension of all 'political' work. Its leadership urged members to devote their energies to the relief of distress occasioned by the war as this was the best way that they could come to their country's aid. Leith Hill WSS members began collecting funds for national initiatives. Members joined local committees for the relief of distress and supported refugees from Belgium. A special fund was set up to support girls who had lost their jobs as a result of the declaration of war.

For Emmeline Pethick-Lawrence the cause of international peace was a natural extension of her fight for women's rights; to her, the outbreak of war was confirmation of the folly of leaving political power solely in the hands of men. Mrs Pankhurst and Christabel were essentially conservative, but for social revolutionaries like Sylvia Pankhurst and Fred and Emmeline, whose political sympathies lay with the Labour movement, the vote was not an end in itself but a means to an end. War did not bring an end to injustice, poverty or suffering but exacerbated it; the campaign for the vote, therefore, with its promise of social change, would go on.

Late 1914 saw an influx of disappointed WSPU members to the United Suffragists. They were joined by pacifists and others who questioned the necessity of war. Fred and Emmeline's transfer of 'Votes for Women' to the United Suffragists in August 1914 gave the organisation a higher public profile, just as the better-known WSPU ceased campaigning. Unlike the WSPU, the United Suffragists was not a one-issue organisation: it campaigned on wider terms, and 'Votes for Women' addressed employment and other issues of social justice during the war years. The organization also undertook philanthropic work. By 1917 the United Suffragists' membership comprised a broad spectrum of ex-WSPU activists and non-militant NUWSS supporters. Meanwhile Sylvia Pankhurst continued to work for social change and labour rights through her East End Federation and spent the war working to combat its devastating effects on working families, providing soup kitchens and nurseries.

War put an end to Emmeline's plan for a suffrage speaking tour of the world. But in October 1914 she was invited to address a mass meeting at Carnegie Hall in New York to inaugurate a new suffrage campaign in the United States. She saw this as an opportunity to enlist the support of the suffrage movement in neutral America in the cause of peace in Europe. She sailed on October 19th and arrived in New York on the 26th, staying at the Women's Cosmopolitan Club. She found many American women keen to combine the campaign for the vote with a commitment to keep the United States out of the war. The women's peace movement grew from the coming together of those two aims, aired and discussed at Emmeline's meetings and lectures. In November she told a New York audience that the campaign for the vote must go on in Britain and America. She did not claim that the war would not have happened had women had the vote; but she believed that women's influence could work to prevent war in general. In correspondence she began to formulate plans for the promotion of a movement to establish what she called an 'eternal commonwealth'.

She also took time to study the way that New York children's courts worked, and how the city dealt with its prostitutes, and met Madeleine Doty, a campaigning

MRS. PETHICK LAWRENCE IN AMERICA

The American papers are full of Mrs. Pethick Lawrence's tour, conducted through the States on behalf of an international women's peace movement which shall tend to prevent wars in the future and insist upon the immediate enfranchisement of women as well as men.

In an interview with the New York *Evening World*, Mrs. Lawrence spoke of the Suffrage movement in England. "Unless something unforeseen brings us the victory, militancy must go on," she is reported to have said. "The war is a thing apart, which has brought only a temporary truce. Ah! you American women hardly appreciate your good fortune! Here, with your slogan of 'Victory in 1915' [this refers to the movement in New York State] and a real possibility of that victory, you have only to educate the public and the vote will be yours. But with us the public is already educated, yet we are to all appearances no nearer success than before."

Asked if she thought that with the vote English women could have averted the war, Mrs. Lawrence replied: "Ah! hardly that. But they could do much to prevent another war—woman's influence in all countries must work for that."

Emmeline's tour of the United States is reported back at home. Asked if she thought that if English women had had the vote, war might have been averted, she said she thought it unlikely, but that women could do much to prevent another war.

157

lawyer who had voluntarily and anonymously gone to prison to experience life there on being appointed a prison commissioner.

Emmeline was scheduled to travel on from the United States to Japan but she found herself in such demand as a speaker that she abandoned her onward travel plans. Before setting off with the National Women's Peace Party on a tour billed as Women's War on War, Emmeline resigned her position on the committee of the United Suffragists. She wished to be able to speak freely on international issues, unconstrained by the policies of any campaign group. At the end of October she suggested that Fred come out to join her and add his voice to the campaign. Plans were put in place to travel to Boston, Montana and Nebraska. In November she spoke in Washington, visited Chicago with Jane Addams, and travelled to Milwaukee, St Paul and Minneapolis; in December she was in West Virginia. At large public meetings she urged governments to enfranchise women in order to completely democratize their nations so that they might make a constructive peace when the war was over. Fred spoke of the stupendous cost of the war in lives and economic waste.

Emmeline's progress in the United States was reported in 'Votes for Women', which Evelyn Sharp now billed as the *war paper for women'*. In April 1915 Emmeline returned to Europe on the liner 'Noordam' with the American delegation to the International Women's Congress for Peace in The Hague. Hosted in a neutral country, the conference brought together women from neutral and combatant nations to discuss a response to the war, which, it was now clear, was not to be the quick and decisive engagement that all had hoped for, but which had settled into stagnant trench warfare across a 600 mile front. The British government was deeply opposed to British women travelling to talk about peace in a neutral nation. It made strenuous attempts to prevent British delegates attending, closing down the ferry service to the continent and refusing to issue passports to travel. Emmeline was one of only three British delegates to reach The Hague; the other two had gone out earlier as organizers. Evelyn Sharp was one of those refused a passport. Forty-four delegates attended from the United States, alongside 28 from Germany, 16 from Hungary, and four from Austria. Other delegates came from Belgium, Denmark, Sweden, Norway, Italy, Spain, Russia, Poland and Brazil.

Fred wrote detailed reports on conference proceedings for 'Votes for Women'. Of particular interest to his readers was the conference demand that women should share all civil and political rights and responsibilities on the same terms as men. He concluded one report with the hope that the harmony shown amongst the women, even from belligerent nations, might be a good augury of the effect that women would have on international relations should they take their place with men in the democracies of the world.

The Women's International League was formed at the conference. Emmeline, with her international reputation, became treasurer of the British group that was affiliated to the International Committee of Women for Permanent Peace. (The committee is now known as the Women's International League for Peace and

Emmeline Pethick-Lawrence (far left, holding the banner) on the liner 'Noordam' on her way from the United States to The Hague women's peace conference in April 1915. She is pictured with the US delegates, including Jane Addams. (Library of Congress)

Freedom.) On her return home she spoke at public meetings and wrote long pieces for 'Votes for Women' on the conclusions of the conference. In a speech at Kingsway Hall in June 1915 she found parallels between men's suppression of women and the use of force in international relations. The women's movement had challenged the supremacy of material things, she said, and instead asserted the sacredness of the human body, of the divinity of the human soul, and of the liberty of the human spirit. Women had opposed the notion that force gives men the right to take what they want from women and to keep them in a position of subordination. Women would now oppose the acceptance of the rule of force in the political world as a legitimate means of settling international issues. For the rest of the war she campaigned for a negotiated settlement between the warring nations. She also opposed conscription when it was brought in in January 1916. Charlotte Marsh, who also followed Emmeline to the United Suffragists and worked for a while as Lloyd George's driver, joined her on the staff of the Women's International League.

In Holmwood the Mascot became a refuge for Fred and Emmeline's war-haunted London circle. Emmeline's brother Harold returned from Canada and left his wife, Evelyn 'Evie' at The Mascot when he enlisted. Dr Marie Pethick took refuge there to recover from the stress of repeated night calls during air raids; Emmeline was devastated when she collapsed and died unexpectedly whilst taking casualties to the Euston Road Women's Hospital. Mary Neal succumbed to the stresses of overwork; the shock of the Silvertown explosion near her home in East London precipitated a nervous breakdown. And the couple's London home at Clement's Inn suffered war damage. They relocated to a pair of apartments in nearby Lincoln's Inn, which they occupied for the rest of their lives, one serving as living accommodation, the other as office space.

Alongside her work for peace, Emmeline continued to campaign for women's suffrage, in print and at public meetings. Had women like her, and magazines like 'Votes for Women', not kept the issue in the mind of politicians, it is likely that the cause would have slipped from the political agenda during the war years. Emmeline was keen to ensure that that should not happen despite accusations that to carry on campaigning was unpatriotic and a distraction from the war effort. Many who abandoned the campaign in the early days of the war returned to the cause in later years, disappointed that, as Julie Spring Rice wrote to Lord Farrer in 1916: *'the very statesmen who asked and advised us to do nothing on account of the war now say there is no sign of our wanting the vote'.*

In some ways the war played into the hands of campaigners. For decades women had been told that they did not need or could not have the vote because they did not play a major part in civil society or they did not encounter the dangers of war in the way that men did. Now, with increasing demands that women leave the home and take on economic and community roles, and with zeppelin attacks bringing the dangers of war to civilians, neither argument applied. 'Votes for Women' was not slow to point out how the needs of war had undermined the position of those who refused to countenance the vote for women. Satirical magazine covers highlighted the irony of government telling women that their place was in the home only for ministers to now demand that they join the workforce. They also pointed out the hypocrisy of women being encouraged to play a major part in the war effort and the war economy, but without being rewarded or incentivized to do so, either by any commitment to allow them the vote, or by offering equal pay for taking on male roles. As women moved into the workplace in higher numbers, discrimination against them became more evident, at a time when government wanted women to move into employment.

'Votes for Women' addressed economic and social issues arising from the war from a female perspective. Many of the issues it covered - poverty, low pay, child mortality - were long-term concerns of Emmeline and Evelyn Sharp, though they were exacerbated by the deprivations of war. Though its editor, Evelyn Sharp, was a pacifist who later became a member of the Society of Friends (Quakers), the magazine was not overtly opposed to the war, though some of its content was. Its editorials were opportunistic in their interpretations, happy to promote what women were doing for the war effort and their advances out of the home in support of the argument for the vote.

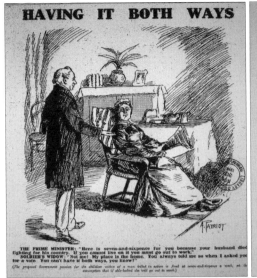

HAVING IT BOTH WAYS

THE PRIME MINISTER: "Here is seven-and-sixpence for you because your husband died fighting for his country. If you cannot live on it you must go out to work."
SOLDIER'S WIDOW: "Not me! My place is in the home. You always told me so when I asked you for a vote. You can't have it both ways, you know!"

(The proposed Government pension for the soldier widow of a man killed in action is fixed at seven-and-sixpence a week, yet the assumption is that if able-bodied she will go out to work.)

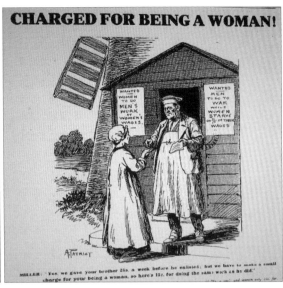

CHARGED FOR BEING A WOMAN!

MILLER: "Yes, we gave your brother 25s. a week before he enlisted; but we have to make a small charge for your being a woman, so here's 15s. for doing the same work as he did."

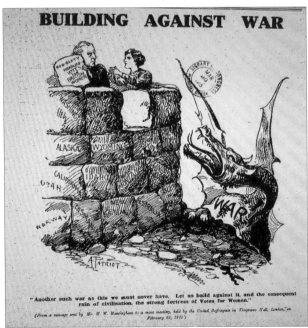

BUILDING AGAINST WAR

"Another such war as this we must never have. Let us build against it, and the consequent ruin of civilisation, the strong fortress of Votes for Women."

(From a message sent by Mr. H. W. Massingham to a mass meeting, held by the United Suffragists in Kingsway Hall, London, on February 25, 1915.)

Above left: A cover from 'Votes for Women' draws attention to the irony of the same voices who had told women that their place was in the home now demanding that they go out to work. When Mr Asquith tells a soldier's widow that she must work if she cannot live on her meagre pension she tells him that her place is in the home, as he has always told her when she demanded the vote, and that he cannot have it both ways. In another cartoon cover the anti-suffrage squire's wife tells a young mother that her place is no longer in the home but in the turnip field. Above right:' Votes for Women' highlights the injustice of employers taking the opportunity to reduce wages by requiring women who step up to fill labour shortages to work for less pay than men. For many the war only confirmed their commitment to fighting for women's involvement in the political process. Below: In this optimistic cover from 'Votes for Women' the states and nations that have granted the vote to women form a wall against the beast of war. A woman tries to plug the gap by wresting the last block, engraved with 'Votes for British women' from Mr Asquith. The cartoon is signed by A. Patriot; this was the signature of artist Alfred Pearse (1855-1933). (Library of Congress)

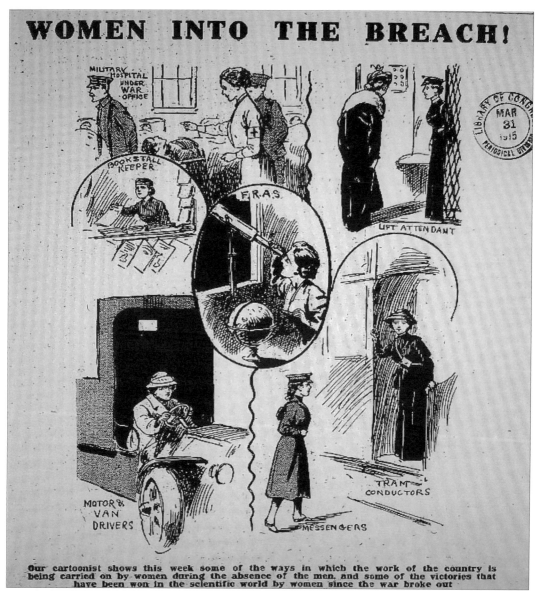

A 'Votes for Women' cover highlights the variety of work now being undertaken by women (including the running of War Office hospitals), and the advances made by women since the outbreak of war. (Library of Congress,)

The editor of 'Votes for Women' was not alone in spotting the opportunity for women to win respect through their contribution to the war effort. The Brackenburys of Peaslake were involved in an overt initiative to prove women's worth at the same time as carrying out work of indisputable importance. In 1914 two militant suffragette doctors, Louisa Garrett Anderson (1873-1943) and Flora Murray established a military hospital solely staffed by women. Louisa was the daughter of Dr Elizabeth Garrett Anderson (1836-1917), the first woman to qualify in England as a doctor. Louisa had been involved with Nurse Catherine Pine's London convalescent home for WSPU hunger strikers. In 1914 she joined Fred and Emmeline in the United Suffragists when the Pankursts gave up campaigning. Unable to obtain permission from the military authorities to set up a hospital in England on account of their criminal records, she and Dr Murray set up in Paris, then in Wimereux near Boulogne, with the French Red Cross. Anderson and Murray adopted the WSPU's motto *'deeds not words'* as a declaration of their intention to convince the authorities of women's competence to establish and manage a military hospital, and by extension, to vote. After their success in France, they were invited to establish a hospital at Endell Street, near Drury Lane in London's Covent Garden. The Endell Street Military Hospital was staffed and run entirely by women and eventually had 573 beds. Over 25,000 patients were treated there. Emmeline's Pethick-Lawrence's sister, Marie, worked as a doctor at Endell Street, and Peaslake's indomitable Hilda Brackenbury, was singing to patients at the age of 86. Murray and Anderson educated those who came to work for them and those who passed through the hospital on the ethos and justice of the campaign for the vote.

It was not the only such initiative. The NUWSS supported the Scottish Women's Suffrage Hospitals initiative, and a meeting was held in Dorking to raise funds to support it in July 1915; by September £20.4.2 had been raised by the Reigate and Redhill society and £25 by the Leith Hill society. In 1914 Dr Alice Hutchison had taken a team of female doctors and nurses to establish a field hospital in Serbia and been held as a prisoner of war in Austria until an exchange of prisoners. In May 1916 she came to Dorking public halls to speak to the women of the Leith Hill and District WSS. The proceeds from the night were donated to the London Women's Suffrage Society which was coordinating efforts to support similar units. The success of such initiatives, as well as work undertaken by women in towns and villages all over Britain, did much to expunge the memory of the excesses of the militant campaign.

As men left for the services, manpower grew scarce and women took over community organizations, from bell-ringing to businesses. In the towns and villages of the Surrey Hills they moved into areas of work that been previously reserved for men. In 1914 Frances Morris became temporary head teacher at South Holmwood School; Lucy Strudwick saw the school through from 1916 to the end of the war. Newdigate

Alice Hutchison came to talk to the Leith Hill and District WSS about her experiences in hospitals in Serbia and as a prisoner of war in 1916. (Reproduced by permission of Scottish Women's Hospitals www.scottishwomenshospitals)

School also appointed its first female head teacher. Women became postal workers, munitions workers, station 'masters' and shop workers. They took over the running of areas of life from which they would have previously been excluded: Maggie Worrow, wife of the landlord of the Norfolk Arms hotel on the road south of Dorking, took on the role of treasurer to the local branch of the Ancient Order of Foresters, (as well as running the business), when her husband was called up. Ralph Vaughan Williams was surprised to find 17 year-old Ann Stewart installing his telephone at Leith Hill Place. Some even lost their lives whilst on war service.

Some were sceptical of women's abilities. In 1916 the 'Dorking Advertiser' reported the Home Secretary's expression of doubt *'that the public would have confidence in women drivers of taxicabs and motor omnibuses'* in answer to the suggestion that he bring in women to undertake such work. A farmer's wife from Newdigate wrote to the paper: *'Woe betide England if the land falls to women to cultivate!'* But others seized the initiative. On the national level, Millicent Fawcett, leader of the NUWSS, was talking to government about heading up a scheme to get women into work as early as 1915. In Dorking her niece, Bessie Rawlings, urged women to come forward to replace men.

Submarine warfare and declining imports led to food shortages. The nation needed to produce more food, but with a reduced male workforce. Villages appointed registrars to recruit for the War Agricultural Service for Women. Constance Aston of Sondes Place, representing Dorking Rural District Council on the Surrey Committee for Women and Farm Labour, called upon women to come forward to work on the land so that schoolboys could finish their education. After training with the land army, women were issued with a masculine uniform of breeches and boots and a green armband with a red crown. Their efforts were celebrated: women who had earned an armlet for working more than 30 days (or 240 hours) on the land were invited to tea at St Martin's by the Dorking District Committee of the Women's Branch of the Board of Agriculture and presented with stripes in recognition of their work at the Public Halls. In October 1918 the 'Dorking Advertiser' reported that demand for land army women far exceeded supply and that farmers employing the women were *'practically unanimous in their praises'*.

The war changed what was thought acceptable or even possible for women. More than one local woman died as a result of their changing roles: Grace King of Abinger died in France whilst serving at the Cantine des Anglais in Paris. Closer to home Lisma Feilding of Betchworth took over running her family's estate and died when her skirts got caught in machinery. And Daisy Wadling, was given a full military funeral at Dorking cemetery. Daisy was the daughter of Lieutenant Colonel Wadling of Townfield. Her sister, Ellen, was a nurse at St Thomas's Hospital who crossed to France with the British Expeditionary Force; she remained there for the duration of the war, was mentioned in dispatches for gallant conduct, and was awarded the RRC and the Mons Star. Daisy was serving as a driver in the Army Service Corps when she caught a 'cold' whilst driving to Chatham on duty. The cold turned out to be influenza. Daisy developed pneumonia and was transferred to the

Women in the Surrey Hills saw their lives and opportunities transformed by the war. They volunteered as VAD nurses, and took over businesses, voluntary organizations, and community services, adopting more practical dress styles then pre-war fashions. Many middle-class women had never worked outside the home before the war. Top: Female land workers on Box Hill; Bottom left: Mrs and Miss Turner of Dorking dressed for 'war work' at a butcher's on the High Street; middle: Edith Sheppard was one of the first women stationmasters, first at Ardingly in West Sussex and then in Dorking; right: Nellie Peters from Dorking in the uniform of the Chilworth Gunpowder works. (Dorking Museum)

Endell Street Military Hospital, where she died in September 1918. Her coffin was covered with a Union Flag and carried, with her military cap on top, to her funeral in Dorking by Army Service Corps bearers. After the funeral service a firing party of local volunteers fired in salute. It would have gratified the women of the Endell Street Hospital to see the local paper comment that: *'We cannot but feel that the services so nobly rendered by the women of England for their country are worthy of all honour and gratitude.'* That a military funeral could be held for a woman in a small market town indicates the changes in women's lives, and the acceptance of their emancipation, that the war brought.

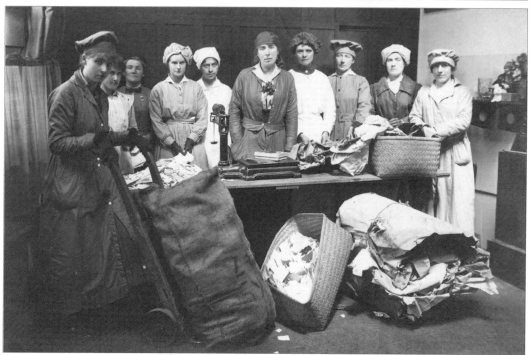

Members of the Leith Hill Women's Suffrage Society volunteering with the Dorking Waste Paper Depot at Nower Lodge. The recycling depot was established in 1917 to raise funds for the Dorking Hospital Supply Depot established by fellow suffrage-supporter, Lady Evangeline 'Eva' Farrer, above left, with Violette Wood. (Images reproduced by permission of John Molyneux and the Farrer family.)

At the end of the war many women returned to traditional roles, but they had changed attitudes towards women's capabilities. And towards women's suffrage. As early as November 1916 a 'Dorking Advertiser' editorial recognized the involvement of women in every aspect of national life: *'It is unthinkable that they – numbering half the nation and vitally concerned in every phase of national activity – should remain without any direct influence on the levying of those taxes and the making of those laws,'* it announced.

The Representation of the People Act 1918 was not initiated by any overwhelming need to give women the vote. It primarily addressed the anomaly whereby male householders who had served their country were effectively disenfranchised at the coming election as they had not resided at their address for the qualifying period of a year. The women's vote was peripheral to the necessity of ensuring that those who had fought could vote. But its achievement owed much to the general re-balancing of the relationship between the individual and the state at the end of the war. The state had resorted to conscription, and it had encouraged women into civil life; and towards the end of the war there was a questioning of what the state owed to its people and what their stake in it should be. In the main this focused on men of military age, and for the first time the country provided individual graves and memorials to non-officers and working men. There was an acknowledgment that the country had changed. The era of the volunteer army was over; men had been required to fight and to die, and in the post-war election many of them would not have the vote, either because of their youth, their status, or because they had been out of the country so long that they no longer satisfied the residency criteria. It was inconceivable that men who had been forced to fight, should have no say in their government. Men and women demanded a return for what they had done. And that women had played their part in a time of crisis could not be denied because women like Emmeline Pethick-Lawrence and the United Suffragists had made sure that the message never faltered. Because of their efforts, the question of the vote for women was on the table when government planned an extension to the franchise.

Emmeline Pethick-Lawrence had repeatedly warned against dropping the campaign for the vote during the war years on the basis of vague promises of reform after the war was won. And the United Suffragists had continued to press the government. Cartoons in 'Votes for Women' had mocked politicians for first exhorting women to cease campaigning and support the war effort as a matter of patriotism, and then using evidence of them having done so to conclude that there was no longer a desire for the vote. One cover likened Emmeline's warning to women to take care of duplicitous politicians to the crow in the fable who drops the cheese he has snatched to the flattering fox.

In 1917 government proposed a conference to discuss electoral reform. In March Lady Farrer chaired a meeting of the Leith Hill and District WSS at Oddfellows Hall. The women were accused of ending the truce in political campaigning that had been agreed at the outbreak of war. But Lady Farrer argued that it was government that had raised the issue of electoral reform, and as it had done so, women must know what was proposed. They must not, she said, find themselves too busy with everyday activities to forget to lift up their eyes to the horizon *'where some day the sun will rise on a country nominally at peace, but in reality with every kind of difficulty in front of it, and... women must have a role in the settling of these difficulties'*. Women must not be caught sleeping, she said, or there was a danger that their claims would be laid aside. They must push now for the vote, or see it once again sidestepped. Speaking after Lady Farrer, Geraldine Cokke warned of the dangers of prolonged discontent and unrest amongst women. She was not, she said, referring to the militant methods of the pre-war years, but to women who were engaged in work for social good, but who came up against laws that they could not influence; if this continued after the war, she warned, dissatisfied women might defect from useful work and return to campaigning. The meeting agreed that nothing should be done to hamper the running of the war effort, but that the society should be ready to take action, should it be needed. Members then approved a motion to support the granting of the vote to women aged 35 and over.

Women's war work is often credited with having achieved in a few years what generations of peaceful campaigning and a decade of militancy had not. However, it is unlikely that the vote would have been granted were it not for the campaigners of the United Suffragists and others who kept the issue on the political agenda throughout the war years, and to the small branches like the Leith Hill and District WSS, who had announced their readiness to take up campaigning again should they need to. Though the militant campaign had engendered resistance to the vote for women by 1914, as the war drew to a close politicians had no desire to go back to the struggle against militancy that would likely recommence on the outbreak of peace. The recognition of women's war work reflected a change in public perception of women, but it also provided a face-saving rationale for granting the

---

Robert Calverly Trevelyan

The poet Robert Calverly Trevelyan (1872-1951) was a good friend of Fred Pethick-Lawrence from their time together at Wixenford School. The brother of the historian GM Trevelyan, before the war he had travelled to India with the novelist EM Forster. During the war he was living at Shiffolds in Holmbury St Mary.

A member of the Society of Friends (Quakers), Trevelyan was a pacifist. The prominent anti-war campaigner, mathematician and philosopher, Bertrand Russell, stayed with him at Shiffolds in December 1915. When conscription was introduced in 1916 Trevelyan sheltered fellow poet John Rodker who had refused to be conscripted and gone on the run. Rodker was eventually caught in April 1917 and imprisoned in Dartmoor.

vote without appearing to give in to militant tactics.

There were many factors at play in the decision to give women the vote in 1918. The more sympathetic David Lloyd George was now Prime Minister, and the increase in number of Labour MPs meant that the old Liberal/Conservative balance that had been so threatened by the prospect of the female vote, no longer held. When the Act passed into law on 16th February 1918, the vote was granted to women over the age of thirty who were householders, who were married to householders, or who occupied property worth over £5 in value, or who were graduates. Men were entitled to vote from twenty-one; those who had served in the forces during the war could vote at nineteen. The fact that women were not granted the vote on a like-for-like basis with men ensured that men remained the electoral majority until 1928. Far from rewarding the primarily young, single women whose work on the land and in the munitions factories had been so celebrated, the vote was given to older, primarily married, women.

Had the United Suffragists not continued to campaign throughout the war, and particularly in the run up to the reform, it is unlikely that even such a concession as this would have been achieved. Campaigners were not content with the inequality of the 1918 act, but they were not about to push for more and risk ending up with nothing once again. And to demand complete equality was problematic for married women were not householders in their own right, so if the vote was granted on terms of strict equality married women, who under the 1918 act claimed a right to vote through their husbands' status as householders, would be disqualified. It was an argument that had another ten years to run.

On the cessation of hostilities on 11th November 1918, anti-suffrage campaigner Bertha Broadwood wrote one of her poems:

Whom have we British fought? The Devil incarnate.
First temper, then forceful driver of a slave,-
A would-be tyrant over kingdoms, Church and state, -
A maniac: manacled 'gainst mercy's sign to save!
How have we fought? - Beside our foes of but ten decades past,
Starting mere thousands! Despised of many-millioned enemy
Who dreamt of crushing Britain's power, then France at last -
After some forty years of 'peaceful' pushing treachery -
with all his devil-master's will to spoil and damn,
Through abuse of Heaven - born laws of science and of art,
Regardless of honour's faith towards God, or man,
Fiendishly confident to cowe, or kill man, body, soul and heart.

And God our hope, wearied by braggart's blasphemies
Has justified His word, as each free nation now rejoicing sees.

There is no sign in Bertha's tortuous verse of any appreciation of the changes that the war had brought, or anticipation of the changed circumstances that its aftermath would bring, either in its poetry or imagery, or in its social structures and political allegiances. As far as Bertha and many others were concerned it was 'job done' and back to normal. For the Pethick-Lawrences and other social and economic reformers, and for millions of newly enfranchised women, the vote was a first step to changing their world.

At the end of the war both Emmeline and Fred saw their future in Parliament. Fred had stood as the 'Peace by Negotiation' candidate at a by-election in Aberdeen South in 1917; he was defeated by the Liberal candidate. In early 1918 he was selected to stand for Labour in Hastings in the general election of December 1918. But in the euphoria of expected victory, there was hostility towards those who had not fought and who had favoured a negotiated settlement. Letters to the Hastings papers mocked the Labour party for selecting a candidate who had supported 'compromise peace' negotiations. Referencing his wife – *'a persuasive, suave type of public speaker'* – and his work for women's enfranchisement, one writer asserted that thoughtful women voters would know that anyone who considered compromise with *'the obscene and brutal Hun'* was no friend of women. *'We do not wish to add to the very small but very loudly assertive group of Pacifists in our Parliament'*, he concluded. Another called it an insult that the Labour party wished to bring a pacifist to Hastings and urged Fred to enlist if he wanted to win. With no prospect of winning, Fred withdrew his candidacy. His planned parliamentary career, so long put on hold while he gave his energies to the suffrage campaign, was further delayed by his stance on the war.

Emmeline stood as the Labour candidate for Rusholme in Manchester. She advocated a just settlement with Germany as a necessity for the achievement of permanent peace. Esther Knowles was her campaign secretary. It was the first election at which women could stand and had she been elected she would have been amongst the first women MPs. She was unsuccessful. She turned her attention instead to campaigning with Evelyn Sharp to raise the blockade on Europe and to feed its displaced people. Deploring the Versailles settlement from the beginning, Fred predicted another war.

Only one woman was elected to Parliament in the first election in which women were eligible to stand. Constance Markievicz nee Gore-Booth (1868-1927) was elected for Sinn Fein in Dublin St Patrick's. She did not take her seat.

After the war Fred and Emmeline decided to simplify their lives and to live without live-in staff. The Mascot was suffering from the increase in motor traffic through Holmwood, and in the spring of 1920 they put the house, The Sundial, the garage in Norfolk Road, the three tenanted cottages facing Holmwood Common, and the two in Buckingham Road, up for auction in five lots. Fred and Emmeline moved to the more isolated village of Peaslake. Mr Rapley went with them; a score of old associates would soon join them there.

Fred, conscription, and the Dorking Military Tribunal

Like Emmeline, Fred opposed the war and believed that the warring nations should work towards a negotiated settlement, rather than fighting for all-out victory. He served as treasurer of the Union of Democratic Control, the leading anti-war movement to which many left-leaning politicians, journalists and intellectuals were affiliated. For many on the left the war was not a war of working people, who, they argued, had more in common with the working men of Germany and Italy than with the upper classes in their own country, and who stood to suffer most in terms of losses and to gain little by victory.

In 1918 conscription was extended to men under the age of 50; at 46 Fred was liable to serve. He applied for an exemption on the grounds that he was an objector, of a political rather than a conscientious kind, stating that he was not opposed to war on principle, but that he believed this war to be immoral. Old anti-suffrage opponent Alfred Keep was a member of the Dorking Military Tribunal which awarded the exemption on condition that he did work of national importance. An application on behalf of the chauffeur and gardener William Rapley was refused and he was called up for employment on the land.

The authorities seemed unsure what to do with Fred once his exemption had been established: whether to punish him or to make use of his offer to be of use in a non-military capacity. He was offered a labouring job at 35 shillings a week by old comrade FE Green at Baringsfield, but though the proposal was approved by the Committee for Work of National Importance, it was judged by the local Tribunal to be of insufficient importance. The Rev Fred Hankinson stepped in and arranged a job at 27 shillings a week with Mr Batchelor of Wattlehurst Farm in Capel. Fred speculated that the difference between the two placements was that the latter farm was partly in Sussex and therefore perceived as being of greater inconvenience, so satisfying Tribunal members that the work also encompassed an element of punishment.

Fred bicycled to the farm every day and made himself useful to the farmer, helping out with his form filling. Of his Newdigate associates, John Aitcheson also obtained an exemption. FE Green was too old to serve, and continued to campaign against child labour and low agricultural wages.

Fred continued to take an interest in the lives of his neighbours. Just after the end of the war he took up the cause of Holmwood's commoners at the instigation of fellow suffrage-supporter Anne Garrett of Holm Cottage. When industrialist M. Aguet of Mill House proposed enclosing a piece of common next to his home and replacing it with an area some distance away, so depriving local residents of their rights to use it, Fred took up their case with the Duke of Norfolk's agent and with fellow suffrage campaigner, Lord Farrer, who was president of the Commons and Footpaths Preservation Society.

John Langdon-Davies and The Sundial

The practical humanitarian spirit of the Pethick-Lawrences was matched by that of the journalist and war correspondent who bought The Sundial from them in 1921. John Langdon-Davies (1897-1971) was from a Quaker background. Like Fred, he refused to fight in the First World War; his stance lost him his Oxford scholarship and brought him a prison sentence. He probably met Fred and Emmeline through the Union of Democratic Control. In May 1921 he and his wife, Constance, travelled with them through France and Andorra to Spain.

The Langdon-Davies were also involved in Labour politics. They supported Sylvia Pankhurst's Ethiopian campaign and he covered the Spanish Civil War. His experiences in Spain turned him from polemicist to activist. He witnessed huge numbers of refugees in Santander, many of them children. One boy had a note pinned to him saying *'This is Jose. I am his father. When Santander falls I shall be shot, whoever finds my son, take care of him for me.'* Langdon-Davies founded 'Foster Parents Plan for Children in Spain' with Eric Muggeridge to care for and educate such children. PLAN now works in 45 countries.

Langdon-Davies was a prolific writer on history, politics, and science. During the Second World War he was recruited by Tom Winteringham, ex-commander of the British Battalion of the International Brigade in Spain, into the Home Guard South Eastern Fieldcraft School – an organization suffused with the socialist spirit of the Spanish veterans. He wrote the 'Homeguard Fieldcraft Manual' and 'Homeguard Warfare'. His son, Robin, was a founder of the Oxford Fund for Famine Relief (Oxfam).

Langdon-Davies often walked from The Sundial to visit EM Forster in Abinger and the Pethick-Lawrences at Fourways. When he went to live in Spain with his second wife, Patricia, Fred and Emmeline joined him as clients on his historical tours. *(Langdon-Davies with his sons in the 1950s, by permission of Patricia Langdon-Davies)*

Max Plowman and May Start – celebrating peace in 1919

May Start (1882-1957) began life in the London millinery trade and went to work for Fred and Emmeline in 1901. As the couple's housekeeper she was responsible for the practicalities of life at Clement's Inn and The Mascot and for the care of visitors. During their imprisonment in 1912 May and Mary Neal kept the households running. Like Mr Rapley, May was part of the couple's close circle and she knew her employers' associates well. When Adah Stuart Franks of Peaslake, whose brother was a colleague in the settlement movement, died in 1916 she left remembrances to her friend May. Often referred to by Emmeline as Mai Mai, May married Wilfred Walter in 1925. The couple took the surname Start-Walter.

The Pethick-Lawrences' friend Max Plowman (1883-1941) was the only serving member of the armed forces to be court martialled for refusing to return to fight after announcing his opposition to all war. He wrote a volume of poetry and a pamphlet denouncing the society that had perpetrated such a war, followed by a war memoir. After the war he edited the socialist journal, 'The Adelphi', and ran a commune and socialist summer school which housed Basque refugees during the Spanish Civil War, then elderly evacuees, and conscientious objectors in the Second World War. He was general secretary of the Peace Pledge Union. Plowman died in 1941. His wife, Dorothy, travelled with Emmeline and often stayed with her at Fourways.

Left to right: Max Plowman, Wilfred Walter, Christopher Plowman, Emmeline, May Start and Fred picnicking on Holmwood Common in 1919. The photograph was taken by Plowman's wife, Dorothy, who sent it to Fred and Emmeline as a Christmas card. The Plowmans' son Christopher died at 11. (Museum of London)

'Maiden ladies' country: Peaslake

A grocer's boy[18] described Peaslake in the years between the wars as *'maiden ladies country'* where there were *'spinsters by the score'*. He probably did not realize just what ladies, however. A favourite with artists before the war, in the 1920s and 1930s the village attracted many new residents who had been involved in the campaign for the vote. By the 1940s there was something of a colony in the village, many of whose members, including the Pethick-Lawrences, carried the fight for equality for women into new areas.

In 1919 Mrs Pankhurst rented a cottage in the village with Catherine Emily Pine (1864-1941). Mrs Pankhurst knew Peaslake through her convalescence with the Brackenburys before the war, and Catherine Pine had nursed her at the sisters' London home. In 1915 Mrs Pankhurst had decided to set up a home for some of the many 'war babies' who languished in orphanages, the result of liaisons between unmarried women and soldiers. Unable to persuade what remained of the WSPU to back her

Nurse Catherine Pine (right), who accompanied Mrs Pankhurst and her adopted girls on a six-month stay in Peaslake in 1919. She is pictured here before the First World War, attending to a fainting Mrs Pankhurst, with the composer, Ethel Smyth. Pine had nursed Mrs Pankhurst's son, Harry, during his final illness. She ran a convalescent home at Pembridge Gardens in Notting Hill where she had cared for suffragettes on release from prison. (Library of Congress)

[18] Harry Daley (1901-1971) delivered to the village for Kinghams of Dorking between 1916 and 1925. He later joined the police force and became the lover of the novelist EM Forster.

scheme, she had informally adopted four small girls: Kathleen King, Joan Pembridge (who was named after Nurse Pine's convalescent home), Mary Gordon and Elizabeth Tudor. Gomshall's Cecily Hale had helped prepare for their arrival and Nurse Pine and two of Annie Kenney's sisters took practical charge of the girls. In 1919 the household moved to Peaslake. Visiting from Woking, Ethel Smyth, who had opposed the idea of a woman with no income taking on the responsibilities of the state, was unimpressed. She took Mrs Pankhurst to task at the girls' affected manners as they flitted about like fairies, kissing the hands of guests.

Mrs Pankhurst did not stay long. Her life became peripatetic; she moved to Canada, then to France, where she and Mabel Tuke took on the unlikely, (and unsuccessful), business of running a teashop. The adopted girls found themselves parceled out amongst her erstwhile supporters. Mary Gordon remained in Peaslake, offered a home at Mackies Hill with Marion Wallace Dunlop; she was often referred to as Dunlop's 'ward'.

Wallace Dunlop's long term collaborator, Edith Elizabeth Downing, came to live in the village after spending the war working with Sylvia Pankhurst's East End Federation. When Sylvia set up the East London Toy Factory in Bow in 1914 to provide work at fair rates to East End women, Edith Downing had designed toys which were sold to Selfridges. After the war she took up residence at Robin's Rough.

Another ex-suffragette, Elizabeth 'Betty' Clara Brewster nee Giveen (1887-1967), moved into the Brackenburys' staff accommodation at Brackenside. Originally from Birmingham, she had been a WSPU organiser in Norwich and on the south coast. With Kitty Marion (1871-1944)[19], (a stone-throwing accomplice of Dorothy Pethick), Giveen had set fire to the Grand Stand at Hurst Park racetrack in June 1913. Arrested in Richmond and tried in Guildford, Marion and Giveen had been sentenced to three years penal servitude. After the usual hunger strikes, Marion had escaped whilst out on licence under the 'Cat and Mouse Act'. In her memoir she recalls being rushed to *a friend's house in the beautiful Surrey hills'*, where Betty Giveen was waiting for her. There she was cared for until she could *'slowly crawl about the garden the lanes and hills with the aid of a stick'*. On another occasion she found refuge in a secluded cottage inaccessible by road, one, she recalled, of a network of safe houses let out by sympathetic non-resident owners. Betty Giveen returned to the village that had given her refuge. In 1914 she married Philip Brewster in Oxfordshire. Her sister-in-law, Bertha Brewster, was also a suffrage supporter who had served on the committee of the United Suffragists with Evelyn Sharp. In Peaslake, Betty Brewster became active in the newly-formed Women's Institute.

On their arrival in Peaslake Fred and Emmeline rented a cottage named Redroofs (Merriedown) whilst a new *'labour saving cottage'* was built on a plot of

---

[19] Kitty Marion was the assumed name of German-born Katherina Maria Schafer, a successful music-hall singer. She had been a beneficiary of Nurse Pine's care. When deportation of German nationals was ordered after the outbreak of the First World War, friends, including Emmeline Pethick-Lawrence, raised funds to pay her fare to the United States.

Fourways, the 'labour-saving cottage' in Peaslake, (Dorking Museum)

land at the end of Rad Lane. It was well away from the road, facing open farmland. When the foundations for Fourways were laid on March 24th 1921 some coins and a ration card were placed beneath the floor, in keeping with ancient tradition. Fred and Emmeline then set off for India whilst building work proceeded.

In 1915 Fred and Emmeline had lunched with Mohandas Karamchand Gandhi (1869-1948) in their Clement's Inn apartment. The Indian lawyer had been on his way home from South Africa, where he had employed tactics of civil disobedience in fighting for civil rights for the Indian community. He had followed the campaign for the vote in Britain with interest, noting tactics, which he discussed with the erstwhile suffragette leaders. His subsequent campaign for the independence of India was influenced by the tactics of the WSPU. With his opposition to colonialism and to the domination of one race over another, Fred in particular, sympathized with the Indian cause. He remained in touch with Indian campaigners for independence and women's rights in India, meeting with Tara Cherian, the first female mayor of Madras, and frequently entertaining Amrit Kaur and other prominent Indian political figures in London. The couple also visited the United States where Emmeline shared a platform with Eamon de Valera at a protest meeting in Washington over British treatment of the Irish playwright and hunger-striker Terence MacSwiney. (MacSwiney died whilst on hunger strike in October 1920.) Many years later de Valera told Emmeline that he would not forget her support for Irish Independence.

On their return from their travels Fred and Emmeline placed the Indian 'symbol of life' by the front door; it had to be carved out when the swastika was adopted by the Nazis. The couple moved into Fourways in October 1921. The house had four bedrooms, a billiard room, gardens of two acres, a bowling green, a tennis court, a miniature putting green, and a copse of three acres. There was a separate cottage for Mr Rapley, the gardener/chauffeur. There were no 'live-in' staff but eventually there were at least eight people working there - gardening, cooking, cleaning, chauffeuring and taking dictation. Emmeline had little experience of house-work; the cook later recalled with satisfaction that her employer had never bothered her in the kitchen.

Abandoning thoughts of a parliamentary career, Emmeline turned her attention to wider questions of women's equality, in the workplace and in society generally. She gathered a circle of ex-comrades about her and a constant stream of activists, reformers and political thinkers passed through Fourways. In her fifties by the time of the move, she did not return to the social work of her pre-suffrage youth, but she retained her interest in young people. For a while she was a prominent member of Fellowship of the Kibbo Kift, a youth organisation that was politically engaged and which attempted to bring together people of different classes and of both sexes in a way that other fledgling youth movements, (notably the Boy Scout and Girl Guide movements), did not.

In 1924 Gladys Groom arrived to work for Emmeline; her sister had been a WSPU office girl. Like Fred's secretary, Esther Knowles, she stayed with the couple for the rest of their lives. The two women were devoted to

Poster for the Reigate Division of the Surrey Conservative and Unionist Association 'Women's Rally'. Billed as the 'event of the summer', the rally took place at Broome Park in Betchworth on 21ˢᵗ July 1927. The MP for Reigate, Major The Hon WGA Ormsby-Gore, is billed to appear; the following year he opposed the extension of the vote to women under thirty.

Fred and Emmeline and both worked hours well beyond their terms of employment. Gladys often found herself at Fourways at the weekend, typing at the kitchen table.

Fred and Emmeline worked in their offices at 11 Old Square in Lincoln's Inn during the week and decamped to Peaslake every weekend. Taking the Friday afternoon train from Waterloo to Clandon they were met by Mr Rapley and chauffeured to Fourways. On Saturdays and Sundays they would have local friends over - Kathleen Coxeter of Keeper's Cottage in Gomshall, whose husband played tennis with Fred, or Rhodes Cullis - and Emmeline would work in her garden. Ada Plaw, who lived at Eastview in the village, came in to cook lunch, though Fred often took care of meals at weekends. He also made jam, and claimed that cookery was an extension of his chemistry experiments at school. Then on Monday morning they would return to London. On occasion they would dictate notes to one another in their respective offices, (Fred probably had in mind a means of countering Emmeline's legendary forgetfulness, as well as providing a carbon for his own files).

The campaign for equality of voting rights for women continued throughout the 1920s, though without the intensity of the pre-war years. Emmeline spoke and wrote for the United Suffragists and for the Women's Freedom League (WFL), both of which continued to campaign. One of her closest associates of these years was Lady Rhondda, who lived close by at Churt Halewell in Shere. As Margaret

Emmeline Pethick-Lawrence (top left) with her neighbour Viscountess Rhondda on a delegation to New York in the 1920s (Library of Congress)

Mackworth, Lady Rhondda had burned letterboxes during the suffragette campaign. She had now inherited her father's title and took the initiative to drive the struggle for women's rights beyond the achievement of equal voting rights. In 1921 she founded the Six Point Group. Through her journal 'Time and Tide' the group campaigned for political, occupational, moral, social, economic, and legal equality: for female hereditary peers like herself to sit in the House of Lords, for equal rights for women as parents, for the professions to be fully open to women, and for equal pay for female workers. She and Emmeline Pethick-Lawrence collaborated closely: Emmeline was a vice-president of the Six Point Group and she accompanied Lady Rhondda on deputations to the Prime Minister. And under Emmeline's leadership the WFL broadened its remit to campaign on more general issues of women's inequality, along the lines of the Six Point Group, calling for equal pay and for the professions to be open to women. In 1926 Emmeline was one of the founders, with Lady Rhondda, of the Open Door Council, which pushed for equal economic opportunities for women. In 1928 she, Fred and Lady Rhondda spoke at a demonstration in Hyde Park in support of equal citizenship: Emmeline on behalf of the WFL, Lady Rhondda on behalf of the Six Point Group, and Fred on behalf of the Trades Unions.

In July 1928 women finally achieved the vote on equal terms with men. The WFL held a victory breakfast at the Hotel Cecil in London. Emmeline presided *'in joyous mood.'* Suffragettes, she said, were not usually in the habit of thanking governments but on this occasion she thanked the Prime Minister, Stanley Baldwin, the Home Secretary, the government and both houses of Parliament. *'We have fought the good fight,'* she told her fellow celebrants. Responding to one who said *'Oh here you are, in at the death!'* she replied: *'No, I'm in at the beginning'.* For to Emmeline the vote was to be but the beginning of women's achievements.

There was a pause in the celebrations in memory of those who had not lived to see the final victory, particularly of Lady Constance Lytton and of Emmeline Pankhurst. Mrs Pankhurst's funeral had taken place on the day of the Bill's final reading in the House of Lords; Fred and Emmeline, Lady Rhondda and Evelyn Sharp had all attended. Three of the pall-bearers at the funeral were neighbours from Peaslake: Georgina and Marie Brackenbury, and Marion Wallace Dunlop; a fourth, Marie Naylor, had come down to speak during the Holmwood campaign.

Emmeline Pethick-Lawrence was followed onto the speakers' platform at the victory dinner by the Labour leader, Ramsay MacDonald, then by Lady Rhondda who thanked the men who had supported the campaign. Fred's appearance on the platform was greeted with shouts of *'For he's a jolly good fellow!'* A breakfast celebration, he told the audience, was most appropriate as celebratory breakfasts had been a common occurrence when the prison gates were unbarred and this victory represented a great unbarring for women and liberty for all.

Emmeline also spoke at Charlotte Despard's victory party and at the Equal Political Rights campaign's victory lunch and reception, at the Hotel Cecil and Caxton Hall, on 24th October 1928.

WOMEN'S FREEDOM
• • • LEAGUE • • •

VOTES
FOR
WOMEN

DARE TO BE FREE

Above left: Emmeline in the 1920s. (Library of Congress)
Above right: Women's Freedom League banner (LSE Library)
Below: The programme for the victory breakfast held by the Women's Freedom League on 5ᵗʰ July 1928 to celebrate women finally achieving the vote on equal terms with men. Emmeline lead the speeches, and was followed her neighbour, Lady Rhondda, then by Fred and Millicent Fawcett, the leader of the non-militant campaign. (LSE Library)

CHAIRMAN

Mrs. Pethick-Lawrence

(Thanks to The Prime Minister and The Government for introducing The Equal Franchise Bill, and to Members of all Parties and both Houses of Parliament, for defeating the opposition to it by overwhelming majorities and carrying it into Law)

SHORT SPEECHES

The Right Hon. J. R. Ramsay Macdonald, M.P.
Sir Robert Newman, Bart, M.P.
Frank Briant, Esq., M.P.

The Viscountess Rhondda, J.P.
"THE MEN WHO HAVE HELPED US"

F. Pethick-Lawrence Esq., M.P.
WILL REPLY

Mrs. Stedman
"THE PIONEERS"

Dame Millicent Fawcett, G.B.E., J.P., LL.D.
"THE WOMEN OF THE FUTURE"

Mrs. Despard
"THE WOMEN'S FREEDOM LEAGUE"

180

In the 1920s Fred finally embarked on the parliamentary career that had been put on hold throughout the campaign for the vote and the war years. In 1920 he published *'Why Prices Rise and Fall'*, signalling a return to his interest in finance and economic issues. In 1923 he stood for election to Parliament against Winston Churchill in West Leicester; he was finally returned as a Labour MP at the age of 52, over 20 years after renouncing his Liberal candidacy on meeting Emmeline. Though his main political interest was in finance, Fred never wavered in his commitment to equality: his maiden speech was on widows' pensions and he contributed to debates on equal pay in the 1930s and 40s. He was no great speaker, however, dubbed *'pathetic Lawrence'* by opponents for his dry delivery.

The extent of the esteem in which the couple were held and their popularity can be gauged by the celebrations held to mark their silver wedding on 2nd October 1926. Four functions were held to accommodate all their comrades: a dinner and dance for friends, a supper at Mansfield House, a reception at de Montfort Hall in Fred's Leicester constituency, and a dinner in the Holborn Restaurant hosted by the WFL. There, on 8th October, they were toasted by Millicent Fawcett, William Wedgwood Benn[20], Henry Nevinson and Evelyn Sharp.

Fred and Emmeline then embarked on a 'silver honeymoon' visit to India where they met up with old suffrage comrade Victor, 2nd Earl of Lytton, (brother of Lady Constance), who was now Governor of Bengal. They also stayed with the poet and philosopher Rabindranath Tagore (1861-1941). This was their second visit to India and they attended the annual meeting of the Indian National Congress and re-established contact with Gandhi who conversed with them over a dinner of raisins and milk. On their return a stream of high-profile Indian contacts met up with them in London. In 1928 they took Motilal Nehru (1861-1931), father of the man who would become India's first prime minister, to dinner at the House of Commons. And in 1931 Fred worked with Wedgwood Benn, who was Ramsay MacDonald's Secretary of State for India, to secure Gandhi's attendance at the Round Table Conference on the future of British India in London. During a break in the

Gandhi with Fred Pethick-Lawrence. (LSE Library)

---

[20] Captain William Wedgwood Benn (1877-1960) was the father of Labour politician Tony Benn. He began life as a Liberal MP in 1906 but resigned from the party in 1927 and re-entered Parliament as a Labour member. He was raised to the peerage as Viscount Stansgate in 1942.

discussions Gandhi visited Peaslake. Eyewitnesses recall Gandhi and Fred walking arm-in-arm around the garden at Fourways.

Sylvia Pankhurst was a frequent visitor to Fourways. She shared Emmeline's concern for the welfare of the working classes, particularly women and children. Unlike her mother and sister, Sylvia remained a radical into later life. In 1928, at the age of forty-five, she gave birth to a son whose father she had no intention of marrying. While Christabel blamed her sister's news for precipitating their mother's death, Emmeline Pethick-Lawrence contributed towards Sylvia's stay in a nursing home for the birth. Sylvia named the baby Richard Keir Pethick Pankhurst, after her father, Keir Hardie, and Emmeline respectively. This gave rise to speculation from some quarters that Fred was the baby's father, Sylvia having refused to name her Italian partner, Sylvio Corio. Pethick, however, was Emmeline's name.

Fred and Emmeline on a visit to the United States. (Library of Congress)

In 1930 Fred Pethick-Lawrence and Lady Rhondda joined the Prime Minister, Stanley Baldwin, to address the crowd at the unveiling of Mrs Pankhurst's statue in Victoria Tower Gardens. At the unveiling ceremony the composer, Ethel Smyth, conducted the Metropolitan Police Band in an arrangement of 'The March of the Women'. To coincide with the occasion Sylvia Pankhurst paid tribute to the part the Pethick-Lawrences had played in the movement in an article in 'The Star'. The couple, she said, had supplied the WSPU with the very qualities that her mother had lacked. For one thing, her mother had had no great organising ability. And '*Mrs Pethick-Lawrence had... the gift of making the most of her co-workers; she took the lead in weaving an atmosphere of ardour and romance about the personality of Mrs Pankhurst and other leaders of the suffragette movement.*' The break of 1912, she said, had been a matter of deep regret.

Emmeline encouraged Sylvia to write her mother's biography, suggesting that it would be better that she did it than Christabel. '*Christabel's idea of Mother - and also of Herself,*' Sylvia wrote, '*is that of the ultimate triumph of a vindicated*

Christ returning to rule the world as a benevolent despot.' It is hard to tell whether that comment was made in bitterness, in candour, or in jest; whichever, it is clear that she and Emmeline were close enough to correspond on family matters with openness. Through the years Emmeline supported Sylvia financially: sending her away with Richard on holidays, paying for housing, supporting her through libel claims, and clearing her debts. She also supported her causes, in particular that of Ethiopia. Emotionally, she became something of a surrogate mother.

Another of the couple's close associates was the novelist EM Forster, who between 1925 and 1946 lived at West Hackhurst in nearby Abinger. A Cambridge man, like Fred, Forster had been a member of the Men's League for Women's Suffrage. He and Fred also had a common interest in Indian affairs; Forster published his best-known novel, 'A Passage to India' in 1924. Both were involved in PEN, the international writers' organisation. The novelist was a frequent visitor to the house in Peaslake and Fred and Emmeline to his.

The 1920s were years of great optimism. After the horrors of the First World War Emmeline confessed her hopes for progress and peace, and for the end of the great military institutions, to her suffragette friend, Georgiana Solomon. She was active in the Women's International League for Peace and Freedom that had been formed at the Women's Peace Conference in 1915. The League's American secretary, Madeleine Zabriskie Doty (1877-1963) became a close friend. Trained as a lawyer, Doty had campaigned for the vote in the United States and on prison conditions. She worked as a journalist in Russia during the Revolution and devoted the rest of her life to promoting peace, through journalism and teaching. She stayed at Fourways more than once.

In 1929 Emmeline wrote of the great spiritual and moral awakening that she believed would be the legacy of the First World War. She had great hopes for women as people of all classes broke free of their bonds and sought a life of freedom from the constraints of gender and class. The dashing of those hopes for a future more equitable and less militaristic in the 1930s was a huge disappointment.

From 1929 Fred served as Financial Secretary to the Treasury in Ramsay MacDonald's second minority government. But he deplored Macdonald's policies in response to the depression of the early 1930s, and declined a ministerial position in his old friend's coalition government. It has been speculated that had Labour won the election of 1931 Fred might have been appointed Chancellor of the Exchequer; but Labour were routed and he lost his seat.

Fred and Emmeline took the opportunity to travel, both for pleasure and in promotion of their causes. They went to Russia, Egypt, Syria, Turkey, Scandinavia and Spain. In 1930 Emmeline travelled to South Africa and Rhodesia with her sister, May to promote suffrage and peace; whilst the sisters were there the vote was conceded to white women. In 1932 Fred toured Russia with Hugh Dalton and a group of left wing intellectuals with a view to studying how a Socialist system might be introduced. The following year he sat for a portrait by Henry Coller. As a member of the Socialist League, alongside Stafford Cripps, (who would later accompany him with the Cabinet Commission to India), he pressed for the implementation of socialism. In 1935 he was returned to Parliament, this time for Edinburgh East. Under party leader, Clement Attlee, he became Labour's chief financial spokesman. In 1936 he and Emmeline celebrated their 35th wedding anniversary; they received a portrait of themselves by Dame Laura Knight from their friends.[21] In his annual missives to Emmeline Fred still wrote appreciatively of his wife's body, and of her hands, her loving eyes, little nose and unruly hair.

Dr Marie Carmichael Stopes (1880-1958) lived at Belmont Road in Leatherhead and then at Norbury Park. The palaeobotanist, who became a pioneer birth control campaigner, was a guest at Fourways and Fred wrote her a letter of introduction when she went to India. Emmeline contributed an article on old friend Havelock Ellis to her Birth Control Review. (Library of Congress)

Two years later, at the suggestion of the Australian campaigner for women's equality, (Emma) Linda Palmer Littlejohn nee Teece (1883-1949), Emmeline published her autobiography, 'My Part in a Changing World'. She was assisted in its preparation by Stella Newsome (1889-1969), who came down to live in Peaslake, renting Appletree Cottage at the end of the lane from Fourways with her companion, Daisy Bedder. A former teacher, Newsome had left the National Union of Teachers as a young woman when the local branch refused to discuss a motion on votes for women; she stormed onto the stage and demanded her subscription back. She had left the WSPU in disgust when Mrs Pankhurst wound up campaigning on the outbreak of the First World War and joined the United Suffragists. Later, she had been an associate of Emmeline's at the WFL. Advance recommendations for the book came from Vera Brittain, Laurence Housman and George Lansbury. It was reviewed in 'The Times' by Henry Nevinson.

For fifteen years Newsome and Bedder met the Pethick-Lawrences every weekend. Fred, she later recalled, was a trusted friend and companion who *'did more for me than any other person ever did in restoring my faith in 'man' which*

---

[21] Fred had also been painted by Henry Coller in the 1930s; after Emmeline's death the artist sent Fred a drawing of her. In 1949 Fred sat for a sculpture in wood by Albin Moroder.

had become rather shattered' by her experiences as a suffragette.

As the era of the fight for the vote passed from memory into history, the way in which the struggle would be represented to future generations became a matter of concern to many of those who had been involved in it. The Suffragette Fellowship had been set up in 1926 to preserve the memory of the militant campaign and to *'keep alive the suffragette spirit'.* By the 1940s Newsome was its president. She was largely responsible for the collection of memoirs, journals and scrapbooks of the Suffragette Fellowship Collection now in the Museum of London. The Fellowship championed the achievements of militancy, particularly arguing for the efficacy of imprisonment and the hunger strike. Its purpose was ultimately self-justifying; celebratory rather than analytical. It is largely as a result of the efforts of its members that militancy is accorded such attention by history. (Suffragette memoirists seldom consider whether their militancy might have been detrimental to the cause, nor do they give much credit to the possible efficacy of other methods of campaigning.) When the Fellowship decided to set up an archive room, Emmeline joined the committee with Helen Archdale, Charlotte Marsh and Lady Rhondda.

Christabel Pankhurst was created a Dame of the British Empire in 1936. Whilst working on Emmeline's memoir, Stella Newsome began a campaign to secure an honour for Emmeline. She contacted old suffrage luminaries, friends, and female MPs in the hope of petitioning the prime minister. She was supported by Lillian Baylis and Sybil Thorndike, Elizabeth Robins, Ruth Cavendish-Bentinck, Mavis Tate MP, Evelyn Sharp and Henry Nevinson. However, many women in politics, including the MPs Eleanor Rathbone and Ellen Wilkinson, and writers Rose Macaulay and Rebecca West, though they revered Emmeline, felt unable to support the campaign because of their general opposition to the honours system, or to the way in which it treated women.

Never a 'pacifist' in the strict sense, Fred put his faith in the League of Nations as war loomed. In 1933 Emmeline had written an article for the 'New Clarion': 'A call to Socialist women: Unite to resist fascism and war'. She was to be disappointed at the failure such peace efforts. Though she was elected president of the newly-formed World Women's Party in 1939 and invited to write its manifesto, she had little hope of its effectiveness seeking to avoid war. The lighting of the flame at the party's headquarters in Geneva in July 1939 would be, she wrote to Fred, the *'last great demonstration of world union before the outbreak of war'.*

In her seventies, increasingly deaf and unable to manage the stairs down to the air-raid shelters at Lincoln's Inn, she 'exiled' herself (as Evelyn Sharp put it) in to Fourways with Gladys Groom, visiting London only occasionally. Ironically the garden at Fourways, where there was no air-raid shelter, was hit by a firebomb.

Fred acted as official leader of the Opposition in the House of Commons between January 1942 and February 1943. (He was one of three Labour politicians who took the role during the coalition government of 1940-45 to allow Parliament to function as normal, despite Labour politicians sitting in government with the

Emmeline in 1938 and Fred in 1940. (The Master and Fellows of Trinity College, Cambridge)

Conservatives.) In 1943 he published his autobiography, 'Fate Has Been Kind'. It was edited and proof-read by Evelyn Sharp and dedicated *'to my wife by whose constant inspiration my life has been enriched.'* In February that year he and Emmeline spoke at a celebratory dinner marking the passage of 25 years since women had gained the vote. In characteristically idiosyncratic style she kept her spirits up through the deprivations of the war years by refusing to mention the conflict in conversation, instead concentrating her mind on eternal beauty. It was a stance with which Evelyn Sharp, subject to the nightly bombing of London, found it hard to relate. Emmeline looked ever to the future, however. She ran a union of the League of Nations in Peaslake and invited EM Forster to address the gathering. And in August 1944 she hosted a celebration for the centenary of Edward Carpenter's birth in her garden; again, EM Forster was the speaker.

Fred commuted weekly from Peaslake to Lincoln's Inn, but Emmeline was not alone in Peaslake. In 1940 her old friend Mary Neal left Littlehampton and came to live at The Retreat, a short distance along Rad Lane. She had her own rooms, but took her meals and spent her days with Emmeline, the two women reverting to the closeness of their youth. (Fred, observers recalled, was not keen on the arrangement as both he and Neal liked to have the last word on any given matter and they clashed at weekends.) Emmeline's standard of living was not obviously diminished, despite wartime labour shortages, as the two elderly ladies were still able to surround themselves with an eclectic collection of 'staff'. In addition to Esther and Gladys, there was a housekeeper and cleaner in London, Mrs Plaw the cook in Peaslake, a Czech refugee (once a member of Emmeline's Women's International League) who cleaned in Peaslake, and two gardeners. All were either over military age or aliens not required to contribute directly to the war effort.

Peace was celebrated at Fourways with flags. On 8th June 1946 Esther and Gladys went up to London to the victory parade. Emmeline was entitled to a seated ticket but stayed in Peaslake. The village, she reported to Fred, had refused to cooperate with Guildford in planning celebrations and there was little enthusiasm until the event. For herself, she said, she was *too appalled by the tragedy of the millions of homeless people... to feel anything but certainty of Judgment to come.* The weary despondency of her outlook was shared by her campaigning neighbour, Dorothy Buxton, who called in to discuss the famine in Europe.

Emmeline's was a relatively cosseted old-age. Indulged by staff and husband, she grew increasingly moody. Untidy, absent-minded and disorganised, she missed engagements, crying off with pleas of ill-health, leaving the dutiful Fred to cover for her. She dictated letters rather than write them. She remained, however, warm, generous and spontaneous, and her staff, now almost family so long had they been together, were devoted. In contrast Fred's observance of routine grew more obsessive: he disliked telephone calls that might delay lunch even by a minute or any change to his pattern of meals. Nonetheless he inspired affection and loyalty, and, though the rigour of his personality might suggest an emotional inflexibility, he was considerate of his staff at Fourways. Unlike many political campaigners who fought for humanity in the abstract but were careless in their dealings with individuals, Fred seems always to have put in a word or given of his time, whereas Emmeline, so spontaneous and relaxed, often would not notice the discomforts of those around her.

Fred retained something of the 'Godfather' role that he had played within the WSPU; in 1942 and again in 1945 he interceded with the authorities on behalf of American-born suffrage campaigner Elizabeth Robins who had been denied passage to return to her home in England. In 1945 he pulled strings to obtain permission for EM Forster to travel to India when all but essential travel was almost impossible. Forced to appeal to a *'friend in high places'* in order to retain her telephone on moving flat at the end of the war, Evelyn Sharp commented ruefully: *'Dear Friend! It is so jolly to think that, after all he has lost in getting me my vote (to say nothing of some millions of others) he can now be asked by me for the favour of a telephone.'*

Emmeline Pethick-Lawrence and the Kindred of the Kibbo Kift

The devastation of the 1914-1918 war brought a questioning of the old order and a desire for change. Such sentiments were behind the foundation of an idealistic movement, the Kindred of the Kibbo Kift.

It was probably Mary Neal who introduced Emmeline to John Gordon Hargrave (1894-1982), the Kindred's founder. A Quaker illustrator/novelist, he had been an early Boy Scout, touted as a successor to Baden-Powell. But his experiences in the ambulance corps during the war lead to disillusionment with Scouting's officer-class leadership. Feeling that Scouting's outdoor pursuits were merely a veneer to militarism, he envisaged instead a movement that would break down social and sexual barriers, leading the nation to physical and spiritual regeneration. His advocacy of social relevance and the regeneration of urban man through the open-air life was a sentiment with which social reformers like Emmeline and Neal might sympathize; less so the socially conservative backers of Baden-Powell.

Hargrave invited Emmeline to the setting up of the new organization in 1920. Unlike existing military and religious youth organizations the Kindred was open to both sexes, with women involved in its leadership. With her commitment to young people, reverence for folklore and pageantry, and belief in the power of the countryside, Emmeline took to the organization with enthusiasm. Once more providing support and resources to a charismatic and autocratic leader, she hosted the Kindred's 2nd Althing (annual 'meet') in October 1921 at her London home. The following year she held a 'pow-wow' there on 'old' May Day.

Like the Scout movement, the Kindred wove together folk and animal lore. Members looked to primitive societies for spiritual inspiration and took mystical names. At the 3rd Althing in 1922 Emmeline was given the name 'Lototsa', meaning *'looking towards the stars'*.

The Kindred's emphasis on peace and brotherhood attracted pacifist ex-members of the Union of Democratic Control; its claims to equality appealed to socialists and socially radical ex-suffragettes. Nor was there any religious bar on membership. Mary Neal and Henry Nevinson sat with Emmeline on the organization's council. At the 1923 Althing Nevinson told tales of Africa around the camp fire and Neal offered her Sussex cottage for the recuperation of Kinsmen and introduced Hargrave to her contracts in the Labour youth movement. (The breakaway Woodcraft Folk was formed when Ramsay MacDonald attempted to bring the Kindred within the Labour fold.) She also introduced him to Rolf Gardiner, an advocate of the healing power of folk dance which the Kindred took up with enthusiasm.

Camping and hiking were integral to the organization. In 1924 'Lototsa' invited the Kindred to an Easter Camp at Fourways. The highlight was a moonlit walk up Leith Hill with camp breakfast at the summit. Later that summer members of the 'Dorian' tribe visited Fourways. In following years she welcomed campers and even a German kinsman. The Surrey Hills, with rail connections to London, were central to Kindred activities. In January 1924 kinfolk camped at Pippbrook Mill, near Dorking. That March the 'Iceni' tribe cycled from Raynes Park to Leith Hill; others hiked the Pilgrims' Way, camping in Peaslake over the August bank holiday. At Easter 1925 30 kinsmen hiked from Westerham in Kent to Box Hill where they ate by the banks of the Mole before hiking via Ranmore to Gomshall to set up camp. In 1927 the women's Spring Festival hike set off form Burford Bridge on Good Friday and participants camped at Coleskitchen near Gomshall. The following year the Kindred hiked from Sevenoaks to Dorking, camping at Bookham. In 1928 the Kindred held a week-long children's camp, known as the 'Dexter Fam', in a field off Coleskitchen Lane. The children hiked to Ewhurst, Abinger, and Silent Pool, swam in the pool in Shere, and marched through Dorking. Two years later the Autumn Festival camp took place at Paddington Farm in Abinger Hammer.

In response to the economic problems of the late 1920s, Hargrave transformed the Kindred into a more politico-economic movement. The singing and hiking, flowing cloaks, and mystical ceremonies by firelight gave way to marching and a military-style uniform By the 1930s, when Hargrave renamed the organization 'the Green shirt Movement for Social Credit', focusing its campaigns in the industrial cities, Emmeline had ceased to be involved.

Emmeline with kinsmen in hand-made 'Saxon' hoods at Lincoln's Inn, 1922; Kinsmen outside Grim's Kitchen tearoom in Abinger Hammer, 1920s; (London School of Economics Library)

Lady Rhondda and Theodora Bosanquet

Lady Rhondda (1883-1958) leased Churt Halewell in Shere from Sir Jocelyn Bray. Born Margaret Haig Thomas, she was an ex-suffragette and committed campaigner for women's equality. Her family had been prominent in the campaign for the vote. Her father, the industrialist and Liberal MP for Merthyr Tydfil, David Alfred Thomas (1856-1918), was a vice president of the Men's League for Women's Suffrage. Her mother, Sybil nee Haig (1857-1941), had been on the executive committee of the London Society for Women's Suffrage with Wilhelmina Brodie Hall and on the executive of the Central National Society for Women's Suffrage with Fred and Emmeline, the Brackenburys, Ethel Smyth and Georgiana Solomon. Sybil Thomas had been amongst the WSPU's biggest donors. During the war she had been vice-president of the United Suffragists and treasurer of Sylvia Pankhurst's East End Federation.

Margaret's artist cousin, Florence Eliza Haig (1856-1952) was also a WSPU member; she took part in the Pantechnicon raid with the Brackenburys and was also close to Marion Wallace Dunlop. Another cousin, Cecilia Wolseley Haig (1862-1912), never recovered from injuries sustained when assaulted and trampled on Black Friday - she died a year later. A third cousin, 'Louisa' Evelyn Cotton Haig (1863-1954), served time in prison. Her Aunt Lottie contrived to ensure that any imprisonment should be in August or December, when her garden least needed her.

As a young woman Margaret Thomas was painfully shy. She failed to find a husband on coming out, and dropped out of Oxford University before marrying Humphrey Mackworth. She was converted to the cause of militant suffragism by Florence Haig who took her to the Hyde Park rally in 1908. She became an organiser in Newport, and a prolific letter-writer and reviewer. She was pelted with herring and tomatoes when she spoke at the Liberal Club in her father's constituency.

Margaret Mackworth went to work for her father, an unusual step for a married woman of her class. She was on The Lusitania with her father when it was torpedoed in 1915. By the end of the First World War she was a director of 20 companies. She carried on her work for women's advancement into the post-suffrage era. Her father was elevated to the peerage in 1916 and she succeeded to his title as Viscountess Rhondda in 1918. She immediately launched a campaign for women peers to be admitted to the House of Lords and established the Women's Industrial League to campaign for equal pay for all women. In the 1920s she campaigned for the vote to be extended to women under thirty, on the same grounds as men.

Lady Rhondda launched the journal, 'Time and Tide', in 1920. It addressed the political and cultural issues of the day and published contributions from Rebecca West, Vera Brittain, Winifred Holtby, EM Delafield, Virginia Woolf and Rose MacCauley. But it never achieved mass readership, and Lady Rhondda subsidized it from her own funds for 38 years. 'Time and Tide's' first editor was fellow ex-suffragette Helen Archdale (1876-1950), but for many years Lady Rhondda edited it herself, using it to promote her own political agenda. In 1921 she founded the Six Point Group which campaigned on six initial issues of inequality: for changes in the laws relating to unmarried women and widows with children, to child assault, to unequal guardianship rights of married parents, and to inequalities of pay and conditions relating to civil servants and teachers. Its aims developed over time to cover six general areas of inequality: political, social, economic, occupational, moral and legal.

In 1925 Lady Rhondda became the first female president of the Institute of Directors. In 1926 she founded the Open Door Council, which pushed for equal economic opportunities for women, collaborating with Emmeline Pethick-Lawrence of the Women's Freedom League, amongst others.

Lady Rhondda shared her homes in London and at Churt Halewell with the writer, literary critic and broadcaster Theodora Bosanquet (1880-?). Of Huguenot descent, Bosanquet was related to the pro-suffrage philosopher, Bernard Bosanquet; his home, Heath House in Oxted, like The Sundial, had been designed by Arnold Dunbar Smith. Her mother was a descendent of Charles Darwin's cousin and confidant, William Darwin Fox. Educated at the University of London, Bosanquet became literary secretary to the novelist Henry James in 1907 and worked for him until 1916. Her memoir of her time working for him was published by Leonard and Virginia Woolf's Hogarth Press. She also wrote studies of Paul Valery and Harriet Martineau. A prolific reviewer, Bosanquet corresponded with the great literary thinkers of the day and for over twenty years served as literary editor of 'Time and Tide', where she commissioned work from new and established writers. She was also known for her lectures and BBC broadcasts on suffrage and literary issues. *(Image of Lady Rhondda reproduced by permission of AV Morgan)*

EM Forster

The novelist Edward Morgan Forster (1879-1970) lived at West Hackhurst in Abinger. In the 1930s he worked with Ralph Vaughan Williams on two pageants, one to raise money for Abinger Church, the other to raise awareness of conservation issues for the Dorking and Leith Hill Preservation Society. After the Munich crisis in 1938 he joined Vaughan Williams on the Dorking Refugee Committee, which helped refugees fleeing from the Nazis in Europe to establish themselves in England. The committee ran a hostel in Dorking and assisted refugees in their dealings with the Refugee Tribunal.

Forster left the area when the lease on his house expired, but Fred often visited him in Cambridge. He was, he told Emmeline: *'very sorry to leave a neighbourhood which I have known all my life and in it so many good friends.'*

The Townsend Sisters

Caroline (left) and Hannah (right) Townsend were amongst the suffragette community that formed around the Pethick-Lawrences in Peaslake. The sisters were teachers from Lewisham. When Hannah Townsend (1868-?) challenged a colleague on the fact that male teachers were paid more than female ones she was told that it was because they needed the extra pay as an inducement to marry. She commented that: *'If the love, services and companionship of women are not sufficient inducement to marry without extra salary men had better remain single'.* Hannah and her sister, Alice, were founder members of the Women Teachers' Franchise Union which met at their home in Lee. Caroline Townsend (1870-1941) had been secretary of the Lewisham branch of the WSPU and the Church League for Women's Suffrage. She had spoken in public, sold papers and paraded with posters. In 1909 she was charged with obstruction on an attempt to reach the House of Commons and served time with Emmeline Pethick-Lawrence. They came to live at Gravelpits Farm in Gomshall. *(Museum of London)*

'A labour-saving cottage': Fourways

Drawing of Emmeline given to Fred by the artist, Henry Coller, after her death. (LSE Library)

The Labour party won an unexpected landslide victory in the election of 1945. With independence for India party policy, Fred Pethick-Lawrence, with his long-held belief in self-governance, was a natural choice for Secretary of State for India. He was elevated to the House of Lords as 1st Baron Lawrence of Peaslake, and in the spring of 1946, at the age of 75, he set off for India with Sir Stafford Cripps and Lord Alexander of Hillsborough (1885-1965).

As he wrote later in the book that he co-authored on Gandhi: *'My friendship with Gandhi was longstanding. Some thirty years previously he had lunched with my wife and myself in our flat in London and had described to us his South African experiences and the active and important part he had played there in the fight for the status of his fellow Indians. In the cold weather of 1926 my wife and I had met him again in India when we attended the annual meeting of Congress in Gauhati. In 1931 I had sat with him at the Round Table Conference and on the Federal Structure Committee held in St James' Palace. Since then we had had some personal correspondence and he had had my good wishes on his birthday, which happened to be the same day of the year as my wedding day.'* In relating his qualifications for the mission, Fred omits to mention that Gandhi had also visited him at his home in Peaslake.

193

The Cabinet Mission's remit was to draw up a constitution for the independent nation with the Indian leaders. Emmeline, in failing health, was unable to travel with Fred, and reluctant to leave her garden. The prolonged separation, as negotiations with the various Indian factions dragged on, was extremely painful to them both. But she wrote frequently and was surrounded with friends: May Start and Charlotte Marsh came to stay and she employed a companion named Lydia. And Mr Rapley was still with them - in 1951 he celebrated 50 years in their employment.

Though Fred headed the Cabinet Mission, Cripps was its driving force. With his lifelong sympathy for Indian independence, Fred felt a bond with the Indian nationalists, referring in correspondence to their shared experience in struggling for a great cause. Mindful of his own prison experiences, he found the assumption of responsibility for imprisoning those campaigning for independence deeply distressing. The climate also proved difficult for an elderly man, weakening him to such an extent that Evelyn Sharp was of the opinion that had he not resigned in April 1947 the job would have killed him. It was with great disappointment at the failure of the Commission to achieve agreement between the religious leaders for the independence of a united India - and at the resultant two-state solution - that he relinquished his position. It was largely through his goodwill and patience, however, that talks had progressed at all. He remained on good terms with many of the leadership of independent India for the rest of his life, in particular the social activist and independence campaigner Amrit Kaur (1889-1964), India's first Minister for Health. And he continued to promote Anglo-Indian relations through the East-West Friendship Council. Despite his commitments in the House of Lords, Fred continued to support his local community. In 1950 he was elected vice-president of The Dorking and Leith Hill Preservation Society alongside President Ralph Vaughan-Williams

In 1946 Emmeline advised on the suffragette scenes in a television production of Howard Spring's 'Fame is the Spur'. In October of the following year she celebrated her eightieth birthday in Peaslake with a cake in suffragette colours. She continued to write, and spoke on Indian Women and on the women's movement in India on BBC radio in 1948. But she left Peaslake much less frequently. In early 1950 she broke her hip in the garden and spent 12 weeks in hospital. Thereafter she was unable to garden and she needed callipers to walk. Elizabeth Kempster was appointed as a nurse/companion. She was adopted into the family. On one occasion she returned to Fourways late at night and rather emotional from a meeting with the fiancée who had abandoned her many years previously, to find the solicitous Fred waiting up in case she was in need of consolation. Always of a mystical disposition - she wrote to Georgiana Solomon about the ability of some to leave their sleeping bodies for their souls to visit the astral world where they could commune with the souls of the dead as well as those of other sleepers - Emmeline grew more so later in life. Her spirituality was of no conventional religion, however.

Fred continued to celebrate their marriage in yearly summaries of what it had meant to him. In 1944 he told Emmeline that '*it has been wonderful to be married to*

194

you for 43 years, it has been delicious to love you and an inspiration to know that you love me'. In 1946 he told her that she was *'my joy and my treasure and the apple of my eye and the blessing of my life'.* As his 'comrade', she had *'planted flowers in the garden of my heart so that my eyes were feasted with colours, my ears were enchanted with music, my spirit infused with good things... whatever else life has brought us of goodwill or ill, one thing it has brought us is of inestimable value – our love for one another.'* *'Bless your darling heart and coaxing ways',* he wrote. *'Bless your eyes, your mouth, your ears and your nose, the locks of your hair. Bless you in your rising and your lying down, your waking and your sleeping.'* In 1949 he recalled that 48 years before she had spoken the word and he and she had been transfigured and nothing had been the same since. And in 1950 he described their marriage as *'a pearl above all price.'*

After her fall Emmeline declined, physically and mentally. By April 1951 she was spending most of the day in bed and Fred feared that she would not make their golden wedding anniversary in October. He did not like to leave her even for a night. But in October they celebrated their golden wedding with a party in London at

Fred (third from left) in the queue at the fishmonger's in Shere. Fred often cooked at weekends when Mrs Plaw had the day off. He also did the food shopping, stopping on his rounds to chat to his many friends in the village. Writing to him in India in 1946 Emmeline passed on greetings from Mr Wood of Forrest's stores who was missing his Saturday visits. (Shere Museum)

195

which Sylvia Pankhurst gave a speech. They returned home to find flowers awaiting them and two golden arm chairs, the result of a collection organised by their friends. Details of the event had been published in the papers, however, and whilst they were celebrating Fourways had been burgled and some of Emmeline's meagre pot of jewellery stolen. Fred refused to call the police, however. (Nor did he believe in insurance.) It had been an extraordinary marriage. Though they had no children, staff and comrades had become family. In later years they donated to between 70 and 80 charities a year and received five to six hundred Christmas cards, all of which were noted and sorted alphabetically, lists being amended and updated with Fred's obsessive meticulousness before being transferred from London down to Peaslake. Both these facts are a testament to the affection in which they were held and to the extent to which they had committed themselves to the causes that they held dear.

Fred was on holiday in the Isle of Wight when Emmeline suffered a heart attack. Elizabeth Kempster had been due to visit a neighbour but had a premonition that all was not well; her appearance at Fourways probably saved Emmeline's life. Emmeline was, said Kempster, *'a wonderful patient'*. She loved to be waited on. With little experience of domestic work, she was capable of making appalling domestic demands but yet she was utterly charming. During her illness Fred kept rigidly to his daily regime, inflexible with well-wishers to the point of rudeness when responding to telephone calls. He and Emmeline's close friend from Peaslake, Kathleen Coxeter, were with her to the end.

Emmeline Pethick-Lawrence died on 11th March 1954 at the age of 87. She had been, wrote 'The Times' obituarist, a true orator with a great power of inducing sacrifice, a fertile imagination and a great sense of the picturesque. *'All the colour and pageantry of the militant suffragette movement were due to her efforts.'* The paper noted her *'fine work'* even before the movement that *'flamed'* her into incandescence and her influence even after the vote was won. *'She was indeed,'* the obituary concluded *'in the main stream of Victorian philanthropy but she brought an individual touch and a sense of mission to her work which gave it permanence and something of greatness.'*

Prime Minister Nehru of India sent a personal message of condolence to Fred and a representative of the Indian government attended the cremation in Woking, where Emmeline's ashes were scattered. Sylvia Pankhurst submitted a long tribute to the 'Manchester Guardian' and on the front page of her 'New Times of Ethiopia' she lamented the loss of a *'dear friend'* of Ethiopia - though Emmeline had only ever had a passing interest in the country[22]. She did not attend the crematorium, claiming to Fred that though she wanted to show her love and admiration for beloved Emmeline, she feared that she could not help crying and would be a burden to others. Giving the

---

[22] Sylvia spent the last twenty years of her life championing the cause of Ethiopia, eventually moving to live there. She was accorded a full state funeral there by the Emperor Haile Selassie on her death in 1960. Fred spoke at her memorial service at Caxton Hall.

eulogy at Emmeline's memorial service, she was inconsolable, breaking into hysterical incoherence.

In her will Emmeline left money to the suffragettes of her youth: to Sylvia Pankhurst, Stella Newsome, Isabel Seymour and Charlotte Marsh.

After Emmeline died, Fourways was sold. Alone in London, Fred often went home at the weekend with Gladys Groom Smith to her husband in Birmingham. He asked Esther Knowles to marry him but was refused. (Emmeline, in her last months, had impressed upon Esther that Fred did not like to be alone and that as she did not want him to be lonely he must marry again.) In 1955 he was honoured in Dorking when the Dorking and District Labour Halls at 85 South Street were named Pethick-Lawrence House. Fred had been a shareholder and first president of the company set up to raise monies to provide a home for the constituency party. On 5th November ex-Prime Minister Clement Attlee and his wife came down to perform the opening ceremony at which Fred also spoke. A dinner followed at Dorking Halls.

In July 1957, three years after Emmeline's death, Fred paid her what he said was the greatest compliment a man could pay to his wife and married again. The second Lady Lawrence, Helen McCombie, had been born Helen Millar Craggs, the daughter of a suffragist. Nearly fifty years earlier Fred had stood bail for her. She rebuffed his proposals several times before agreeing to the marriage. The ceremony took place at Caxton Hall, a place full of resonance for both parties since it had been

Clement Attlee and his wife with the elderly Fred (right) at the opening of Pethick-Lawrence House in South Street in Dorking. (Dorking Museum)

the venue for many suffragette meetings and the starting point for delegations to Parliament. Fiery, less intellectual, but more practical, Helen was no replacement for Emmeline, but the marriage was companionable and affectionate.

The couple lived a busy and purposeful existence. Fred was still active in the House of Lords; he remained a trustee of the National Library of Scotland and a member of the Political Honours Scrutiny Committee; in 1960 he joined the committee of the National Campaign for the Abolition of Capital Punishment. Throughout the 1950s he produced articles and broadcasts for the BBC on India and Indian personalities, on music, and on politics, including a radio series on British prime ministers. As rigorous physically as mentally, he had kept himself physically fit, playing tennis until he was 76. Emmeline's secretary, Gladys Groom Smith, retired on Emmeline's death but when Esther Knowles became ill, she returned to work for Fred. Thereafter the two women shared the secretarial duties. In 1957, at the age of 86, Fred took Helen to India and Pakistan. For the months of November and December they travelled, staying with Nehru and attending lunches, teas and dinners in their honour, (one of them with Agatha Harrison). Fred met with campaigners on women's issues in India and recorded a broadcast for the BBC.

Shortly after his marriage Fred suffered a stroke, but with the help of Helen, Gladys and Esther he was able to continue working and remained politically active in the House of Lords.

Emmeline Pethick-Lawrence and Christabel Pankhurst had corresponded briefly in the 1920s. When travelling with Grace Roe in Canada in May 1922 Christabel professed herself to be overwhelmed on seeing Emmeline's handwriting on an unexpected letter. Ten years of separation, she claimed, were gone as if they had never been. *'Our love,'* she wrote in response, *'united us all the time and only the surface of it was marred. Wasn't that the way? It was like your generous heart to write.'* She fondly reminisced over the *'wonderful years'* that she and 'Godfather' had spent together, and wished herself back with the friends with whom she had lived five years of her youth. *'My heart met yours in all you said... How I long to be in your arms and have a long and satisfying talk about all the essentials.'* But she expressed no regret at the manner of the Pethick-Lawrences' ousting from the WSPU that had occasioned the long separation. Emmeline wrote again when Christabel became a Dame of the British Empire at New Year 1936, to which Christabel replied with assurances that *'there is no inward change in the love which once united us in the service of the same ideal, the same cause... Profoundly the love endures and the value each sets upon what has been seen in the mind and heart of the other.'* And she acknowledged the part played by Fred and Emmeline in the movement; her honour, she said, was *'our honour'*, and that of all who had a part in the campaign, *'ever remembering all you both did to give that movement power'*. But for all the acknowledgments of their shared past, Emmeline and Christabel were never really close after the split of 1912.

A long-distance friendship was re-established between Christabel and Fred after Emmeline's death. Christabel was living in Santa Monica, California, in 1957 when a book and proposed TV programme about the suffrage campaign occasioned a flurry of correspondence between the two about the representation of the movement and of Christabel, her mother and sister. Christabel declined to appear in the programme and charged Fred with overseeing its accuracy and putting the case for militant action. Reminiscing about their holidays together and the *'inspiring days'* with *'the two wonderful Emmelines'*, she was unrepentant about militant tactics.

When Christabel died in 1958 Fred spoke at her memorial service. *'It was generous of you,'* wrote Sylvia, from her home in Addis Ababa, *'as you and Emmeline always are.'* Grace Roe (1885-1979), a suffragette who had only come to prominence in the WSPU after his ousting, and who had been inspired to join the WSPU on hearing Emmeline speak, brought Fred Christabel's unpublished biography. She and Fred prepared it for publication. It is a measure of his generosity that he did so as Christabel made little of his contribution to the WSPU, nor that of Emmeline. (Roe, on the other hand, told Fred that Emmeline had been *'the most perfect honourary treasurer and fundraiser any movement has ever known'*.) He arranged publication of 'Unshackled' through his friend Victor Gollancz. Sentimental as ever, he chose as a frontispiece a photograph of Christabel wearing a hat that he had given her. He also ensured that her name was added to the statue commemorating her mother outside the Houses of Parliament.

With the passing of the Life Peerages Act in 1958, Fred was finally able to welcome the first women to the House of Lords. One of the first four to be appointed was his neighbour, Barbara Wootton Wright of nearby High Barn. She took the title Baroness Wootton of Abinger. Fred was quick to offer his congratulations. Another of the four, Katherine Elliot, Baroness Harwood, told him that it was the fulfilment of his late wife's work. But what, she wondered, would her late brother-in-law, Prime Minister Asquith, have thought?

In 1961, at the age of 89, Fred spoke at the unveiling of a plaque to fellow WSPU committee member, the actress and novelist Elizabeth Robins, at her home at Backsettown in Kent, where, with Dr Octavia Wilberforce, she had run as a refuge for stressed and overworked women. An American citizen, Robins had resigned from the WSPU national committee on Fred and Emmeline's ousting. She continued to support the campaign for the vote through their Votes for Women Fellowship and socialised with them and with Lady Rhondda. In 1937 she had supported Stella Newsome's petition for an honour for Emmeline and at the end of the war Fred had secured her re-entry to the country after she was stranded in the United States. With Dr Octavia Wilberforce (1888-1963) she had founded a sanctuary for women.

Frederick William Pethick-Lawrence died on 10th September 1961 at the age of 90. His secretary, Esther Knowles, recalled that after his last speech in the House of Lords on 27th July he *'folded up'*. She and fellow secretary Gladys Groom-Smith were 'heartbroken'. Helen received hundreds of letters of condolence. Stella

Newsome and Daisy Bedder claimed themselves 'devastated'; Elizabeth Kempster said she had lost a wonderful employer and a true friend. Daisy Solomon summed up his contribution to the women's movement: *'Those of us who went through the suffragette campaign know what he gave to the movement, what sacrifices he made, and his support has never wavered. A man of such moral courage, of such devotion to principle – of such outstanding character – is rare to find and I feel grateful that I knew him'.*

A memorial service was held at St Margaret's, Westminster. When the House of Lords reconvened Lord Hailsham paid tribute to his career. Fred's long-time friend and colleague on the India mission, Lord Alexander of Hillsborough, (who had known Emmeline's father whilst growing up in Weston-super-mare), talked of their playing tennis and billiards together when they shared a bungalow in India; it was all a matter of mathematics, Fred had told him. Lord Layton said Fred was the most religious-minded agnostic. Edith Summerskill said that he was *'oblivious to ridicule and regarded his principles as the light in his life.'* Earl Attlee summed up his achievements thus: *'It is given to very few men to play a leading part in two great movements of emancipation. Pethick-Lawrence did this.'*

'The Times' obituary declared him *'one of the most distinguished veterans of the Labour Party',* a *'historic figure'* who was of a type not uncommon in English political life: *'a man of thought and humane principle who employed his fortunate personal circumstances in the discharge of public responsibility.'* With his *'unaffected warmth, simplicity of spirit and fundamental...moral purpose,'* he was *'never so happy'* it declared *'as in his house in Surrey, where the friendliness to his friends gave light and warmth to the personality exhibited in parliamentary debates.'*

'No one,' wrote Hazel Hunkins Hallinan of the Six Point Group, *'ever did more to channel the women's movement to its present success than Lord Pethick-Lawrence. I do not know of any movement to repay him the respect and love which is due to him or to perpetuate his memory, but I hope, if any move is made, in that direction that we of the Six Point*

Frederick Pethick-Lawrence by John Baker. The portrait used to hang in Dorking's Labour Party Headquarters at Pethick-Lawrence House in South Street. It is now on display at Dorking Museum. (Dorking Museum)

Group will be allowed to express our love and admiration for him.'

It was Grace Roe and the Suffragette Fellowship who took that suggestion forward, organising memorial ceremonies in Dorking and in Peaslake in celebration of the lives of Fred and Emmeline. Reporting them, the 'Dorking Advertiser' said that the couple *'never gave up, never relaxed, never despaired and are an inspiration to generations to come'*. The fund to raise money for permanent memorials in Peaslake and in Dorking, was sponsored by Viscount Alexander, Earl Longford, Baroness Wootton of Abinger and Dame Sybil Thorndyke. Contributors included family members Dorothy Pethick, Thomas Pethick, Nancy and Freda Budgett; employees Gladys Groom-Smith and Esther Knowles; Fred's colleagues in politics Lord Alexander, Earl Mountbatten, Nehru and Barbara Wootton; ex-suffrage campaigners Vera Holme, Betty Brewster, Cecily Hale, Stella Newsome, Grace Roe, Daisy Solomon, Mabel Tuke and Thelma Cazalet-Keir; and local friends Mrs Bamfield, Daisy Bedder, Kathleen Coxeter, Nesta Rhodes-Cullis, Kathleen Ironside, Lorna Nadhar and Daisy Wood. Perhaps most significantly, for according to Gladys Groom-Smith Fred had always hoped for a woman Prime Minister, amongst them was the recently elected MP for Finchley, Margaret Thatcher.

On the afternoon of 7th July 1962 Peaslake flew the WSPU colours. Elderly suffragettes travelled long distances to the village to pay their respects. Amongst them were Mary Leigh nee Brown (1885-1965) who had set off bombs in Dublin's Theatre Royal and who carried with her Emily Wilding Davison's colours; 86 year-old theosophist lecturer Clara Codd (1876-1971) who had stormed Parliament with Emmeline in 1909; Joan Cruickshank nee Dugdale of the Actresses Franchise League; the dancer Lillian Lenton (1891-1972), who had set fire to the Tea House at Kew Gardens, and who had later worked with Emmeline as a speaker for the WFL and as treasurer of the Suffragette Fellowship; and Emmeline's sister, Dorothy Pethick.

At the village hall Lorna Nadhar read tributes from Nehru and Earl Mountbatten. Joan Dugdale gave an account of her life-long friendship with the couple and Clara Codd read out Fred's hymn: *'When my mission is accomplished and my scroll complete thou will break this casket and gather me again unto thyself.'* Baroness

Ex-suffragette Clara Codd (1878-1971) read a hymn at the memorial service in Peaslake. Originally from Devon, she lived in Bath and campaigned alongside Emmeline before becoming a lecturer for the Theosophical Society. (LSE Library)

In Memoriam

Rt. Hon. Lord & Lady (Emmeline) Pethick-Lawrence (Edith) of Peaslake

sponsored by

Viscount Alexander of Hillsborough, Earl of Longford,
Dame Sybil Thorndike, Baroness Wootton of Abinger.

FRED & EMMELINE PETHICK-LAWRENCE
Artist: John Baker of Epsom

At the base of this portrait is a plaque inscribing the following quotation:—

"Children of Freedom"

"O Freedom, beautiful beyond compare, thy Kingdom
is established !

Thou with thy feet on earth, thy brow among the
stars, for ages us thy children

I, thy child, singing daylong nightlong, sing of

Commemorative leaflet put out by the Suffragette Fellowship. The leaflet features the joint portrait of the couple which hangs in Peaslake Village Hall, modelled on a photograph of Fred and Emmeline at Fourways. (Dorking Museum)

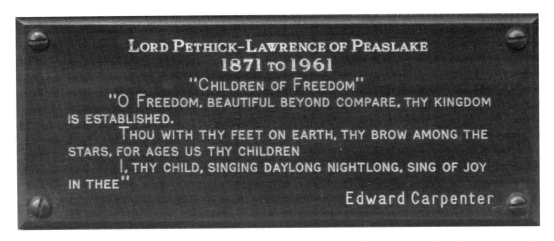

LORD PETHICK-LAWRENCE OF PEASLAKE
1871 TO 1961
"CHILDREN OF FREEDOM"
"O FREEDOM, BEAUTIFUL BEYOND COMPARE, THY KINGDOM
IS ESTABLISHED.
THOU WITH THY FEET ON EARTH, THY BROW AMONG THE
STARS, FOR AGES US THY CHILDREN
I, THY CHILD, SINGING DAYLONG NIGHTLONG, SING OF JOY
IN THEE"
Edward Carpenter

Summerskill (1901-1980) then unveiled a portrait of the couple by the artist John Baker of Epsom at the base of which was inscribed a verse by Edward Carpenter (above). She also presented a commemorative speaker's table to the village as Guildford's Stoughton junior choir sang 'Jerusalem'.

In the evening Bernard Hunt of Dorking's Labour party presided as Lord Longford unveiled a portrait of Fred, again by John Baker, at Pethick-Lawrence House in Dorking. He had never, he said of Fred, met a man who radiated *'a more complete and unmistakable atmosphere of goodness.'* And Vera Brittain announced that her biography of Fred would be published at the end of June 1963, 51 years to the day since Fred's release from Brixton prison.

A plaque was placed on the wall outside the front door, by GH Maynard of Abinger Hammer. It reads: *'Frederick William Pethick-Lawrence born 28th December 1871, died 10th September 1961 / Emmeline Pethick-Lawrence born 21st October 1867, died 11th March 1954 / In loving memory of Fred and Emmeline, Lord and Lady Pethick-Lawrence of Peaslake, lovers of freedom and humanity whose combined work for the emancipation of women and for world peace will be remembered by countless generations.'*

In 1963 the Pethick-Lawrence Memorial Committee put out a pamphlet, 'Memories of Fred and Emmeline Pethick-Lawrence', celebrating the occasion, its cover branded in WSPU purple, white and green. The following year the Committee visited the memorials in Dorking and Peaslake and the two commemorative benches that had been placed, one on Butter Hill in Dorking, the other on Holmwood Common, opposite The Sundial where Emmeline had liked to sit looking at the cottage she had founded more than half a century earlier.

With the coming of the dual carriageway The Sundial is less a rural idyll than once it was. However it is still possible to sit on Holmwood Common, under the great oak tree on the rise opposite the cottage, and to contemplate the extraordinary lives of those who gave so much to the benefit of so many.

Life at Fourways

The Fourways lifestyle was not extravagant; furnishings were sparse and meals tended to be frugal. Food was prepared on an ancient oil stove until Elizabeth Kempster persuaded Fred to exchange it for an Aga that he subsequently loved. He drank little alcohol and did not take coffee or tea. He rose at seven, exercised every morning and ate the same breakfast daily – barley water, toast somewhat extravagantly spread with butter and finished with a spoonful of jam. Thereafter he took a brisk walk around the village, stopping each day to chat with regular acquaintances. He disliked flowers in the house and insisted that meals be taken with precise regularity and without delay or interruption. Though he was absurdly fussy – he could not bear onions, even in the larder – he loved his food. Emmeline, by contrast, was vague and liable to forget to eat altogether. She rose late, and in later years, not at all. She took her breakfast and her post in bed, dictating letters from her bedroom, a chaotic maelstrom in which the loss of papers would drive Fred to distraction. Never one to pay much attention to clothes – unlike Fred, who dressed meticulously – in later years she might not dress all day, returning to bed as the whim took.

Fred's holidays, like his meals, followed a regular pattern. Seldom longer than four nights – he would not go longer without his work – breaks were taken year after year in the same locations and with the same companions. He took an annual fishing holiday with Fred Hankinson. With others he went on golfing trips. Until she was incapacitated Emmeline travelled to conferences and as a guest speaker in Europe and America.

With separate friends, separate holidays and separate rooms, their differing meals and separate meal-times, some might have said that theirs was hardly a marriage at all. But when Fred found Emmeline he had promised her freedom and he was proud to have honoured that promise. Both were aware that they, as others in their circle, were pioneers of a new kind of marriage in which the wife was subject neither to her husband, nor to his routine.

Emmeline inspired devotion: from family, from her Esperance girls, from WSPU volunteers who cherished her into old age, and from friends who moved to be with her. Employees became part of the family, treated more as friends than staff and known by their first names. The couple's chauffeur moved with them to Peaslake, working for them for decades; similarly their secretaries, Esther Knowles, who had grown up with the WSPU and left it on the split from the Pankhursts, and Gladys Groom Smith, who spent more of her time at Fourways than at home with her husband.

In later years Emmeline's housekeeper/companion, Elizabeth Kempster, was treated like a daughter, as had been Christabel Pankhurst. Always referred to as 'Liz' and introduced as a friend, she described Fred as having been like a father. An energetic, self-possessed and sporting young woman, Kempster had contracted polio in her youth, which had deprived her of her fiancée and left her with difficulty walking. She had spent the war years in occupied Jersey and was somewhat horrified at the thought of working for a 'Lord and Lady', but she was quickly absorbed into the Peaslake pseudo-family. With Fred away in London on government business from Monday to Friday, Elizabeth took care of the house and of the increasingly erratic Emmeline, whom she called 'Emmie'.

Though Fred's rigidity could be highly demanding and Emmeline's self-absorption wearing, their staff remained devoted. Chief of Emmeline's attractions seems to have been that, like Fred, she loved people. She was interested in them and in their lives no matter what their class or status. Employees and young people, used to being ignored, dismissed or overlooked, found their opinions asked and their views valued. In a strictly stratified society this inspired intense loyalty. And in Emmeline's case her interest and lack of snobbery was coupled with a flirtatious charm: even as an elderly woman she was capable of inspiring devotion in young male admirers.

Photograph of Fred and Emmeline at Fourways by Wilfred Start-Walter, husband of their old housekeeper, May Start. (The Master and Fellows of Trinity College, Cambridge)

The first women peers – Baroness Wootton of Abinger

Christabel Pankhurst and Millicent Fawcett were each awarded a DBE. Stella Newsome campaigned in vain for an honour for Emmeline. And Lady Rhondda fought and failed to take a seat in the Lords. None of the luminaries of the suffrage campaign was elevated to the House of Lords when women were first admitted under the Life Peerages Act 1958. The first women to be elevated were too young to have played a part in the suffrage campaign. One of them was Barbara Frances Wootton Wright nee Adam (1897-1988) who lived at High Barns in Abinger; she took the title Baroness Wootton of Abinger.

Barbara Adam was the daughter of Cambridge classicists. Though fearsomely gifted, she had had to beg to be allowed to attend school rather than being taught at home, and on reaching Cambridge fought to be allowed to study economics. She married in 1917 at the age of 20 and spent just 36 hours with her husband before his departure for the front; she was widowed within a month.

Barbara Wootton Wright returned to Cambridge at the age of 23, having completed research in criminology and social work at the London School of Economics. She began lecturing at an institution which, as yet, did not award degrees to women. There was no possibility of her being admitted as a college fellow, and she was a JP at the age of 29 – before she was entitled to vote.

Barbara Wootton Wright worked in the research department of the Labour Party and at the Trades Union Congress before becoming principal of Morley College, then reader at Bedford College. She became a full professor in 1948. When she entered the Lords as one of the first four female life peers in 1958 her neighbour, Fred Pethick-Lawrence, was one of those most enthusiastic in his welcome. Baroness Wootton served as a governor of the BBC and on four royal commissions. In 1967 she became deputy speaker of the Lords, the first woman to hold the post. She was on good terms with Fred and Emmeline, and sponsored their memorial campaign. *(National Portrait Gallery, London)*

Gandhi's followers from the Surrey Hills

In 1931 Gandhi was accompanied on his trip to England by his devoted English follower, Madeleine Slade (1892-1982). She had spent much of her youth with her grandfather, James Carr Saunders, at Milton Heath House in Westcott, and was bridesmaid to her sister Rhona at Holy Trinity church in 1913.

Inspired by a biography of Gandhi, Madeleine Slade devoted her life to the man and to the cause of Indian independence. She travelled to India in 1925, learned Hindi, took the name Mira Behn, and lived as in Gandhi's entourage. Eventually she took over all his personal care, washing his clothes and cooking his meals. She also learned to spin, a skill that had symbolic significance in Gandhi's advocacy of Indian self-sufficiency. It is likely that Mira Behn accompanied Gandhi when he visited the Pethick-Lawrences at Fourways in 1931. In her autobiography she recalls passing the gates to her childhood home at Milton Heath at this time, without time to visit. She and the Pethick-Lawrences would have had much in common, for she had spent time in prison for offences relating to the campaign against British rule in India. Fred met her again when he was Secretary of State for India. After Gandhi's assassination in 1948 Mira Behn set up an ashram. She ended her life as a semi-recluse in Austria and was played by Geraldine James in the 1982 film 'Gandhi'.

Madeleine Slade was an inspiration to others. Locally Miss Fairbanks ran a cooperative of weavers at The Old Cottages at Mill Bottom in Holmwood. She set off for India to follow Gandhi in 1930. *Image: Miss Fairbanks on Holmwood Common on the morning of her departure for India.*

Like-thinking neighbours in Peaslake - the Buxtons, Mosa Anderson, and Save the Children

The Buxtons lived close to the Pethick-Lawrences at Whingate in Peaslake. Like Fred, Charles Roden Buxton (1875-1942) came from a wealthy family, was educated at Trinity College, Cambridge and studied for the bar. He believed in education for working people and lectured on literature at Morley College in Lambeth, becoming principal of the college in 1902. Later a Liberal MP, he was a founder member of the Union of Democratic Control (of which Fred was also a prominent member) on the outbreak of the First World War. After the war he joined the Independent Labour party and spent the rest of his life in and out of Parliament; mutual friend Evelyn Sharp worked on his election campaigns. Buxton advised the Labour party on foreign and colonial matters and served as party treasurer. He was a proponent of Esperanto and a delegate to the League of Nations. Like Evelyn Sharp and Agatha Harrison, he was attracted to the pacifist Society of Friends. Having worked all his life for understanding between nations, he, like Emmeline and George Lansbury, was deeply disappointed by the outbreak of the Second World War.

The legacy of Dorothy Frances Buxton nee Jebb (1881-1963) is perhaps more concrete than that of her husband. With her sister, Eglantyne Jebb, she founded the charity Save the Children. Also from a wealthy family, Dorothy studied at Newnham College, Cambridge. She was prevented from travelling to the Hague Women's Peace Conference in 1915 but was a founding member of the Women's International League for Peace and Freedom with Emmeline. During the First World War she organised the publication of news from Europe in translation, with the aim of increasing understanding of Germany and its allies. After the war she was so appalled by reports of children starvation in Germany and Austria, that with her sister and others she set up the Fight the Famine Committee which lead directly to the founding of Save the Children in 1919. Emmeline took an interest in the charity but doubted it would ever raise sufficient funds; Evelyn Sharp was a committed supporter. Later she took on Hermann Goering, haranguing him about atrocities in Nazi Germany. After her husband's death in 1942, Dorothy called often on Emmeline at Fourways to discuss world affairs and to meet mutual friends.

The couple were introduced to Peaslake by Mosa Anderson (1891-1978), who had edited Dorothy Buxton's 'Notes from the Foreign Press'. She lived at Charlton House in Peaslake. Like Dorothy Buxton she was a member of the Women's International League and was on the council of Save the Children. A linguist, she had worked as secretary to Dorothy's husband before setting up nurseries for children during the Second World War and travelling to Poland to organize Save the Children relief work there in 1946.

The second Lady Lawrence – Helen Craggs

The daughter of accountant Sir John Craggs and his suffragist wife, Helen Millar Craggs (1888-1969) had wanted to become a doctor. But she had no parental support so she became a teacher at Roedean. After interrupting a Liberal party meeting at the Albert Hall attended by her mother, home life became difficult; becoming a paid WSPU organizer enabled her to leave her parents' house. Close to Emmeline's friend, Evelyn Sharp, she became responsible for the distribution of 'Votes for Women' in central London.

Mrs Pankhurst's invalid son, Harry, fell in love with Helen in 1908. During his final illness his mother was on a fundraising trip to the United States with Dorothy Pethick; his sister Sylvia arranged for Helen to visit daily. On her return Mrs Pankhurst was less than pleased. Whether Helen was devoted to Harry or just comforting the dying young man is a matter of conjecture. She was, however, at his side when he died in January 1910.

Craggs achieved notoriety in early 1912 when she was arrested after trying to burn down Nuneham Courtney, the country home of Lewis Harcourt. She later married a doctor and trained as a pharmacist, supporting her children on her husband's death by running a jigsaw puzzle business and emigrating for a time to Canada. *(Image: Shere Museum)*

He bailed her out; now he marries her

Select Bibliography and Sources

AJR (ed.): *The Suffrage Annual and Women's Who's Who*, 1913

Balfour, Lady Betty ed.: *Letters of Constance Lytton*, 1925

Balshaw, June: 'Sharing the Burden - the Pethick-Lawrences and Women's Suffrage', *The Men's Share*, Ed Angela V John and Clare Eustance, 1997

Bartley, Paula: *Emmeline Pankhurst*, 2002

Bell, E Moberley: *Flora Shaw (Lady Lugard DBE)*, 1947

Benn, Caroline: *Keir Hardie*, 1997

Black, Ros: *A Talent for Humanity, The life and work of Lady Henry Somerset,* 2010

Blackburn, Helen: *Women's Suffrage*, 1902

Brittain, Vera: *Pethick-Lawrence: a Portrait*, 1963

Bush, Julia: *Women against the Vote - Female anti-suffragism in Britain*, 2007

Callaway, Helen and Helly, Dorothy: 'Crusader for Empire – Flora Shaw/Lady Lugard' *Western Women and Imperialism* Ed Nupur Chaudhuri and Margaret Strobel, 1992

Cazalet-Keir, Thelma: *From the Wings*, 1967

Cowman, Krista: *Women of the Right Spirit, paid organizers of the WSPU*, 2007

Cowman, Krista: 'A party between revolution and peaceful persuasion: a fresh look at the United Suffragists' in Joannou, Maroula and Purvis, June Ed.: *The Women's Suffrage Movement: New Feminist Perspectives*, 1998

Crawford, Elizabeth: *The Women's Suffrage Movement, A Reference Guide 1866-1928,* 1999

Crawford, Elizabeth: *The Women's Suffrage Movement in Britain and Ireland*, 2006

Drakeford, Mark: *Social Movements and their supporters – the Green Shirts in England*, 1997

Eastlake, Lady: *Mrs Grote, a Sketch*, 1880

Essen, RI: *Epsom's Suffragette*, 1993

Fawcett, Millicent Garrett: *What I Remember*, 1924

Fitzpatrick, Kathleen: *Lady Henry Somerset*, 1923

Gawthorpe, Mary: *Up the Hill to Holloway*, 1962

Geddes, Jennian F: 'Words *and* Deeds in the suffragette military hospital in Endell Street', *MH*, 2007

Green, FE: *The Surrey Hills,* 1915

Hale, Cecily: *A Good Long Life*, 1973

Harrison, Brian: *Prudent Revolutionaries – Portraits of British Feminists between the Wars*, 1987

Harrsion, Irene: *Agatha Harrison: An Impression by her sister*, 1956

Himsworth, Sheila: 'As Good as a Son', Bertha Broadwood, *Surrey History* Vol.3, No.5, 1988

Jenkins, Inez: *The History of the Women's Institute Movement of England and Wales,* 1953

Joannou, Maroula and Purvis, June Ed.: *The Women's Suffrage Movement: New Feminist Perspectives*, 1998

John, Angela V: *Evelyn Sharp Rebel Woman 1869-1955*, 2009

John, Angela: *Elizabeth Robins: Staging a Life*, 1995

John, Angela V and Eustance, Clare Ed: *The Men's Share, Masculinities, Male Support and Women's Suffrage in Britain 1890-1920*, 1997

Jones, Mervyn: *The Amazing Victorian – a life of George Meredith*, 1999

Judge, Ray: 'Mary Neal and the Esperance Morris', *Folk Music Journal* vol5 no5, 1989

Keen, Hilda: *Deeds not words, the lives of suffragette teachers*, 1990

Kenney, Annie: *Memoirs of a Militant*, 1924

Law, Cheryl: *Suffrage and Power – the women's movement 1918-1928*, 1997

Lawson, Marian Ed.: *Memories of Charlotte Marsh*, 1961

Lewin, Col TH, Ed.: *The Lewin Letters 1756-1885*, 1909

Liddington, Jill: *The Militant Suffrage Movement, citizenship and resistance in Britain*, 2003

Liddington, Jill and Norris, Jill: *One Hand Tied Behind Us, the Women's Suffrage movement*, 2000

Liddle, Helen Gordon: *The Prisoner, A Sketch*, 1911

Lytton, Lady Constance: *I, Constance Lytton*, 1987

Lytton, Lady Constance: *Prisons and Prisoners,* 1914
Mackenzie, Midge: *Shoulder to Shoulder*, 1975
Mackworth, Margaret: *This was my World,* 1933
Mitchell, David: *The Pankhursts*, 1970
Montagu, Lily: *My Club and I*, 1941
Morgan, Kevin: *Ramsay MacDonald*, 2006
Murray, Flora: *Women as Army Surgeons*, 1920
Neal, Mary: *'A Tale that is Told – the autobiography of a Victorian Woman'* (unpublished)
Newsome, Stella: *The Women's Freedom League 1907-1957*, 1957
Overton, Jenny and Mant, Joan: *A Suffragette Nest – Peaslake 1910 and after,* 1998
Pankhurst, Christabel: *Unshackled*, 1959
Pankhurst, Emmeline: *My Own Story*, 1914
Pankhurst, E. Sylvia: *The Suffragette Movement*, 1931
Pankhurst, Richard: *Sylvia Pankhurst, Artist and Crusader*, 1979
Pankhurst, Richard and Bullock, Ian: *Sylvia Pankhurst from artist to anti-fascist*, 1992
Pethick-Lawrence, Emmeline: *My Part in a Changing World*, 1938
Pethick-Lawrence, Frederick: *Fate has been Kind*, 1942
Pugh, Martin: *The March of the Women*, 2000
Pugh, Martin: *The Pankhursts,* 2001
Pugh, Martin: *Votes for Women in Britain 1867-1928*, 1994
Pugh, Martin: *Women and the Women's Movement in Britain 1914-1959*, 1992
Purvis, June: *Emmeline Pankhurst*, 2002
Raeburn, Antonia: *The Militant Suffragettes*, 1973
Romero, Patricia W.: *E. Sylvia Pankhurst, Portrait of a Radical*, 1987
Rosen, Andrew: *Rise Up Women! The Militant Campaign of the WSPU 1903-1914*, 1974
Ross, Ellen: 'Disgruntled Missionaries': the Friendship of Mary Neal and Emmeline Pethick at the West London Mission', *Ramapo College of New Jersey*, 2009
Rubinstein, David: *A Different World for Women: A Life of Millicent Garrett Fawcett*, 1991
Slade, Madeleine/Mira Behn: *The Spirit's Pilgrimage*, 1960
Smyth, Ethel: *Female Pipings in Eden*, 1933
Spence, Jean: 'Working for Jewish Girls': Lily Montagu, girls' clubs and industrial reform 1890-1914', *Women's History Review vol.13, No.3*, 2004
Strachey, Ray: *Millicent Garrett Fawcett*, 1931
Strauss, Sylvia: *Traitors to the Masculine Cause, the Men's Campaign for Women's Rights*, 1982
Taylor, Rosemary: *In Letters of Gold, the Story of Sylvia Pankhurst and the East London Federation of the Suffragettes in Bow*, 1993
Tickner, Lisa: *The Spectacle of Women - Imagery of the Suffrage Campaign 1907-14*, 1987
Van Wingerden, Sophia A.: *The Women's Suffrage Movement in Britain 1860-1928*, 1999
Wainwright, David: *Broadwood by Appointment*, 1982
Wootton, Barbara: *In a World I Never Made*, 1967

Archive material

Dorking Museum: general papers; Shere Museum: Bray papers; The Women's Library: Emmeline Pethick-Lawrence letter collection & interviews with suffragettes by Brian Harrison; London School of Economics Library: Kibbo Kift archive & the Letters of George Lansbury; Surrey History Centre: Memoir of Harry Daley SHC 7832, papers of Bertha Broadwood SHC 6973/5/10 and 2185/BMB, papers and letters of Lord Farrer of Abinger SHC 2572, papers and letters of Lucy Etheldred Broadwood SHC 2185/LEB & scrapbook of Helena Auerbach SHC 3266; Bodleian Library, Oxford: papers and diary of Evelyn Sharp Nevinson and Henry Nevinson mss.eng.misc.d. 668, e.634, 635, 636, b.102; mss.eng.lett.c.278, 279 mss.eng.litt.d.276 and 277; Trinity College, Cambridge: papers of Frederick and Emmeline Pethick-Lawrence; Cecil Sharp House: papers of Mary Neal; The Museum of London: Suffragette Fellowship Collection papers.

Index

213

214